CELTIC
QUEEN

CELTIC QUEEN

THE WORLD OF CARTIMANDUA

JILL ARMITAGE

AMBERLEY

First published 2020

Amberley Publishing
The Hill, Stroud
Gloucestershire, GL5 4EP

www.amberley-books.com

Copyright © Jill Armitage, 2020

The right of Jill Armitage to be identified as
the Author of this work has been asserted in
accordance with the Copyrights, Designs and
Patents Act 1988.

ISBN 978 1 4456 8415 4 (hardback)
ISBN 978 1 4456 8416 1 (ebook)

British Library Cataloguing in Publication Data.
A catalogue record for this book is available
from the British Library.

Typesetting by Aura Technology and Software
Services, India. Printed in the UK.

CONTENTS

PREFACE

Marching victoriously northwards from the Thames valley across the Chilterns and the flat lands of central England, the Roman Army came to a halt on a line running roughly across the country from the Wash to the Chester Dee. This was the southern frontier of Brigantia, the powerful Celtic state that stretched from there up to the Tyne and Solway and beyond. The geographer Ptolemy writing in the 2nd century AD described the lands of Brigantia as extending to both seas – east to west; reaching as far north as Birren in Dumfriesshire and as far south as the River Trent in south Derbyshire.

The tribal federation who inhabited this vast territory were known as the Brigantes. Their relationship with Imperial Rome makes a dramatic story in itself, but we add to this a mysterious, powerful queen named Cartimandua. She ruled over this enormous region that covered most of northern England during a period of major turmoil, captured a rebel prince and lived a life of luxury on Roman wealth. When she took her husband's former armour bearer as her lover, she shocked even the Romans, but her husband intended to seek revenge.

Cartimandua is one of the few female rulers known to history, yet she didn't get a chance to tell her story; she left no written word. We can only find her in the narration of prejudiced Roman historians writing for a purpose – propaganda. To go some way toward countering this imbalance, we tell the story of Cartimandua and her lifestyle as a first-century Celtic Queen from the pointers we can find. Today we have archaeological finds, folk lore and legends from which to build a truer picture.

I

WAS CARTIMANDUA A QUEEN BY BIRTH?

A Celtic couple. (British Museum)

Mention the name Cartimandua and most people look blank, yet Cartimandua is the first documented queen to have ruled a major part of Britain in her own right. She was a central player in the drama of the Roman annexation of Britain in the first century AD. This was a time of immense change, the merging of the old and new worlds, the new millennium. The invading armies may have occupied her tribal territory, but Cartimandua kept her lands through skill and tact when many other Celtic rulers were forfeiting theirs in the aftermath of the invasion.

The name Cartimandua may be a compound of the common Celtic roots *carti-* meaning chase, expel or send, and *mandu-* meaning pony. However, it was quite common for the Romans to ignore Celtic names and give Roman names to people and places, so Cartimandua may be a Roman name, and would therefore have a totally different meaning. For example, Caratacus, son of King Cunobelinus and heir to the Catuvellauni kingdom, is the Romanised name of the Celtic Caradoc, or Ceretic/Cerdig/Cerdic. Because he is male, far more is known about him. Women were secondary citizens categorised by their relationship to men – wife, mother, sister, daughter, whore.

We know of Cartimandua principally from the Roman historian Publius (or Gaius) Cornelius Tacitus. Cartimandua is first mentioned in 51 AD when her reign appears to be well established. She was an Iron Age aristocrat; her blood line may have included nobility from a number of the other Celtic tribes which at that time occupied the British Isles (or *Pritani* in the Common Brittonic Celtic language). To hold such a prestigious position, her connections would be wide and powerful but we have no background, no mention of her parentage or how she became queen. Tacitus records that she was '*pollens nobilitate*', powerful in noble lineage, so she was undoubtedly of illustrious birth. Because Cartimandua ruled in her own right rather than through marriage, she may have been heir to the Brigantes through birthright because the male line had failed.

Writing in *Historic UK*, Ellen Castelow states that Cartimandua was the granddaughter of King Bellnorix, but this is only conjecture. Castelow gives no supporting evidence. Other sources are of the opinion that she could have been the great-granddaughter of Addedomoros, King of the Trinovantes. According to Guy Phillips in his book *Briganti*, Cartimandua succeeded her father Dumnoveros or Dumnocoveros, and her grandfather Volisios as ruler of Brigantia. Phillips seems to have come to this conclusion because of the Brigantian gold coins of Cartimandua, Dumnocoveros, and Volisios that he says have been found with Roman silver coins of dates corresponding to the period between 209BC and 41BC. Phillips does not expand on this and gives no indication as to where this information can be checked so perhaps the information is questionable.[1]

Early Coinage

The first coins appeared in Britain from the continent around 150BC but the first British coins were not produced for almost another hundred years, probably to pay the soldiers who went into battle when Caesar invaded in 55 and 54BC. Early minting was highly sporadic and localised, and the coins were uninscribed until around 45BC when King Commios of the Atrebatic/Regnan tribe started the practice of placing his name on them. Other rulers followed suit and later coins feature the name Volisios, who Phillips said was Cartimandua's grandfather. Unfortunately, the name Volisios is known only through inscriptions on coins.

The name Volisios appears together with names of two other presumed sub-kings, Dumnocoveros and Cartivelios, in three series minted *c.* 30–60AD. Phillips stated that Dumnocoveros was Cartimandua's father, so if his name appears alongside Volisios, could this be proof that one succeeded the other and they were father and son? But if Volisios and Dumnocoveros were Brigante tribal kings, why do they appear on coinage with Cartivelios, who was believed to be a Corieltavian tribal king? The Corieltavian tribe was due south of Brigante territory and their capital was *Ratae Corieltauvorum*, known today as Leicester. The two tribes were neighbours, there would have been trade between them, but tribes did not share coinage.

Although it's a long shot, is it possible that the name Cartivelios was a Romanised version of the Celtic name Cartimandua? As we've already stated, 'Carti' may be a compound of the common Celtic root meaning chase, expel or send; 'vellios' means fixed in opinions, firm in friendships and square in dealings; one who possesses organisational skills and is persuasive. Such assets would certainly be qualities needed by a tribal leader. The coins bearing the three names could depict three generations of Brigante rulers. It's highly speculative yet feasible, if we can build on the information given by Guy Phillips.

Almost all Celtic coins featured at least two names, suggesting they had multiple rulers, but the names on the earliest coins are so abbreviated as to be unidentifiable. For example, for one hundred and twenty years a coin type was wrongly attributed because the inscription was read as CAM. This was interpreted as being short for Camulodunon (Colchester), capital of the Catuvallauni tribe, but recently the letters CAM have been re-interpreted as CAR and been ascribed to the previously mentioned Caratacus (Celtic name Caradoc). A viable alternative would be to suggest that CAR could be short for Cartimandua.

According to Nicki Howarth in her book *Cartimandua, Queen of the Brigantes*, gold and silver staters dating from the first half of the 1st century with the name VOLISIOS on the obverse and CARTI-VE on the reverse were found in West Yorkshire in the 19th century. Because this was Brigante territory it wasn't hard to make the connection. CARTI was claimed to be a shortened version of Cartimandua and this exciting find seemed to link the two names Volisios and Cartimandua as joint leaders, or a leader and his/her beneficiary. Surely here was proof that Volusios was an early Brigante leader who was succeeded by Cartimandua. The VE further supports the claim because this was believed to refer to Cartimandua's husband Venutius. Then another gold stater bearing the same inscription was found in 1999, but by then modern analysis had questioned the CARTI-VE and it was decided that it didn't stand for Cartimandua and Venutius, it stood for Cartivellaunos. If this is another version of the name Cartivelios, we have circled back to the previous question – does this refer to a Corieltavian leader or Cartimandua?

There is a connection between the three names in coinage indicating that they were all leaders but we can't be sure of anything more. The names Dumnocoveros and Volisios are some of the earliest personal names ever recorded from the region but they may have been common names in that period and some historian simply linked them with Cartimandua. Sadly, at present all we can say is that there have been no finds of coins minted in Brigantia showing the actual name Cartimandua in full.

Was Cartimandua an Elected Queen?

Unable to ascertain her lineage we should consider if Cartimandua was an elected queen and not a ruler as a result of birth. The oldest male child or female in the absence of a male heir of a Celtic tribal chieftain may not have automatically succeeded as leader. Kings and queens could have been chosen by the gods, their decision interpreted by the Druids of the tribe. Succession was a matter of the highest importance for the continuing survival and well-being of the tribe, so the people would have looked to their gods for guidance in choosing their leader. These prehistoric people believed that all things needed the blessing of the gods, they were very influenced by pagan beliefs, superstitions, spirits and omens.

It's possible that Cartimandua was a chosen leader because the people believed that she was the reincarnation of one of her forefathers. The writings of the Poseidonian and Alexandrian schools of history, as well as Caesar, support the possibility that the Druids generally practised and taught a belief in reincarnation. Instances of reincarnation are described in insular literature. Reincarnation was thought to transpire in the case of exceptional people, and there was a belief that

Stone sculpture of Brigantia from Birens, Dumfriesshire. (National Museum of Scotland)

the spirit could pass from one member of a family to another. The evidence, although not substantial does exist (see more in later sections).

It is possible that Celtic women practised polyandry because some early Celtic groups recognised the primacy of the matrilineal descent, in which an individual's status depended upon the identity of the mother rather than the father. The Roman writers were men, and were not comfortable giving Celtic women powerful roles like tribal chieftain or queen. But one of the few observations that Tacitus made on the subject was that 'Britons make no distinction of sex in their appointment of commanders.'

Cartimandua was a native woman thriving in a man's world and she managed it in a civilised way, using force to put down trouble without the need for all-out war. These early writers must have had a grudging respect for such achievements but it's doubtful that their descriptions of female rulers in Britain provide an accurate picture. Women in antiquity were largely defined by their relationship with men. Although some Celtic noblewomen were pawns in the dynastic marriage arrangement by which noblemen sealed alliances, compared with their Greek and Roman contemporaries they enjoyed considerable personal freedom and even power, a situation that wasn't accepted readily by Roman writers. Celtic noblewomen could and often did play a part in politics; they were priestesses and rulers in their own right; carried arms and were often present on the battlefield.

Early Roman writers like Tacitus were anxious to under-represent the role played by Celtic women, acknowledging them only as playing small parts, and giving them unflattering, stereotypical images. Tacitus showed women in a negative light and if he was trying to discredit Cartimandua he did a good job. Because she was a staunch Roman ally, he couldn't criticise her as a ruler, so he concentrated on her faults as a woman. In the *Histories*, he describes her as 'cruel, treacherous, scheming and immoral'. The Roman propaganda machine written by a male chauvinist was never going to give an impartial report of Cartimandua. However, by examining popular Celtic culture, living conditions, their gods, beliefs, art and symbolism we get a more rounded picture. Add to this the archaeological evidence, mainly from the hillforts that could have been Cartimandua's headquarters, and we gain an intriguing insight into the life of this fascinating woman and the Romano- Celtic world in which she lived.

Queen of the Mountain?

Cartimandua was queen of the Brigantes, a name believed to be derived from the Gallo-Brythonic word 'briga' meaning high hill. So they could be defined as highlanders. The word is cognate with the English 'burg' or 'berg', and the German 'birg', all meaning mountain, although this later came to describe a fortified settlement. When a tribe took its name from a geological feature such as 'briga' there are likely to be several tribes of the same name and here we find the Brigantii tribe in the Alps and the Brigantes of Ireland. Although there is nothing to indicate that these tribes were in any way linked other than in name, according to Guy Phillips in his book *Brigante,* the Northern England tribe had a colony in Ireland.[2]

An alternative suggestion would be that the tribe was not named after a geographical feature but obtained its name from the Celtic goddess Brigantia whom they worshipped and continued to worship until the early third century at least. For thousands of years, many religions existed that worshipped a female creator, the mother goddess. Brigantia was a cult figure known variously as St Briget, Brigid, Brig, Brid and Bride, making it relatively safe to assume all these names are cognate and derived from the same Celtic origins.

Altar to the goddess Brigantia found in 1895 south-west of the fort at South Shields. The dedicator is Congennicus, a Gallic name. Drawn by Jacqui Taylor. (From *Roman Britain*, Patricia Southern)

There are places named after Brigantia, St Briget, Brigid, Brid and Bride throughout the Brigantia region. In Cumberland there is Bridekirk with a church of St Bridget; there's St Bridgets Beckermet on the coast, and the ancient church of St Briget at Bessenthwaite. At Kirkbride is a pre-Conquest church described as 'dedicated to St Bride', and just across the Solway Firth, but still in Brigantia, is Brydekirk. To the north east of Leeds, ancient tracks meet and cross the River Washburn at a place called Bride Cross, and there's a place called Bride on the Isle of Man.

According to Guy Phillips there is a dedication to Brigantia from Irthington, east/north east of Carlisle, not too far from Birrens, (see the statuette dedicated to Brigantia) and an invocation at Corstopitum (Corbridge) on the River Tyne.[3] In Edmund Bogg's book *Lower Wharfdale*, written in 1900, a drawing by A. Sutton entitled 'Querns found at Wetherby' includes a Roman type altar which is inscribed 'DEAE V C / TORINE/ BRICANT / ADAURS / FAI PLRNV.

The mother goddess was familiar to the Romans as *matres domesticate,* and in both her iconography and descriptions by the Romans, Brigantia resembles the Roman goddess Minerva, goddess of wisdom and the sponsor of arts, trade and strategy. While the Mediterranean civilizations of Greece and Rome had goddesses of love, wisdom, peace etc, the Celtic female divinities seem to have been strongly associated with the reproductive sequence and procreation. As essentially farming people, crop yields and the reproductive capacity of their flocks and herds probably took precedence over everything else. Brigantia's areas of concern were protecting the tribe, ensuring prosperity and fertility in the home, and inspiring success in the learned arts, especially poetry.

In 1731, a female statuette carved in buff sandstone was discovered in the ruins of a building outside the Roman fort at Birrens, Dumfriesshire. It stands in a gabled niche about 90 cm high and 45 cm wide (36" x 18") and once had traces of gilding, but that has worn away long ago. She is winged, crowned like a tutelary deity, has a Gorgon's head as a pendant hanging on her breast and wears a plumed helmet encircled by a turreted crown. In her right hand she holds a spear, in her left a globe; to her left stands her shield, to her right an omphaloi stone. An omphalos is a powerful symbolic artefact, the navel of the earth – the centre point from which terrestrial life originated. Her attributes equate her with Minerva Victrix. She wears Minerva's symbol of the gorgon's head as a pendant but there is no doubt who she is because the base of the statue is inscribed with the name Brigantiae. It reads:

> *Brigantiae s(acrum) Amandus arc(h)itectus ex imperio*
> *imp(eratum) (fecit)*
> *Sacred to Brigantia: Amandus, the engineer, by command*
> *fulfilled the order. (R.I.B. 2091)*

It was common practice for the Romans to link their gods with native deities, a process known as *interpretatio Romana*. This is a term derived from Tacitus, *Germania*, 43. Roman soldiers in faraway lands would worship their own gods but would also pay homage to the powerful local gods just to be sure.[4]

According to Henig, the Birrens relief was dedicated to the goddess Brigantia sometime around the mid to late Severan period, AD193–235. Since 1857, the statuette has been in the National Museum of Scotland, Edinburgh (the former National Museum of Antiquities).[5]

The Goddess Becomes Britannia

This Brigantian statue shows the ancestor goddess of the Brigantes serving a dual purpose. The warrior aspect shows her as a figure of strength who will protect the tribe, as well as a guarantor of fertility, a woman who will give them potency and prosperity. The goddess featured heavily in the everyday life of the tribe and according to Ziegler, it is possible that Cartimandua was the living symbol of the tribal goddess Brigantia. That's an interesting theory that can't be easily dismissed. If this can be proved, it's an amazing accolade.[6]

We can take this a stage further. Brigantia the ancestral goddess of the Brigantes would eventually become Britannia, the symbol of the British Empire. After the Roman conquest of the island, the Roman province was given the Latin name Britannia and the natives became Britons. The name Britannia long survived the end of Roman rule and came to be used as the embodiment of Britain.[7]

On coins issued in the 2nd century, Roman Britannia came to be personified as a beautiful, helmeted goddess armed with trident

A 50p coin still showing the image of Britannia on the reverse.

and shield, and wrapped in a white garment with her right breast exposed. On coins issued under the Emperor Hadrian, Britannia is a more regal-looking female figure usually shown seated on a rock, holding a spear, and with a spiked shield propped beside her. Sometimes she holds a standard and leans on the shield.

On another range of Roman coinage, Britannia is seated on a globe above waves depicting Britain at the edge of the then known world. Although the archetypical image of Britannia seated with a shield first appeared on Roman bronze coins of the 1st century AD it was not until the late seventeenth century that Britannia re-appeared on British coins. In 1672, during the reign of Charles II, a loosely draped, bare-headed Britannia holding up a spray of leaves in her right hand and a spear propped by her side in her left appeared on a British farthing. She is sitting on a globe on which is propped a shield, and her right leg is bare to the knee. The farthing had the value of a quarter of an old penny, and later in 1672, the image of Britannia appeared on the halfpenny. For 336 years, Britannia, the British cultural icon has featured on all modern British coinage until the major redesign in 2008.[8]

The name Britannia, symbolising Britain and British patriotism, has been adopted for a variety of purposes, including naming cars, companies, trains, planes, naval and other sea going vessels, pubs (82 recorded in 2011) and poems. *Rule Britannia* is a poem composed by James Thomas and set to music in 1740 by Thomas Arne for a royal masque. It has become perhaps the best-known patriotic song ever. The song *Rule Britannia* assumed extra significance in 1945 at the conclusion of World War Two and now, in an orchestral arrangement by Sir Malcolm Sargent, it is traditionally performed at the BBC's annual *Last Night of the Proms*.[9]

If Cartimandua was the living symbol of the tribal goddess Brigantia who is depicted as Britannia, this Celtic queen has been part of our history in a very tangible sense for two thousand years. That's some tribute, but this was no ordinary woman. She must have been one of the most powerful of her time ruling what was probably by far the most important section of Celtic-speaking Britain both before and during the Roman occupation. Historians argue about its exact borders, which must have fluctuated like any other frontier, but generally it included Lincolnshire, Yorkshire, Durham, Northumberland, Cumberland, Westmorland, Cheshire, Lancashire, Derbyshire, and part of Nottinghamshire. In some periods it also extended into the Scottish Lowlands.

2

WHO WERE THE CELTS?

Celtic roots are deep in European antiquity but when dealing with pre-history, it's never easy to find a starting point. How far back did the Celts actually go? No one can say how long ago Brigantia began as a divinity or as a political unit because just as the tribal borders are vague but extensive, so are the borders of time. Broadly speaking the period we are dealing with represents the end of the Bronze Age in Britain, but there would have been a Celtic population residing in the Brigantia area who originated from the Iron Age and the even earlier Stone Age because the proto-Celts were given the name of the materials they worked in. These proto-Celts can be traced back to beyond the beginnings of literate civilization in the lands they dominated north of the Alps, but the term Celt was applied only to people living in continental Europe. Prior to the 1st century BC and before the Roman invasion of Britain in AD43, (ignoring Julius Caesar's raid on Britain in 55-54BC), it was the materials the people used that defined the period.

The earliest history of Britain is written in stone, bone, wood and clay, as the people learnt to produce tools and weapons from chipped and flaked stone, wood and bone. Evidence of the people who lived at this time is extremely rare, but what are believed to be the earliest cave dwellings in Britain are to be found at Cresswell on the Derbyshire/Nottinghamshire border on the very edge of Brigante country. By about 40,000BC, flint was being mined and at Cresswell, tools made from flint and quartzite dating back over 30,000 years have been found. Miners dug shafts and climbed down timber ladders or ropes to the flint beds found in layers of chalk deep underground. They used picks made of deer antlers to dig out the flint that was carried to the surface in baskets to be chipped and flaked. Saws using small flint flakes like teeth glued with resin into handles of wood or bone were made from about 12,000 BC. These saws were used to cut through bone and wood. Flint was used to make knives, axes and spear heads.

These early Stone Age people were nomadic hunters and used all the parts of the animals they killed – meat for food, skins to make clothing, gut to make thread, bone to make needles and other tools, and fat to make grease and lamp fuel. Flint scrapers would be used to scrape the flesh off the hides. The people set up camps as they travelled, using natural shelters like trees and caves. A typical Mesolithic encampment from around 7600BC has been found at Star Carr in Yorkshire. It was built in a birch forest, beside a lake and boggy land alongside the River Derwent. The settlement was home to about 250 people with a territory of around 25 square kilometres. Archaeologists excavating the site found evidence that the people hunted big wild cattle called aurochs, wild boar, elk and red deer. Archaeologists found twenty-one red deer antlers and skull parts that had been bored with holes. The most likely explanation for this was to enable them to be tied onto the head, probably to have been used during religious rituals or dances. Many early gods were depicted with antlers, so wearing an antler head-dress could have been in tribute to those gods. Whether with stag antlers or the horns of a bull or ram, fertility and strength is implied and tribal warriors later invoked the strength of the horned god by fashioning helmets with horns attached. There are some artefacts that are specific to the territorial Brigantia, and which date from the Bronze Age, like a pre-Roman artefact known as the horned god found at Isurium Brigantium (Aldborough) in Brigante territory. (see later section on Cartimandua's headquarters) It is made from a copper alloy, possibly originally enamelled, and was a common representation of a local deity in pagan tribal worship.

The Great Stones

It was during these proto-Celtic years that the great stones of mystery were erected in the British Isles and other parts of Northern Europe. These megaliths could weigh as much as 26 tonnes each and were

The remains of a stone henge at Arbour Low, near Buxton.

quarried by being cracked with stakes, fire, water and hammers. Some pillars were placed on their own and may have been used to mark tribal boundaries or ceremonial routes, while others were arranged within oval ditched enclosures called henges. These seem to have been observatories, used to mark the appearance of the sun at midsummer or midwinter, or to track the movement of the stars. They were sacred places where religious rituals were carried out, and one prime example is Arbor Low, known as the Stonehenge of Derbyshire. Many more henges in Brigante territory will be mentioned throughout this book.

Because Brigantia was an area that exhibited a continuity of culture stretching back thousands of years it is no surprise to find a series of henges that have been given derivatives of the name of the goddess Brigantia. On the bleak limestone plateau of Sleight's Moor, just south of the lane from Goathland, are two distinct groups of stones known as High Bridestones and Low Bridestones. Most of the stones have now fallen. On the North Yorkshire moors there are two unconnected groups of standing stones, each known as Bride stones. Although the group south east of Chop Gate village looks like a small stone circle, the Bride Stones are actually the kerb stones of a robbed round barrow. The body of the mound has been removed leaving a double ring of slabs about 10 metres in diameter, some fallen, some still standing.[1]

Bilsdale is the most westerly of the steep-sided dales of the North York Moors. It stretches about ten miles from Clay Bank, on the Cleveland escarpment, south to Newgate Bank where the road climbs onto the tabular hills and heads for Helmsley. In addition to numerous tumuli, there is an impressive stone circle known as the Bride Stones that stand on a prominent ridge near Tripsdale. The remains of a Celtic field system are found on the moors to the west.

Another group of stones gives its name to Bride Stone Moor, north of Todmorden on the Yorkshire/Lancashire border of the Pennines. There are Bride stones at Congleton, Cheshire, that also mark a barrow or burial ground with a long chamber. All have similar legends attached that could date back to the days of human sacrifices when a young woman was slain to pacify the gods, but the modern twist is a bride who was slain for infidelity.

On the far north-eastern side of the Wirral Peninsula, Merseyside is Bidston Hill where there are two sets of rock carvings of indeterminate date. There is a 1.4-m (4½-ft) long carving of a sun goddess with outstretched arms. The head of the goddess faces the direction to where the sun sets on Midsummer's day. There is also a carving of a cat-headed Moon goddess with a moon at her feet. Although it's thought that these carvings were done by Viking settlers in the 9th century, there is evidence that they are much older and could date from the 1st century. Guy Phillips refers to these as bride carvings, and quotes the description of by S.G. Wildman, author of *The Black Horsemen*:

> … a woman is executed in dots, arms outstretched, something dangling from her right hand, no breasts but large sexual orifice, standing on a rayed sun. This I think is Brigid, and nearby is a much cruder stick woman of the same type but standing on a moon, and nearly worn away.[2]

In their classic work, *The Geology of Yorkshire*, Kendal and Wroot point out that at Rosedale, the 'dogger' iron ore underlying the

North Yorkshire Moors changes to what was formerly a very rich deposit of magnetite, the iron ore known as lodestone. If a long narrow piece is suspended on a thread to allow freedom of movement, or a fragment is floated on water, it will point to magnetic north. This formed a very early portable compass used for astrological or geomantic purposes, and there would have been many north/south alignments that were laid down by lodestones. Early man would have used lodestone to find direction, to orient their henges, the dwellings of the living, or the interments of the dead. The east/west lines could have been laid down at any period by the equinoctial sunrise or sunset, spring or autumn.

The New Stone Age Farmers and the First Factory Systems

Invaders and traders from the European mainland brought livestock and seeds, and farming spread throughout the British Isles from about 4,000BC. This marks the period known as the Neolithic or New Stone Age, but before crops could be grown, clearings had to be cut through the forests that covered huge swathes of the country. Stone was polished and ground to make axes for clearing these forests, and in areas like northern Derbyshire and Yorkshire which were later to become the territory of the Brigante tribe, stone was, and still is, plentiful. Field stone was easy to collect but stone would have been quarried, and here we find evidence of the first recognised factories where axe heads were produced in bulk at factory sites and exported the length and breadth of the British Isles.

Once the forests had been cleared, the Stone Age people became farmers, cultivating crops and tending animals. Farming changed the way people lived. Until then, every man, woman and child had been a hunter-gatherer, but now crops were grown and surplus grain could be stored. It could also be exchanged for other goods or services, allowing people to specialise as traders, craft workers or labourers. People no longer had to live as nomads. They could stay in one place, building permanent settlements. (Though there is a counter-theory that farming exhausted the soil and actually forced people to move on after a period.)

Skilled stoneworkers could turn their attention to making domestic appliances like hand mills called querns, for grinding grain into flour.

On top of a circular, flat base stone was placed a deeper stone of similar diameter anchored with a central wooden shaft. The top stone had a central hole into which the grain was poured, and a handle that enabled the stone to be turned. As it turned, the grain was ground against the bottom stone and flour spilled out from between the stones. It's very likely that small particles of stone were also ground into the flour, making it necessary to grade the flour and price it accordingly. Only the rich could afford the finest flour.

Skilled craftspeople produced baskets, jewellery and from about 4500BC pottery, then metals were discovered. The British Isles was rich in ores – rocks containing metal, but first the metal workers had to heat the mined rocks until the ore melted, a process called smelting. Copper was found in western and northern Britain, tin was found in Cornwall, and mining became an industry in these areas.

Mixing a combination of tin and copper produced bronze. Metals melted together make alloys, and bronze was the most prized. It was used to make spearheads and axes, tools and weapons that were much sharper than those made of stone and harder than those made of copper. To form these objects, the molten metal would be poured into sandstone moulds smeared with soot and grease to give a smooth finish. Bronze could be beaten into shape and used for items such as sculptures, jewellery, medical instruments and wire.

It is from this time that many grave finds have survived, especially in the graves of chieftains who were buried with personal possessions made of gold, bronze and copper. Amongst such finds are rings, tweezers, jewellery, cauldrons and harnesses for horses.

In his book *Bronze Age Metalwork in Northern England. c.1000 to 700BC*, Colin Burgess and his metallurgist colleague Dr R.F. Tylecote relates that in Northern England (presumably Brigante territory), in the middle and late Bronze Age there was a considerable time-lag compared with southern England, in the adoption of new bronze-making techniques. The northern smiths were still making tin bronze while those in the south were making lead bronze. This seems rather strange because lead was plentiful in the Pennine hills that ran through the Brigante region while tin had to be carried from south-west England, so it should have been the other way round.

To emphasise his point, Burgess states that the cairns known as The Three Men of Gragareth, near the summit of Gragareth Mountain west of Ingleborough, mark the route followed by the traders carrying tin from Cornwall to the north.[3]

Copper and bronze continued to be used but in the British Isles around 600BC smiths were extracting a new metal from the rocks and hammering out glowing bars of iron. The Iron Age had arrived. Iron was much tougher and harder than copper or bronze and was ideal for making swords, spears, axes, hammers and horseshoes. Iron was found in peat bogs and because the peat bogs provided iron and fuel, the people threw offerings into the bogs in thanksgiving to the gods. (See sections on bog finds at Llyn Cerrig Bach, and on Lindow Man) People believed that iron was magical and even today iron horseshoes are a symbol of good fortune.

The Celtic Name

At this time, there was a European-wide network of trading routes by land and sea, so it's frequently assumed that during this period Celtic-speaking groups migrated to north-western Europe, then to the British Isles. These regions would already be populated by the native people creating a shifting mosaic of autonomous tribes and states. Britain was not a united kingdom.

Although the Celts may have existed much earlier, the name Keltoi first appears in Greek texts dating to around 500 BC and means barbarian, a term used to refer to the illiterate societies on the northern fringes of the Classical World. They were certainly not illiterate, just different to the people in the Mediterranean civilizations, the Greeks, Phoenicians and Romans. When tribal warfare erupted and Rome was sacked in 390BC, the Romans called them *Galli*. When they attacked Greece and possibly sacked Delphi in 279BC, the Greeks called them *Keltoi* or *Galatae*. During the later third and second centuries BC, the Celtic lands were beginning to come under attack by the Germans and Romans, but the greatest blow to the Celts was the Roman conquest of Gaul in the 50s BC, and the conquest of the whole of Spain before the turn of the millennium.

In the early written Greek and Roman histories, scribes such as Herodotus (450BC) and Polybius (200BC) refer to ethnic groups they called Keltoi or Galli dispersed as far south as the Iberian Peninsula and as far north as the Scottish Highlands. Although this might point to a shared language or at least links in terms of linguistics and culture, it does not unite them. It just points out that they were not part of the Graeco-Roman world.

The idea of referring to these people under the collective title of Celts only came about when Renaissance scholars revived the interest in both the Graeco-Roman world and in the native cultures of lands such as Britain and France. They discovered that Gaulish, spoken by the ancient Gauls of France was related to other languages like contemporary Irish, Welsh and Scottish Gaelic. This led to the ultimate conclusion that for at least five hundred years before Rome conquered the known world, Britain, Ireland, France, Spain, southern Germany, Bohemia, Italy, the Balkans and central Turkey shared a common language, customs, art and culture.

The Celtic people may have had a universal or exclusively material culture and they may have had much in common in terms of social structure, religion and material culture, but there were also enormous variables. Beyond their related speech, the ancient Celts had no concept of a shared identity or indigenous ethnic unity. It's possible that certain tribes were nomadic, which resulted in a crossing and merging of dialects and ideas, but they were not a homogenous people and they did not inhabit a Celtic empire.

Yet there is a general agreement that a distinct Celtic language, different from that spoken by the Celtic tribes living elsewhere, was spoken in Britain from around the middle of the first millennium BC up until the arrival of the Romans in the first century AD. Linguistic researchers and historians work on the hypothesis that the Celtic languages of the British Isles, the earliest tongue of our ancestors, evolved independently from the Celtic languages of Europe.

Historians have researched the subject of the Celts extensively for years and because of the lack of evidence, all are of the same opinion, the Celts left no written records that show what their language looked like. We are told that they had little use for writing and although that seems true in Britain, we find a few exceptions in Gaul dating from the later Iron Age. This writing used Greek characters for census records of the lands that Caesar captured. The Gauls were also known to have placed letters to the dead on funeral pyres, and some funerary inscriptions have been found in southern Gaul.[4]

Undoubtedly, Rome would have required similar census records covering Britain. These would have shown the structure of a Celtic community with the privileged classes, the chief – whether king or queen – and the warrior nobility. Then there were the artisans, who not only had the ability to make tools and equipment but also much of the finery that the Celtic lords and ladies wore to express their wealth and high rank. Then came the farmers, the labourers, peasants and slaves. All would have been recorded by the Roman census.

There were also those with special skills including the bards, seers and diviners. This group probably shared the role of living repository of oral tribal history and tradition, maintaining the identity of the people. They would promote the gods and the dead, and sing praises extolling the virtues of the nobility. According to Diodorus Siculus, 'amongst them are also to be found lyric poets whom they call bards. These men sing to the accompaniment of instruments which are like lyres, and their songs may be either of praise or of obloquy.'⁵

The Druids, The Bards, and Ogham

Amongst this group were the Druid priests, although Druidism was probably limited to Gaul and the British Isles. The Druids were probably an itinerant class and would have had the freedom to move around between the various tribal groups. The word Druid is possibly derived from a mixture of languages. The Greek word *Drus* – means oak tree, which is sacred to Druidism, and *wid* from the Indo-European language root meaning to know. The name has clear links to the Gaelic word *Druidh* – meaning wise man or magician.

According to the Roman Emperor Julius Caesar, the Celtic Druids were an elite group of scholars. A Druidess would be trained in the healing arts while the position of priest, wise counsellor and judge (presumably male roles) required as much as half a lifetime of learning. Some people remained under training for twenty years. They probably wrote in Latin and Greek as well as Celtic using Latin script. Trading links with the empire were strong, so to speak and write their language was expedient, yet we are told that the Druid's vows forbade them from committing any of their knowledge to paper. They trained their memories and did not rely upon the written word, but we only have the Romans' word for that. Maybe the Celts did write down

Climbing Ashover Fabric, believed to go back into prehistory as a Druid Temple site.

their history but it was destroyed by the Romans, and anything that might have slipped through the Roman census would have long ago dissolved in the sodden mires of England.

The Roman writings are the only ones we have of the Celtic people, and the Roman writers were writing for a Roman audience. The conquering nation wanted to be entertained at the expense of the opposition There's always been them and us, the good guys and the bad guys, black and white with very little shading. So with nothing to contradict the early historians, classical writers continued in the same vein, neglecting to question their source.

We have evidence that people wrote on small portable tablets made of wood with a hollowed-out rectangle that held wax. Writing was done in the wax with a pointed metal tool called a stylus. When the message was no longer needed, the wax was heated and smoothed over and the table re-used. Writing styli were made by turning a piece of metal on a pole lathe, powered by a foot pedal that worked a long, springy wooden pole. Once the stylus was perfectly rounded, the worker took it to the forge where the end was made pointed.

People would correspond using very thin veneers of local alder, birch or oak wood with one smooth side as a writing surface. They wrote in ink made from a mixture of carbon, gum arabic and water applied with a reed pen. After writing the message, the user would fold the veneer in two to protect the message and seal it, like an early form of letter. Archaeologists have discovered writing tablets about the size of postcards and as thin as 2mm at Vindolanda (Chesterholm) a fort and civilian settlement just south of Hadrian's Wall. These writing tablets (more than 700 of them) were preserved because of the exceptional anaerobic soil, but they are fragile and need careful conservation and the use of infra-red photography before they can be read. These are now in the British Museum, but there is a museum on the site at Chesterholm showing replicas.

Cartimandua would have been a legend in her own lifetime. The bards would have honoured her in song and verse. She would have employed her own bard to compose sonnets and songs, rather like an oral diary. The bards had a winning formula weaving a patchwork of fact and fiction into the culture of the day. They were the reporters of the time who recorded everyday events with uncanny accuracy. These news carriers were entertainers and would be found in every chieftains' round house throughout the kingdom. Cartimandua's activities would be related in rhyme and rhythm; they would be the pop songs of the day, soon learnt, easily retained, enthusiastically recalled and sung by the people to ease the pain of daily labour. Yet none have survived!

In a training that lasted twelve years, the Celtic filid (fil'ee) or oracle poets were expected to learn the equivalent of a whole library of stories, grammatical lore, prosody and historical precedent. They maintained their status by virtue of this verbal dexterity, their formidable memories, and their ability to define the meanings of the unseen world. If it was not for the oral traditions that survive in legend and stories, the Celtic traditions would be lost, but even their stories that were passed on orally in ballads are woefully depleted. The Romans were determined to root out the Celtic culture and obliterate any reference to it. They succeeded in England but we still have a rich supply of Celtic, Irish yarns.

The oracle poets were masters of the spoken word, their sharp ears could catch both the surface and the metatext. They were accustomed to speaking the *dordacht*, or the dark language to each other, obscuring what they were saying from the uninitiated. The task of the oracle poets was to remember complex ancestral and traditional lore, and forgetfulness is of course the enemy of such knowledge. They needed a means of recording such details, an encoded language that would confound the ignorant, and here we encounter ogham. It's been described as the tool of the guardians of the oral Celtic wisdom.

The Ogham alphabet may be the closest we can get to what the writing of the Celts at this time may have looked like. According to Derek Hyatt, prehistory is the world before the written words and ogham is the first sound byte. He based his theory partly on the probability that the Celtic oracle poets named it after Ogma, the god of poetry and eloquence. 'The alphabet rather resembles notation for music: a visual code for sounds that become names and stories and folklore.'[6]

We do not know who invented the Ogham alphabet or how old it actually is. There are various conflicting theories as to the reason for its creation and use. It could have been a primitive counting method because the symbols bear a close resemblance to ancient tallying systems. It's highly possible that it was the Druids who designed and used Ogham as a secret language to transmit information in a form that could not be understood by the Romans.

According to Roma Ryan, in ancient Celtic belief, trees had spirits within them and were considered sacred. Trees enter the earth with their roots and the sky with their branches to find replenishment and wisdom. They are the keepers of memory and lore. The Druids gained their knowledge by interpreting the messages received from the sacred spirits that resided in the trees and they in turn recorded that wisdom by means of the secret Ogham alphabet, carved into wood.[7] Og;ham was used for divination purposes too (*see* page 170).

Ogham's use by the oracle poets to preserve complex ancestral lore is backed by a delightful story. When the god Lugh prophesied the future line of succession of the kings of Tara, the poet Cesarn found it difficult to memorise the incantation. He was aware that such an important set of prophecies needed to be secured for future generations, so he inscribed them in Ogham on four rods of yew. Each of these yew rods was twenty-four feet long (seven metres) and had eight sides making them rather unwieldy to transport or hide, but at least Cesarn ensure that the prophecy was remembered long after he was dead.

Ogham is often referred to as the Celtic Tree alphabet, not just because of the previously stated reason, but because originally each of the twenty symbols/letters corresponded to the name of a tree. Although the ancient letters were all represented by trees, trees are now only one set of criteria by which the alphabetic names are remembered. Just five trees are symbolised in the Ogham letters – beith (birch) fearn (alder), saille (willow) duir (oak) and coll (hazel). The other fifteen letters have names like gort (field), uir (earth) and straif (sulphur). The twenty Ogham symbols that were used until the 5th century, when extra letters were added, consisted of a series of lines or slashes stemming out from or crossing a vertical line called the 'druim', meaning spine. Further reminding us that they are the tree alphabet, they look rather like branches off a central stalk or stem. The system is divided into four sets of five symbols according to the point at which they cross or stem from the vertical stroke. These groups are sometimes referred to as aicmi, or tribes. The first three groups contain consonants and the fourth group contains vowels. The B tribe (B L F N S) all have their strokes to the right of the druim or stemline. The H tribe (H D T C Q) are to the left, the M tribe (M G NG STR R) are diagonal to the stem, and the A tribe or vowels (A E I O U) pass left to right across the stem. It's rather like an early form of Pitman's shorthand.

Since Ogham uses ridges or edges, early examples would have been inscribed with a knife or chisel on wood, so like the four yew rods inscribed by Cearn, haven't survived the ravages of time. But early Ogham has been found on personal objects such as brooches, knife handles and weaving swords as a mark of ownership. Traces of Ogham carvings are found on around four hundred stone inscriptions and stone monuments dotted throughout southern Ireland, Wales and England. Most of these date from between the third and sixth centuries. When translated, the majority of these Ogham scripts seem to be names of people or places and appear to have been used as boundary markers to divide territories, or were memorials to the dead.

Ogham seems to have been used as a system that was not just inscribed, but could also be signed. If each stroke corresponds to the fingers, it's possible to convey a message by signing, and there are references to foot, nose and palm Ogham. These are thought to have been transmitted by placing the fingers of the hand across the shinbone, nose or palm to indicate the shape and number of strokes. Medieval Cistercian sign language is based on Ogham. But there are no references to the Celts using Ogham in this way.

The origins of this simple runic alphabet used by the Celts were either buried by the Romans or drowned out by the dialects of the Germanic tribes who settled in England in the 5th century, after the Romans withdrew. They gave us the first British alphabet, but with no documentary sources and written material pertaining to the Celts, we must rely upon the writings of others.[8]

Greek and Roman Historians

During the Roman occupation of Britain, Latin became the official language of the state and of governance. Celtic Britons from the higher social strata would have been familiar enough with the Latin language to be able to use it when required, and understood enough words to trade. Some coins exist from before the Roman invasion with the names of Celtic leaders on them, but the ancient sources available to us give few clues as to the amount of trading that occurred.

In comparison to Greek historians, only a small proportion of the works of Roman historians have survived the hiatus in culture and learning that followed the decline of the western half of the Roman Empire. A Roman historian was first and foremost a historian of Rome, the basic aims of which were to preserve the memory of Rome itself and to transmit to future generations the exploits and characters of her famous men. This history was not just secular, it also concerned Rome's relationships with the gods who watched over her growth and prosperity as revealed in the portents by which the gods communicated with mortals, and the cult practices that were the mortals' answer to them.

The most inspiring topic for a Roman historian was Rome's phenomenal rise to dominance. Their version of conflicts was a useful adjunct to foreign policy. In repeating the story of the founding of Rome by Romulus, the historians were following the poets in glorifying Roman virtues. Cato was a pioneer in turning history into a political weapon, a trend which other politicians followed and which led to Caesar's commentaries. Roman historians like Polybius put Rome firmly at the centre of world history, In the late second century, a distinction was drawn between *annales,* in the strict sense of a chronicle of events year by year, and *historiae.* The term *historiae* was used by Sallust and Tacitus for works about their own lifetime, while *annales libri* tended to mean ancient history. Antiquarian history flourished as never before, expanded with material culled from a variety of genuine and forged documents. These sources, supplemented by frequent stereotype inventions, led writers such as Livy to wonder how various conquered races had had enough men to be slaughtered in such numbers and so often by the Romans. Some lamented this rough and shapeless mass of material.[9] The fragments of the work of early annalists include the commentaries of Julius Caesar on his Gallic and Civil Wars that tell of the expansion of Roman power. Caesar's soldiers are of course heroes and he defends his own actions according to traditional values.

Sallust became a historian about the time of Caesar's murder. Patriotically he gives Roman military glory its due but contrasts this with the moral corruption which attended the expansion of the Roman Empire. For him, vice and decadence were as important subjects as virtues and victories.

Titus Livius is the first annalistic writer whose work survives in any quantity, although the chronicles make up only thirty-five of the one hundred and forty-two books attributed to him. Livy carried his history down to 9BC, a mammoth work never to be emulated, not least because the republic became a dead subject. His great annalistic history of the Republic was the last written in Latin. Some historians who chronicled the transition from republic to monarchy maintained their independence from the new regime while writers such as Cremutius Cordus had his books burnt under Tiberius and later reproduced under Gaius in a censored edition.

Augustus, who historians typically refer to as Octavius (or Octavian) was born with the given name Gaius Octavius in 63 BC until his adoption by Julius Caesar in 44 BC. After Julius Caesar's death, he took Caesar's name and became Gaius Julius Caesar Octavianus in accordance with Roman adoption naming. After Augustus' time most emperors did not seek major new conquests. Changes in administration at home and abroad, the growth of cities, the spread of citizenship and Graeco-Roman culture was not the stuff that had interested historians in the past and did not lend itself to pathos and sensationalism. Yet this was the era of Tacitus, Rome's greatest historian, who lamented the lack of military material available to him but made up for it in other areas.

Most of the information we have on the early Britons comes from the early Roman historians Publius (or Gaius) Cornelius Tacitus and Dio Cassius Cocceianus, a Greek born in AD150. Like Tacitus, Dio was not contemporaneous with the period and had no personal interest in Britain, so neither account is full or varied enough to be a true account of the time.

Tacitus was born in 56 or 57AD around the time of the Roman conquest. He progressed through senatorial ranks under the Emperor Trajan in the middle of the first century AD and reached high office to become a provincial governor during the Flavian dynasty. He married the daughter of Julius Agricola, one of the Roman governors of Britain. Tacitus wrote mainly under the Emperor Trajan, and one of his early works was a version of a funeral panegyric about his father-in-law Agricola who died in 93AD. It was simply entitled *Agricola*. Tacitus no doubt learnt a lot about British affairs from Agricola and other old soldiers. He may also have had access to official reports or documents in Rome's imperial archives because his writings covered the period from the time of the Roman conquest of England. But he was probably writing about the conquest thirty or forty years later, so the accounts could be Agricola's version of events. His *Histories* covered the years 68 to 96AD – but only the years 68 and 69AD survive. His *Annales* covered the period 14–68 AD but many sections and even whole books are missing.

Tacitus was not a military historian and tends towards the literary. It is known that he exaggerated the foibles of leaders in order to appeal to Roman tastes. That's probably why his work has survived. He was a storyteller. Tacitus has left us two major historical works – The *Annales* on the Julio-Claudian dynasty AD14–68 and the *Historiae* which deals with the Flavian period (AD69–96). Although he gave those who were destroyed by emperors their due, he reserved his greatest admiration for those like himself and his father-in-law Agricola who survived. As a historian for the Empire, Tacitus denounces the corruption of Roman rule and puts the case for the opposition, highlighting courageous independence and resistance to the blandishments of soft Roman civilization. He agreed with the captured British leader Caratacus when he said 'If you wish to rule everyone, does it follow that everyone should accept slavery?' A feature of that slavery were 'the amenities that make vice agreeable – porticoes, baths and sumptuous banquets'.

Tacitus attributes a very revealing comment to a Roman commander rejecting a plea from a tribe to be allowed to settle in Roman territory. 'Men must obey their betters; the gods they invoked had empowered the Romans to decide what to give and what to take away, and to tolerate no judges but themselves.' Tacitus claimed that history in general was corrupted in two ways, by flattery of the present emperor and detraction of his predecessors. 'I think it a particular function of annals that virtues should not be passed over in silence, while those responsible for wrong actions and words should be threatened with disgrace in the eyes of posterity.'

Tacitus seems to have had genuine doubts about the free will of men. He believed the world was a realm of pure chance unmitigated by divine providence or by the planets. Tacitus said little of religious ceremonies, and his treatment of portents was equivocal. In his lifetime, literary fashion was turning from history to biography of the Roman Emperors. Biographers would spice up the official careers with succulent details of private lives. Tacitus' younger contemporaries created *Historia Augusta*, a collection of imperial biographies whose authorship and reliability were both disputed. The flow of Roman history dried up after Tacitus, and the next great history of Rome was written in Greek by a Roman senator Dio.[10]

Cassius Cocceianus Dio was a Roman senator born in Turkey in AD150 and the author of some eighty volumes on Roman history, from the founding of the city to the history of the Empire into the 2nd century AD. Like Tacitus, he had no personal interest in Britain. His views were just as biased. Through these writers, Celtic noblewomen scandalised Roman opinions by their alleged promiscuity. Roman women saw themselves as civilised and enlightened, but according to Dio, in sexual relations Celtic women were much more open and independent than Roman women. The Romans were told that British women frequently slept with men other than their husbands. Dio relates the story of the wife of the Caledonian chieftain Argentocoxus who, when challenged by the empress Julia Augusta about her morals, replied, 'We fulfil the demands of nature in a much better way than do you Roman women, for we consort openly with the best men, whereas you let yourself be debauched in secret by the vilest.'

The chronicles of the early Roman writers like Julius Caesar, Tacitus and Dio are contradictory and confusing. We must take into account that their writing is only one person's viewpoint. Human errors, misunderstanding and mistakes were undoubtedly made in the original manuscripts, The Medieval monks who copied the original Latin papers introduced more errors. Then subsequent male-orientated cultures interpreted the texts, which led to more problems and errors.

The 19th-Century Reinvention of the Celts

One of the most celebrated episodes in the reinvention of the Scottish Celts was the so-called discovery of the works of Ossian. Supposedly the creation of a Highland bard, the whole text was an elaborate forgery, based on Irish material and a vivid imagination, written by James MacPherson in the 1760s. He hoodwinked a whole generation, including the great historian Edward Gibbon. Iolo Morganwg, the 18th- and early 19th-century Welsh Celticist, created numerous so-called Druidic and Celtic manuscripts which convinced the academic world for a long time. They were fakes, but perhaps one day the genuine article might surface because there was certainly learning here and artistic exuberance.

Rowter Rocks was believed to be a Druid temple, reputedly remodelled between 1680 and 1710 as a Druid folly by the Reverend Thomas Eyre of Rowter Hall.

The rocky outcrop of Catcliffe Tor, like other rocky outcrops, would have acted as a distinctive landmark for users of the ancient Celtic highway known as The Portway.

During the later eighteenth and early nineteenth centuries, the 'discovery' or virtual invention of the Celts as an ethnic entity was seized on by the Romantic movement, who were fascinated by the concept of the noble savage, nature, primitivism and mysticism. The Celts were re-interpreted and even deliberately falsified to create the powerful romantic images we have today. The Romantic movement nurtured the popular concept that the Celts were flamboyant, warlike and courageous. This image has only the most tenuous links with the reality of earlier times.

3

THE TRIBAL GROUPS OF THE PRETANNIC ISLES

In Britain at the time of the Roman conquest, the Romans put the British Celts into thirty-three tribal groupings. They gave them names such as the Icini and Silures, which may have had only a vague resemblance to their original names. These tribal factions were probably temporary and unstable, fragmented or fusing according to outside influences, but each individual tribal chiefdom had its own hierarchy and chieftain.

The map shows the approximate location of the major tribes who lived in Britain at the time of the Roman Conquest of Britain in the First Century AD. The sole source for the existence and location of these tribes are Roman writers who visited Britain. Two of the best observers of the tribes were Tacitus and Ptolemy, a Greco-Roman mathematician, astronomer, astrologer and poet who wrote a description of Britain, listing the names of the many British tribes.

In the first century there were no divisions between England, Scotland and Wales but just for ease of understanding where the tribal lands lay, throughout I have referred to them. Likewise, there were no counties, the historic counties of England were established for administration purposes by the Normans. In many cases, they were based on earlier kingdoms and shires created by the Anglo Saxons, and these in turn may have been loosely based on the Celtic tribal areas. To cover the country and identify the tribal areas, I have started in the very north and worked in a sort of methodical maner south, so we begin in the Scottish Highlands.

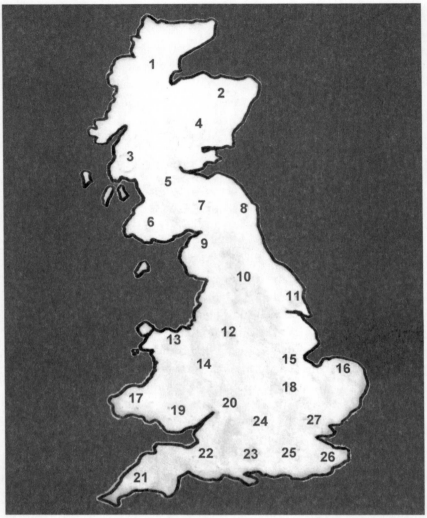

01: Caledones	10: Brigantes	19: Silures
02: Taexali	11: Parisi	20: Dubunni
03: Epidii	12: Cornovii	21: Dumnonii
04: Venicones	13: Deceangli	22: Durotriges
05: Damnonii	14: Ordovices	23: Belgae
06: Navantae	15: Corieltauvi	24: Atrebates
07: Selgovae	16: Iceni	25: Regni
08: Carvetti	17: Demetae	26: Cantiaci
09: Votadini	18: Catuvellauni	27: Trinovantes

Map of Britain showing the Celtic tribal sections. Brigantia is 10.

Caledones (1), Taexali (2), Epidii (3) Venicones (4) Dumnonii (5) Novantae (6), Selgovae (7) Carvetii (8)

The Romans used the name Caledones to describe all the tribes living in the Scottish Highlands and Islands, but among later-identified tribes were the Caereni, who lived in the far west of the Highlands; the Carnonacae and the Creones in the Western Highlands; the Vacomagi around the Cairngorns, the Smertae and Cornovii who probably lived in Caithness in the far north of Scotland, and other unknown tribes. The Anavionses, Caereni, Carnonacae, Creones, Vacomagi, Cornovii and Smertae were smaller Scottish tribes, which are not identified on the map. The Cornovii share their name with a tribe that lived in what are today the modern counties of Staffordshire, Shropshire and Cheshire, but there is no reason to think that these two groups shared any common ancestry. The Venicones (4) and Taexali (2) lived in what is today Tayside. The Epidii (3) lived in the modern region of Kintyre and probably the islands of Arran, Jura and Islay. Warriors from many of these Scottish tribes came together to resist the Romans under a leader called Calgacus at the Battle of Mons Graupius in AD84, and although the Romans won this battle, they never successfully conquered or permanently occupied the Highlands. Scotland was left to the Caledonians but the details of the battle were immortalised in AD98 when Tacitus published his biography on his father-in-law, *De vita Iulii Agricolae*. According to Tacitus, the Romans admired the Caledonii for their ability to endure cold, hunger and hardship, and described them as red-haired and large-limbed.

Further south in the low-lying and fertile parts of eastern Scotland in what today is Grampian was the territory of the Taexali and their neighbours the Venicones. Although the Roman army campaigned several times in their territories the tribal lands of Scotland were never conquered or permanently occupied and they remained independent of Rome. Around AD150 Roman influence extended up to the short-lived Antonine Wall, now visible as a bank and ditch of impressive dimensions between Glasgow and Edinburgh. This was the most northern frontier of the Roman Empire.

The Damnonii (5) lived in the central part of Scotland around what is today Glasgow and Strathclyde and for many years their territory was occupied by the Roman army. But the Romans slowly withdrew to the Solway–Tyne isthmus where they remained for the next sixty years famously building Hadrian's Wall, a more permanent structure constructed between Newcastle and Carlisle. This marked the edge of Roman civilization in Britain.

The Novantae (6) were a little-known tribe who lived in what is today south-west Scotland alongside their neighbours the Carveti (8) who lived in what is today Cumbria. A recent discovery also mentions the Anavionses, who are assumed to be part of the Novantae on their border with the Brigantes. The Roman geographer Ptolemy places the Selgovae (7) tribe in the Southern uplands of Scotland, although some scholars place their location as the upper Tweed Basin. Like their neighbour the Votadini (9) whose territory straddled the present day border between England and Scotland, the Selgovae (7) and the previous mentioned tribes were conquered in AD79–80 by the Roman army.

Votadini (9) Brigantes (10) Parisii (11)

The Votadini (9) were a very large tribe probably made up of a number of unknown tribes that lived in the south east of Scotland. Their territory started at Edinburgh and the Firth of Forth and stretched as far south as Northumberland in northern England where it bordered the land of

1 Brigantia
2 Carvetti
3 Votadini
4 Parisi
5 Corieltavi
6 Cornovii

Map of Brigantia showing neighbouring territories and their position in relation to modern cities.

the Brigantes (10). The Setanti, Lopocares, Corionototae & Tectoverdi were believed by historians to be smaller tribes who made up the vast Brigante tribe. It's not clear where the boundary between the Votadini and the Brigantes was, although it probably frequently shifted as a result of wars and as smaller tribes and communities changed allegiances. The Brigantes, like the Votadini, was a very large tribe made up of a federation of smaller tribes that covered most of Yorkshire, Cleveland, Durham, Lancashire, Cheshire and Derbyshire. It stretched from the North Sea in the east to the Irish Sea in the west, and as far north as Scotland where both the Novantae (6) and the Carvetti (8) tribes might have become part of the larger federation of the Brigantes. We know the names of some of the other smaller tribes that made up the Brigantes at the time of the Roman Conquest; they include the Setanti in Lancashire, the Lopocares, the Corionototae and the Tectoverdi around the Tyne valley. The Parisii (11) in east Yorkshire were a small, but distinctive group of people who farmed the chalk hills of the Yorkshire Wolds and for the most part remained separate from their large, powerful neighbours, the Brigantes. After the Roman Conquest they were made into their own small civitas with their capital at Petuaria (modern Brough on Humber). Although unrelated, there was a Parisii tribe in France that gave their name to the French capital Paris.

Cornovii (12, Deceangli (13), Ordovices (14), Corieltauvi (15) Iceni (16), Demetae (17), Catuvellauni (18) Silures (19)

The Cornovii (12) tribe probably lived in what are today the modern counties of Staffordshire, Shropshire and Cheshire. Given that they lay well within the boundaries of the Roman province and their civitas capital, Wroxeter, was one of the largest in Britain they are a surprisingly obscure tribe. The Cornovii share their name with a Caledonian tribe who lived in the far north of Scotland but there is no reason to think that this group shared any common ancestry with the group in Caithness. The large Corieltauvi tribe (15) combined groups of people living in what is today the East Midlands. Before about 50 to 1BC, archaeological evidence suggests two different groups or tribes lived in this region. One lived in what is today Lincolnshire, the other in what is today Northamptonshire. The Corieltauvi tribe appears to have combined the two and was only created shortly before the Roman Conquest of Britain. It offered no resistance to the Romans and was quickly turned into a civitas (an administrative district equivalent to a modern county) with its capital at the city of Leicester.

The Deceangli (13) and the Ordovices (14) lived in the mountains of what is today north and mid-Wales. However, in prehistory Wales, England and Scotland did not exist as distinctive entities in the way they have for the last 1000 years. The Deceangli (13) probably included the people who lived on the Isle of Mona (Anglesey). Known to be the stronghold of the Druid priesthood who played an important role in encouraging the recently conquered Britons to resist the Roman Conquers, the Romans targeted Mona (Anglesey) for destruction. The Ordovice (14) territory covered much of the mountains and valleys of what is today mid-Wales. They were the Southern neighbours of the Deceangli (13) and northern neighbours of the Demetae (17) and Silures (19).

The Iceni (16) tribal territory was in the modern counties of Norfolk and parts of Suffolk and Cambridgeshire. The Iceni Queen Boudica led the most successful revolt against Roman rule in the history of Roman Britain. The Demetae (17) lived in the fertile lands of Pembrokeshire and much of Carmarthenshire in southwest Wales. They were friendly towards the Romans and quickly adapted to Roman rule, unlike their more warlike and scattered neighbours in the mountains of Wales, the Silures (19) in south east Wales, the Brecon Beacons and south Welsh valleys, and the Ordovices (14). The Demetae (17) tribe was incorporated into the province of Britannia and became a civitas (an administrative unit) within the Roman province with its capital at Carmarthen (Moridundum Demetarum).

The Catuvellauni(18) were the tribe that lived in the modern counties of Hertfordshire, Bedfordshire and southern Cambridgeshire. Their territory also probably included tribes in what is today Buckinghamshire and parts of Oxfordshire. The Catuvellauni were one of the most pro-Roman tribes who very quickly and peacefully adopted Roman lifestyles and Roman rule. They became one of the first civitas in the new province, Verulamium (St Albans?) becoming one of the first and most successful cities in Roman Britain.

Dubunni (20) Dumnonii (21) Durotriges (22) Belgae (23) Atrebates (24) Regni (25), Cantiaci (26), Trinovantes (27)

The large Dubunni tribe (20) lived in the southern part of the Severn Valley and the Cotswolds, and occupied or ruled an area as far south as the Mendips. They may have been one of the first tribes to submit to the Romans, even before the Romans reached their territory. The Dumnonii tribe (21) occupied the whole of the South West peninsula and parts of Southern Somerset. They were probably a group of smaller tribes that lived across the large area of Cornwall, Devon and Somerset, and although they accepted the Roman conquest this area never fully adopted Roman ways of life.

Centred in Dorset, the Durotrige (22) were also found in southern parts of Wiltshire and Somerset and western Dorset and seem to have been a loosely knit confederation of smaller tribal groups at the time of the Roman conquest. After the conquest they were made into a civitas with their capital at Durnovaria (Dorchester) in the mid-70s. Later a second Durotrigean civitas was created, administered from Lindinis (Ilchester).

The Belgae (23) were probably not a British tribe as such because the Romans applied the name Belgae to a whole group of tribes in northwest Gaul. They probably introduced the name Belgae to an area where they administered a civitas. The civitas of the Belgae was therefore most probably an artificial creation of the Roman administration, like the neighbouring civitas of the Regni tribe, and was created at about the same time. Its administrative capital at Winchester was known as Venta Belgarum, and was an important settlement before the Roman conquest.

According to the Roman geographer Ptolemy the territory of the Belgae included Bath, which the Romans called Aquae Sulis, an as yet unidentified settlement called Ischalis, and Winchester, called by the Romans Venta Belgarum meaning town of the Belgae. It's been suggested that Ptolemy made an error since the resulting shape of the territory of the Belgae would bear little resemblance to pre-Roman tribal geography. If the civitas was actually focussed around Winchester (Venta Belgarum) this would have caused an administrative nightmare. There is still a problem, since this area seems to have been part of the kingdom of the Atrebates.

The Atrebates (24), a name that means settlers or inhabitants is another British tribe that shares a name with a tribe in pre-Roman France. They had many contacts with France, were related by marriage to people from French tribes, and Commas, a French leader from the French tribe fled to Britain during Julius Caesar's conquests of Gaul. It can't be coincidence that his name then appears as the ruler of the English Atrebates.

They were the second most powerful group in southern Britain at the time of the Roman Conquest. Their territory stretched from what is today West Sussex, Hampshire and Berkshire. They were probably a group of tribes ruled by a single dynasty, and after the Roman Conquest, their territory was divided into three separate civitates. Here we encounter the name Regni (25) but this is not a tribe known at the time of the Roman conquest. It's therefore been suggested that the Romans created this civitas (an administrative unit within a Roman province), possibly around a smaller tribal group that were part of the Atrebates (24). There were major settlements at Silchester (Calleva Atrebatum), near Reading, and Chichester comparable in size to the settlements at St Albans, Colchester and Stanwick (in Brigante territory).

From about 15BC, the Atrebates (24) seem to have established friendly relations with Rome, and it was an appeal for help from the last Atrebatic king, Verica, which provided Claudius with the pretext for the invasion on Britain in AD43 and served as one of the bases for the Roman Conquest of Britain. The ruler of the area was King Togidubnus, who is associated with the great palace at Fishbourne, outside Chichester. Because of his help to the Romans, Chichester at least remained a client Kingdom and not part of the new Roman province until Togidubnus' death in about 80AD.

The Cantiaci (26) lived in north and east Kent, and like other tribes in southeast Britain at the time of the Roman conquest, they were very open to influences from France and the Mediterranean World. After the Roman conquest the Cantiaci became a civitas, an administrative unit within a Roman province, based on their principal settlement/capital at Canterbury (Durovernum Cantiacorum).

The Trinovantes (27) are the first British tribe to be mentioned by a Roman author, appearing in Caesar's account of his invasion of 54BC. By this date they seem to have been already involved in a power struggle with the neighbouring tribes to the west who were to be forged into the kingdom of the Catuvellauni (18). The king Cunobelinus absorbed the two tribes into one larger kingdom and he or his predecessors established *Camulodunon*, known today as Colchester, as a new centre. It was Colchester that became the target for Claudius' invasion in AD43, became an administrative centre and colony within the new Roman province, then was the first of the three major civitas that Boudica destroyed in AD61.

4

THE CELTS IN LOWLAND FARMSTEADS

Modern surveys using aerial photography and searches that might indicate traces of settlement have located farms, hamlets and larger agglomerations in their thousands. Not all of these were occupied at once, but recent estimates have put the Iron Age population of Britain as high as 3 million.

The majority of the tribal inhabitants of this pastoralist Iron Age culture lived communally in lowland farmsteads that comprised one or more roundhouses inside a compound which was ringed by a ditch and low bank topped with a wooden perimeter fence. The buildings would be made of timber, wattle, daub and thatch, and would offer communal living and sleeping areas. Within the compound would be other smaller structures such as a granary, animal enclosures, haystacks and storage pits, and outside the perimeter fence would be paddocks and adjacent fields. The perimeter fence would keep livestock and children in, and scavenging and dangerous animals out, but it would have no significant defensive purpose. These farming people relied on the protective umbrella offered by the local chieftain and warrior aristocracy at the hillforts. These smaller satellite hill forts would have been fortresses where the people from the dispersed settlements fled when under attack by rival tribes.

A lowland farmstead populated by a family of freemen might include an extended family of three or four generations. The family would farm the land and work it jointly, and would pay a tax or tithe to the chieftain or to one or more of the warrior aristocracy at their local hillfort. Each farmstead would be separated from its neighbours by one or two miles, and the surrounding area would be kept clear of trees to give look-outs a clear view of the surrounding area in case of attack.

These people lived in harsh conditions, but the Iron Age farmers established a complex and sophisticated proto-feudal society based on sustainable agriculture, rearing their flocks and herds, coping with relentless menial tasks and the daily grind of hard labour.

The rivers provided fish, hens and ducks provided eggs, and geese provided an early warning system. It was unlawful to eat hares, fowl and geese, as they were reared for pleasure and amusement. Bees both wild and domesticated were kept for honey for sweetening and wax for making candles. A popular drink was honey beer, or cyser made from fermented apples sweetened with honey. Beer would have been made using grain, wine was imported and only drunk by the wealthy. According to the Roman writer Diodorus Siculus, traders would receive a slave in payment, though we don't know for what quantity.

Sheep were common, providing meat and wool. The preferred breed was small with long legs and horns and could be mistaken for goats (like the Soay breed). This breed is capable of jumping fences six feet high. Their meat is remarkably fat-free and tastes like venison, and the wool is short and was probably plucked off the animal using bone combs before being spun into yarn and woven.

Small, tough goats were also kept, but goats are capable of eating anything and might have been a disadvantage. Domestic pigs were kept and fed off waste. They could be turned out into the fields to root in the stubble and would leave good quality manure behind. They could also be left to forage in the woodland during winter when food was short and they were prolific breeders. Water vole, badgers, foxes, moles, weasels and hares were common but there were no rabbits. In the woods were red and roe deer, wolves, bears and wild boar. Dogs were used to hunt game.

Meat would have been preserved by smoking, drying in the sun, being packed with salt or put in a barrel of brine. The bones would be picked free of marrow and boiled for stock before being used to make picks, fishhooks, knives, combs and needles.

Cattle were a form or wealth that could be displayed and traded, even invested. Cattle-owning aristocracy would lend their animals to freeman farmers in return for goods and services. Ideally, two cows were kept for milk and a steer to slaughter. Despite its small stature the shorthorn would have been the animal of choice. It's a powerful animal and a pair yoked together could pull a plough and work a hectare (2.5 acres) of land or more in a couple of days.

To prepare the soil, a basic plough called an ard was pulled by a pair of oxen or cows. The ard had a shaft connected to the animal harness with a handle for the ploughman to use and a pointed end that cut a groove through the soil. Made completely of wood with simple joints, it was well suited to light or heavy soil but only produced one groove. The first plough was difficult because the soil was packed hard. To turn the soil the ard was then pulled across the field at right angles to the first groove. This second groove or second plough was easier. This double ploughing produced a criss cross pattern, then the seed was scattered by hand. It would take several months to train a team of oxen to pull a plough, but men would pull the plough themselves if no oxen were available. Land was measured by how much a team of oxen could plough in a year, and was referred to as a caracate. Metal workers may have reinforced the pointed end of the ard with iron so that it did not wear out so quickly. Horses were never used to plough; they were used to pull chariots and were ridden into battle. At the end of their lives, horses would be butchered, but they were never used as plough animals.

The poor lived on a diet mainly of vegetables as meat was expensive. Melde, or fat hen, which tastes like spinach when young, is thought to be the main green vegetable grown in Britain until the introduction of cabbage. Kale was a substitute, with wild mustard and charnock both tasting like cabbage. Brassicas such as cabbage and kale, possibly peas and the Celtic bean were nutritious and common staples, but there were no tomatoes, carrots, broccoli, cauliflower or sweetcorn. The Romans introduced asparagus, leeks, peas, and turnips.

To supplement the supply, fungi would have been available in the woods in season, and parsnips were grown as a root crop. Many wild herbs like garlic were eaten along with plants, roots and leaves from nettles. There were hedgerow finds like hazelnuts, and fruits like blackberries, elderberries and crab apples.

Flax was one of the most versatile crops. Oil can be extracted from the crushed seeds, its leaves are used for animal fodder, and linen is obtained from the stalks by a process called retting. This requires the stalks to be soaked for approximately ten days to allow bacteria to break down the vegetable matter. The plant is then crushed, soaked again and combed out over spikes to extract linen thread.

Crop rotation kept the land healthy and land was also left to rest or lie fallow every alternate year. Manure was used as fertiliser and there were specific times when the Celtic people believed that it was more effective. It had to be spread when the west wind blew, or when the moon was waning, or when it is not likely to rain.

The most commonly cultivated crops were emmer wheat, spelt wheat and hulled six-row barley, all winter-sown varieties. Emmer and spelt wheat have a particularly high protein content – 20 and 19 per cent respectively (dry weight) compared to just 8–9 per cent protein found in modern varieties. Winter sewing had a big advantage in that it spread the labour of harvesting across the year and a crop which ripened early the following year offered a supply of fresh food when supplies stored over the winter might be running low.

Agricultural techniques were simple and labour-intensive. The crops were harvested using a small iron sickle or scythe attached to a wooden stake. After harvesting, the crop would be cleaned, threshed and winnowed. The grain would then be divided into three groups, for human consumption, for seed, and for animal feed, before being stored. The grain for human consumption could be ground to make flour for bread, or could be added to soup to make a gruel. Barley would be used to brew beer. There was obviously a surplus because before the Roman invasion, corn was exported to the Empire. It's ironic that after the Roman invasion, with the influx of so many fighting soldiers in Britain, British agriculture couldn't cope.

It was essential for the people to store their grain throughout the winter or for times of shortage. Hillforts may have had a community storage centre. Surplus grain was stored in four-post granaries with a raised floor to allow air to circulate. In chalk, gravel or sandy areas, surplus grain would be stored underground in storage pits. Varying in size and shape, sometimes they were cylindrical, but mostly they tapered from top to bottom and were called bee-hive pits. The recently harvested grain would be poured straight into the excavated pit, then sealed with an airtight plug of clay. Cats were used to keep vermin at bay, and the remains of yellow-necked and house mice have been found in grain stores from the period.

Seeds, grains and plants do not normally survive over thousands of years unless they are subject to unusually favourable conditions. For example, seeds can become carbonized in a fire, which stops them from deteriorating. Other plants might be preserved in peat bogs or in other conditions where oxygen is excluded – anaerobic conditions. It is from these sources that archaeologists are able to identify the types of grain used by the early Celts.

Celtic Hillforts

As the name suggests, hillforts were strongly defended hill-top sites, protected by ditches, gates and ramparts topped by stockades. Security was necessary in times of inter-tribal conflict, and where there were no natural cliffs, the ramparts, the walls and stockades above them

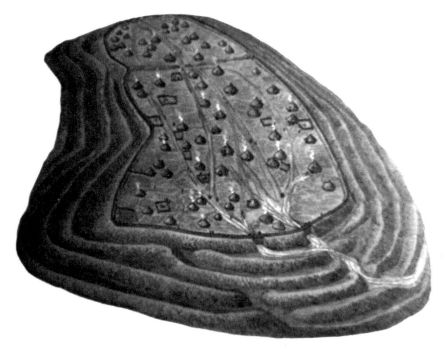

An artist's impression of a Celtic hillfort with ramparts and ditches surrounding the plateau on which can be see the roundhouses of the period.

needed to be substantial. Although the building of hillforts by the Iron Age people was believed to be for defences and a show of strength, it's quite possible that many hillforts were built more as impressive displays of prestige and community identity. The most impressive structure of the hillfort was a massive gateway overlooking the roadway leading up to the settlement. Often, at larger sites, the ramparts are much greater than would be needed as protection from raiding with the gateway a stone and timber construction with a large, four-post timber gate tower and wooden gate. The walls of the gateway contained slots for massive timber beams to keep the doors firmly closed.

Many larger hillforts were placed at the boundaries between areas with different topographies and resources. Flat areas of beaten earth would have been used during communal gatherings such as annual fairs or religious festivals. This is when social bonds were formed and reaffirmed, where diplomatic meetings sorted out agreements and alliances, marriages and general transactions were arranged.

People lived in a grander style in the Iron Age hillforts. They would have been home to the tribal leader and extended family, warrior nobles and craftsmen, clients and slaves. They would have dominated the local area and enhanced the status of the noble owner who was able to demand a great deal of local labour in tithes in order to maintain the buildings and defences.

These forts had to be situated near a fresh water supply, usually a river or its tributary. Near the river was a sullage pit where the occupants could take a wash. If you were the chieftain or a noble, slaves and those captured in battle would collect water from the river and then carry it back in wooden buckets for your use. It would be heated in a cauldron hanging over the central fire then brought to the chieftain in jugs. The latrines were next to the pig compound on the edge of the town, surrounded on two sides by wicker hurdles to give a modicum of privacy.

Within the encircling walls were large round houses with their attendant granaries, barns, stores, workshops and stables often occupying platforms scooped from the steep slopes. The tribal aristocracy would offer patronage to skilled workers who included craftsmen such as blacksmiths, bronze-workers, poets, musicians and genealogists. There would be ironmongers, carpenters, butchers, bakers, sellers of glassware and leather goods.

Archaeology can provide a ground floor plan of the roundhouse but rarely any evidence of the actual structure, but we can assume that on the cut level surface huts were constructed of turf or stone walls with internal hearths and pits.

The roof was the most complicated part of the structure. Usually six or so poles were lashed together at the apex. A ring beam was fixed 5 feet below the centre and ran all round the roof. Secondary rafters were fixed to this. These coppiced hazel purlins were attached to the rafters with wooden pegs. The roof was thatched using straw left over from the harvest, heather or river reed, which was more waterproof and durable, tied or sewn to the hazel supports.

To obtain the subtle branches of willow or hazel to make the wattle partitions, the early Britons must have developed an effective form of woodland management. The branches used in the walls and roof were grown by coppicing – a technique where the main trunk is cut and the stump or stool then sends out numerous shoots. It takes about 7 years for these branches to reach the correct length and thickness.

For the walls, the coppiced hazel branches were woven into a frame which was daubed with a 'plaster' made from a mixture of clay, straw, dung, soil, animal hair and blood. This was spread on the wall with a person working on each side to push the mixture through from both sides. When smoothed off and dry, this was a tough, waterproof wall but needed regular patching.

Wattle and daub was a versatile combination that was also used to build furnaces and bread ovens. Provided it was repaired regularly it worked well, but once the people had moved out, the elements reclaimed these natural building materials and they vanished from the landscape. Pieces of blackened daub are found at many excavation sites.

Amongst the roundhouses in a hillfort would be the women's house, the house of the warriors where the unmarried aristocratic young men of the tribe and leaders of visiting war bands slept, the guest house, the chieftain's house and a feasting hall. Food would be eaten from wooden bowls with wooden spoons and iron, wood or bone knives. Drinking cups were made of wood, metal or pottery that had been known in Britain since the 5th millennium BC.

To show wealth and power, a beaker could have been used for drinking mead. Each roundhouse would be dominated by a central fire and surrounded by wooden benches made from lengths of sturdy tree trunks used both for seating and as low tables. There was no superfluous furniture.

The tribal chieftain's round house would reflect his wealth and position. His great chamber would smell of wood smoke from the logs in the central hearth, but there would also be scented herbs in bowls, crushed grass and hay, the sweet smell of beeswax from the candles, and flowers that stood in silver jugs. There would be no trace here of the sour echo of tallow or the stink of the latrine pits at the edge of the township. Under their feet would be woven rugs with others flung across the seats, along with sumptuous cushions. It would be lit with dozens of lamps

There would be small sleeping chambers around the walls screened by woven wattle and daub 'fences'. These would be furnished with bed boxes piled high with hay or heather mattresses, softly scented and topped with linen sheets, woollen blankets and soft, beautifully cured fur covers. Possessions would be few. Mantles and cloaks hung on pegs on the wall. The tribal chieftain would have the largest of the bed-chambers which would hold such luxuries as a bronze wash basin, carved bone combs, and a bronze mirror inlaid with coloured enamels.

The great feasting hall built next to the chieftain's house was slightly larger but without the smaller rooms round the circular walls. It was a ceremonial space, kept for tribal gatherings and entertainment, where the population of the settlement would crowd in to share the evening's communal meals. Again, the décor would reflect the wealth and status of the chieftain. The room would be richly decorated with colourful woven wall hangings, elaborately carved support pillars and lit by dozens of lamps.

Personal Appearance and Clothing

Fashion did not exist but signs of increasing prosperity and more settled conditions were reflected in the dress of the nobility and social status was defined by it. Wool was the material used for most garments. Skins and fur were used, and for the wealthy linen was available along with some silk. The ruling classes wore more

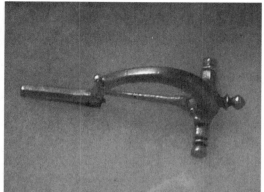

Above left: A selection
of jewellery belonging to
a woman of high rank.
(British Museum)

Above right: A Celtic pin or
brooch formed a practical
and decorative fastener.

Right: A model of a Celtic
lead miner. (Poole's Cavern,
Buxton)

elaborate and decorated clothes with gold thread and embroidery on
hems, sleeves, neck edges and panels down the front of tunics. Traces
of embroidery have recently been found in a grave at Bruton Fleming
in Yorkshire, in the heart of Brigante territory. As in every age,
the poor had neither the wealth nor leisure time to indulge in change
or novelty in their clothing.[1]

The clothes of men and women were similar and based on the
simple lines of a tunic. Later the man's shirt and woman's chemise

both derived from the tunic, but it would be many centuries before people learnt how to shape clothes. Men wore a long, loose, outer tunic with an undershirt of thinner material, *braecci*, breeches or long trousers, all based on simple tube shapes. Belts of leather or chain would hold up the braecci and go around the tunic.

The warrior nobility would wear a sword belt but belts were in general use to hold a pouch to carry personal belongings such as small trinkets and a knife, and also amulets and talismans,. Both men and women believed in spirits and omens, so both sexes carried such objects. The most ancient records of humanity indicate a belief in inanimate objects being endowed with some occult influence.

The terms talisman and amulet are not synonymous. The word talisman comes from the early Greek *telesma* meaning mystery and is an object that brings good fortune and averts danger. The chief purpose would be to bring love, cure illness, increase wealth and bring success in battle or any other undertaking. They usually consisted of carved or inscribed stone, metal, glass or wood, or they could be natural objects such as powdered toad or mandrake root to induce love, or a hyena skin to make one invulnerable. The origins of most talismans are so old that the particular purposes for which they were originally made have been lost. An amulet, from the Latin *amuletum* is solely protective against dangers, both physical and spiritual. It does not bring good fortune. The chief purpose of amulets was to protect the wearer against the evil eye, which was supposed to be possessed by certain men and women. Such a person called a *jettatore* in Italy. The amulets worn for personal protection were very varied. They might consist of a grotesque figure, the object of which was to deflect the look of the *jettatore* from the face of the wearer, or they might be some form of charm hidden in the clothing.

It is possible that the sole function of beads originally was to protect the wearer from evil influences and bring good fortune. Eye beads representing the all-seeing deity were considered particularly lucky and were commonly made from glass or onyx. Amber beads gave protection against and cures for diseases of the throat, made husbands faithful, women bear fine children, and ensured a long life. Beads of coral warded off evil and were beneficial to health. Jet beads inspired hope and courage. The list has expanded over the centuries as the faith in talismans and amulets has continued.[2]

Both men and women wore sandals strapped over the feet, or went barefoot. Bound shoes made from a single piece of tanned leather tied together around the ankle are often only detectable in graves from the metal eyelets and fasteners which survive.

Women wore a long tunic with a full-length, wrap round skirt, or a peplum (peplos), a simple tubular sleeveless dress with shoulder fastenings. The materials would be sewn together with inside seams using needles made from bone, bronze or iron. Women would also wear a belt to give their clothes shape and double as a means of carrying a pouch [3]

Both males and females wore mantles and cloaks fastened with brooches (fibulae) at the right shoulder. The brooches were sometimes made of bronze and decorated with coral, and worked like a modern safety pin with a spring and a catchplate to hold the point. It would seem that the brooch was worn with the catchplate upwards. The cloaks could be lightweight or heavy to suit the weather. To waterproof a hooded cloak, it would be oiled with lanolin or waxed with tallow.[4]

We have no evidence that the Celtic men or women wore underclothes, but the Roman and Greek women did. There is a delightful Roman mosaic showing what would appear to be the first underwear, a young lady wearing two bands of fabric resembling a bikini. The Greeks can probably be credited with introducing the breast band to flatten or minimize the bust. The Romans called the lower garment a girdle or cestus, and the breast band a stophium.[5]

Bathing and Personal Presentation

We are aware of the Roman habit of bathing as a recreational activity but the Celts bathed regularly for spiritual purposes. Bathing and washing have always had a ritual significance that had nothing to do with hygiene. The aim was not to remove dirt, but to remove the invisible stains contracted by touching the dead, by contact with childbirth, murder, persons of inferior caste, madness or disease. Water, preferably blessed beforehand, was of course the most common liquid for ablutions, but cow's urine or blood have been used. The Celts must have bathed to get clean too, as they used soap that they introduced to the Romans who previously used sand and strigils (sticks) to clean themselves.[6]

Men would usually wear their hair long and shaggy. It would be washed in lime to bleach the colour or chalky water to spike it, then combed back from the forehead. Some men used bronze razors and were clean shaven but those of high rank shaved their cheeks and chin but left a moustache that covered the whole mouth. The aristocracy favoured large moustaches. Men were said to shave their body hair, and razors and tweezers have been found in burial sites and are now regularly seen in museum collections.

Men tattooed their bodies with various patterns and pictures of all kinds of animals, using a dye made from woad, a European cruciferous plant cultivated for its leaves which yields a blue dye. Fitness was promoted and if a young man put on weight he was punished. According to Strabo,'they endeavour not to grow fat or pot-bellied, and any young man who exceeds the standard measure of the girdle is punished.'[7] He adds that a fine was imposed on those who became too obese to do up their belts.

Like their menfolk, it's possible that Celtic women also used tattooing as a means of ornamentation. Women may well have used cosmetics as Propertius wrote that the Roman women aped the painted Briton by wearing a fashionable cosmetic called Belgicus colour, perhaps an imported Celtic eye shadow or blusher. Women sometimes dyed their eyebrows black with berry juice, and may have dyed their eyelids too. The cheeks were reddened using a plant called "ruam', probably the sprigs and berries of the alder tree. It is not clear whether it was only women who reddened their cheeks, or men as well.[8]

Among the higher classes, the fingernails of both men and women were kept well-groomed. One warrior is spoken of disapprovingly in a text as having 'ragged nails'. Women sometimes dyed their nails crimson. According to an ancient Irish legend from the Celtic Iron Age, when the beautiful Deirdre laments the deaths of the sons of Uisnech, she says: 'I shall sleep no more, and I shall not crimson my nails: no joy shall ever again come upon my mind.'[9]

Numerous types of hair ornaments were used. Women braided their hair and fastened hollow golden balls at the ends of tresses. They wore hair ribbons made from thin, flexible slivers of gold, silver or bronze. Charioteers wore a golden or bronze fillet (forehead band) around their foreheads. Hair combs were made of bone or horn, with strips of metal strengthening them. Hair preparation took a great deal of time, and chiefs and kings had their own barbers.[10]

It's very likely that Cartimandua would have had her own women to tend her hair and apply her makeup. These could have been free women or slaves but such things did not interest the male writers of this period, so even if they wrote about such things, the details we have are very sparse.

5

COINAGE, MINING, ART

Ancient Celtic society was held together by a complex web of kinship ties and other obligations, such as guest friendships, a bond arising from providing hospitality to an outsider. Within this network individuals strove to attain and retain rank and prestige. Intellectual qualities and personal courage were essential commodities, and success as a warrior was a vital source of prestige, power and the material wealth to sustain them. Warrior lords were renowned for ostentatious public displays of generosity, which seem to have been essential for the maintenance of their place in the social pecking order.

Wealth and power came from the acquisition of clients, people under obligation to support and serve. Artisans making prestige goods would be reliant upon the wealth and power of the nobility for a living, and as the authority of the nobles grew they were able to control trade, agriculture and other forms of wealth generated by the community. In return the increasing number of the free poor became dependent upon them and relied upon them in times of poor harvests or other difficulties. According to Polybius 'Those amongst them being the most feared and most powerful' were those who thought to have the largest number of attendants and associates.[1]

In Iron Age Britain it is believed that land was held communally by the tribe with grazing rights for personally owned stock, or plots for arable farming allotted to individuals or families. The ownership of land was therefore not as important as the control of surplus produce and the possessions of herds. The lords would offer protection to those who did the farming in return for livestock and produce to trade.

Iron currency bars appeared during the 2nd century BC supplemented by gold 'ring money', neck torcs and arm bands of gold, silver and bronze. Then coins minted in Northern France came to Britain around 150BC and continued in circulation for the next hundred years. This would indicate that trade links were being formed across the Channel and although primarily an instrument of trade, coinage had a value for displaying power and status. Coins were used as gifts, dowry payments, ritual sacrifices and storage of wealth, The Greek geographer Strabo (*c.* 60BC–20), whose name means squint-eyed, lists the principal exports of Britain as 'grain, cattle, gold, silver, iron, hides, slaves, and dogs that are by nature suited to the purposes of the chase.'

Until four hundred years ago, nobody knew that Celtic coins existed or failed to mention it, then in 1586, details of British Celtic coins appeared with some woodcuts in *Britannia*. In 1849 the first distribution map was drawn and in 1864 *The Coins of the Ancient Britons* by John Evans was published. A century later Derek Allen wrote *The Origins of Coinage in Britain*. The major contribution to knowledge was the growth of metal detecting as a hobby in the 1990s which meant more finds and an increase in the publication of well-written, well-illustrated textbooks.

The first coins were made in Britain around 80–60 BC and were cast, not struck, in a tin-rich bronze alloy called potin. Coins made of gold followed, but one early problem with gold currency was counterfeiting. Because there was no reliable means of measuring the purity, base metals could be mixed with gold and silver.[2]

It is probable that Cassivellaunos, king of the Catuvellauni tribe who led the campaign against Caesar's invasion in 53BC ordered an issue of gold and bronze coins to fund the campaign. However, the amount seems to have been insufficient: 'They use either gold or bronze coinage or, instead of coinage, iron bars weighed out precisely.'[3]

Before Caesar left Britain in 54BC he imposed a heavy tax on the Celtic coalition tribes to be paid each year to prevent a third Roman invasion. (It obviously worked because they didn't come back again for another 100 years.) This probably prompted an increase in production of coins, but the first fifty years of British minting was highly sporadic and localized. The vast majority of Iron Age coins were produced by a technique known as striking. The process began with the production of a blank, almost certainly produced in a clay mould. Carefully weighed metal would be put into the mould in powder or nugget form then heated to form a blank disc. Many fragments of these pellet moulds have been discovered on late Iron Age sites.

To add a design to the blank, it was struck between two engraved pieces of metal known as dies. All the early coins were uninscribed and bear no distinguishing marks, then around 45BC King Commios of the Atrebatic/Regnan tribe started the practice of placing his name on them. King Addedomaros of the Trinovantian/Catuvelliaunian tribes promptly responded to this display of vanity by emblazoning his entire name across the coins and the practice quickly spread to other tribes. By the end of the millennium virtually all the tribes would have had their own mints and be striking inscribed coins. The Brigante would have been no exception, yet based on current evidence, there are no coins that can claim to be categorically Brigantian. Obviously, coins were distributed over vast areas but gluts of coinage bearing the same names and found in the same area would indicate that they were minted locally and dedicated to the local tribal leaders. However, of all the coins found in Brigante territory, including two hoards found at Lightcliffe near Halifax and Honley near Huddersfield, there are none that can claim to bear the name Cartimandua. (see page 11). It's possible that Celtic coins were melted down to appease the Romans because within a couple of years of the Roman invasion the minting of Celtic coins in Britain was completely suppressed and Roman coinage, aureus, denarii, sesterces and talents, were the only acceptable currency.[4]

Metals, Mining and Minerals

The Celts were experts in the use of timber and made remarkable wooden structures, but if not working on the land or with wood, Celtic men were likely to have been involved in the mining or shaping of metal. Bronze had been worked for 2,000 years and iron for several centuries so the Celts were not just experienced miners, they were skilled metal workers who had mastered the art of smelting.

It is possible to smelt certain metal ores by using wood-fires alone, but to make bronze and iron, the high temperatures reached in the charcoal fire are essential. Charcoal is carbonized wood produced by

Above: Early woodcut of a bole for lead smelting. The name Bolehill, still in use today comes from the early hearths, or boles, set on the hillside to take advantage of the wind.

Right: Stone was used to make a mould into which lead was poured. This mould, clearly, would have produced axe heads.

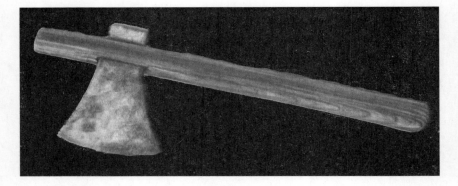

Above: The axe head
secured to a handle ready
for use.

Left: Coin showing a
craftsman at work.

slowly burning off the gases in timber. It takes 3 or 4 tons of wood
to make a ton of charcoal and is a very time-consuming business.
Depending upon the size of the mound of timber, known as a clamp,
it could take days or weeks to fire. The timber would be stacked
tightly leaving the minimum space between each piece of wood, and
the mound would be covered with a thick layer of damp leaves and
bracken, then turf and a layer of soil.

Constant vigilance was essential because as the wood burnt and
turned to charcoal, it would shrink and the clamp could collapse on
itself. If cracks appeared in the soil covering the clamp, oxygen will
get to the fire and destroy the process. Conversely if the fire inside
the clamp seemed to be dying out, small holes would be poked

into the base of the clamp to get the combustion process going. The fire would continue to burn but instead of using oxygen, it consumed the natural gases in the wood.

Most settlements of any size had at least one small roundhouse that would be used as a forge where the forgemaster/blacksmith practised the art of smelting and worked in metal, especially bronze and iron. Iron was five times the price of gold, and small iron items such as dagger blades had such high status they were given as royal gifts. But iron is relatively soft when used alone. Like copper when mixed with tin to form the alloy bronze, the Celts found that iron alloyed with a small amount of carbon produced steel, which gave a much harder cutting edge. Melting the iron produced a lump that was brittle and needed further working to render it strong enough to make tools and weapons, so it was re-heated in the charcoal furnace. When it was white hot it was hammered, then quenched in water. Carbon is absorbed into the surface of the iron during this process, which needs to be repeated several times before sufficient carbon is absorbed. Tempering iron, which hardens and toughens the metal by heating, sudden cooling and re-heating makes it more robust than bronze or other copper alloys.

Practical knowledge was necessary as different varieties of iron had different uses. Some were suitable for making tools and weapons where strength was important; some were more prone to rust; some were more suited for short lengths like hob nails, and some would be turned into knife blades that needed horn or bone handles fitting. Iron heads were mounted on wooden poles to make javelins, but these iron heads had to bend on impact so the enemy couldn't pick them up and re-use them.

Alongside making practical items like coins, horse bits, harnesses and cart fittings using the lost-wax method, the bronze smiths made beautifully crafted swords and engraved bronze mirrors. The lost wax process basically involved making a model of the desired object in wax, and has changed little since those Bronze Age artisans modelled in wax using bone or iron tools, some of which still survive. Many fragments of fired clay moulds and pieces from ceramic crucibles which were used to melt the bronze have been found. Clay would be used to cover the wax object and was built up to form a mould, then the wax had to be removed. To do this, the whole was placed in a kiln or similar, and heated to about 150°C (325°F). The clay would bake and the wax would melt and be drained off through sprues, leaving a hollow cavity. Molten metal was then poured into the shape previously occupied by the wax model, and when the metal had cooled and set, the mould would be broken open. The result would be a perfect replica of the original wax model. Ranging from life-size statues to fine jewellery, lost wax casting gave early artists and craftspeople extraordinary freedom to create beautiful objects in metals like gold, bronze, silver and platinum as well as base metal. Many of the world's most famous statues have been made using this process.

Decorative bronze mirrors from this early period are rare and uniquely British, found mainly in graves dating between 100BC and AD100. A bronze mirror would have been a powerful, almost magical object in a world where reflections could only be glimpsed in water. The bronze plate was highly polished on one side to produce a reflective surface, and on the back, the plate was engraved with a complex design providing an ideal field to display the talents of the engraver. Bronze mirrors such as those found at the site of a Roman villa at Holcombe, Devon, and at Desborough, Northamptonshire, are some of the finest examples of La Tène, or Celtic art, found in Britain.

The Romans are given credit for many things but they can't take the credit for discovering the rich natural resources that lay under the hills of western Derbyshire. The first metal-using people, the Bronze Age and Iron Age people, knew how to work metal and they would have used lead (galena). It was readily available, easily worked and, unlike iron, was resistant to corrosion. It also had the additional benefit of silver, which is often found as an impurity in lead sulphide and which was extracted through a process called 'cupellation'. The metal worker first heated the ore to get rid of the sulphur leaving an alloy of lead and silver. They melted the alloy in a clay crucible called a cupel and blew a strong blast of air across the molten metal. This process separated the silver from the lead.

The hill tribesmen of the Celtic Pennine communities mined the lead which would have been an established economic concern by the time the Romans arrived on the scene, but the mineral wealth was a powerful incentive for them to stay and set up a well-organised lead mining industry. Early lead mining deposits were worked open cast and by means of shafts and galleries. The ore was obtained with hammers and chisels and gathered with wide-mouthed oak shovels into baskets to be taken off for smelting. The dressed lead ore was measured, not by weight but by volume. It would be placed in a circular wooden dish bound by hoops, or a bronze dish before sale to the smelters. It may have been that smelting was a cottage industry carried out by the miners in their roundhouses. The silver would be used for jewellery and ornamentation. Cartimandua would undoubtedly have worn a silver circlet around her head denoting her position as chieftain of her tribe. After the arrival of the Romans, large quantities of lead were mined throughout the Peak district to make water pipes, cisterns, coffins and burial urns. (See later section on Carsington.)

There were lesser known minerals that were mined in smaller quantities and one of these was found on the east coast of Brigante territory around the area we now know as Whitby. During that time, collecting jet was done by beachcombing rather than quarrying. Whitby Jet is a product of high-pressure decomposition of wood from millions of years ago, and the jet found there is approximately 182 million years old. Jet is also found in Poland, northern Spain and Turkey, but Whitby jet is the finest. It's been used in Britain since the Neolithic period, and continued through the Bronze Age when it was used for necklace beads. During the Iron Age it went out of fashion but regained its popularity in Roman Britain when it was used in rings, hair pins, beads, bracelets, bangles and necklaces. It was considered a magical material and was frequently used in amulets and pendants because of its supposed protective qualities and ability to deflect the gaze of the evil eye.[5] Pliny the Elder suggests that 'the kindling of jet drives off snakes and relieves suffocation of the uterus. Its fumes detect attempts to simulate a disabling illness or a state of virginity.'[6]

There is no evidence that Whitby jet was actually worked in Whitby itself but just inland. There is considerable evidence that jet production was centred around Eboracum (York) and was exported throughout Britain and Europe. Dating from the 1st century AD, jet bracelets with grooves in which gold is inlaid have been found in the Rhine region. Now a good selection of early pieces can be seen in the Yorkshire Museum, including a jet cameo around 3cm, depicting the head of Medusa. In Greek mythology, Medusa was a monster, a Gorgon, generally described as a winged human female with living venomous snakes in place of hair. People who gazed at her would turn to stone.[7]

Another semi-precious mineral mined in Brigante territory was Blue John. Not only is it beautiful, it had a rarity value as it was only mined in the caves under the great Celtic hillfort of Mam Tor on the outskirts of Castleton in the Derbyshire Peak District. Blue John is a form of fluorite with bands of a purple-blue or yellowish colour. It has always been mined for its ornamental value, and was known to the Romans as *murrhine*. Pliny the Elder referred to the soft ornamental rock out of which drinking vessels were carved. He describes the mineral as having a great variety of colours, with shades of purple and white with a mixture of the two. This banded fluorite was apparently soft enough to allow one particular man of consular rank to gnaw at the edges of his cup and take a chunk out.[8]

The popularity of Blue John was such that it fetched enormous prices. It's claimed that Blue John vases were found during excavations at Pompeii, and two cups have been found among Roman grave-goods near the Turkish/Syrian border, on the former Persian-Roman trade route. Both cups, known as the Crawford Cup and the Barber Cup, are in the British Museum.

Arts and Crafts

We are told that in comparison to other nationalities, the British tribes were more ostentatious with their wealth – favouring the wearing of gold and brightly enamelled jewellery and accessories. Both men and women wore gold ornaments, and according to the Roman historian Diodorus Siculus: 'Around their wrists and arms they wear bracelets, around their necks they wear necklaces of solid gold, and huge rings they wear as well, and even corslets of gold.' The neck rings, known as torcs were made in gold, silver, iron or bronze, which might have indicated a particular rank or status. Earrings (various hoop styles) and finger rings were worn, as well as fillets (a band of metal or cloth around the crown of the head).

When making a bronze brooch the smith would use a flat-ended planishing hammer and a leather or wooden mallet. He would hammer out a thin billet of metal, repeatedly reheating the metal to keep it pliable as he shaped it into the bow of the brooch. The end of the billet would be stretched into a rod, and wound round another rod to make the complex spring which tensioned the pin when it was hooked into the catchplate, just like a modern safety pin.

Above left: A finely worked, richly coloured Blue John drinking taza, much prized by the Romans.

Above right: Early pots. (British Museum)

Below: A selection of coins. (British Museum)

Few examples are known from the early stages but by 300BC an independent insular style was flourishing. Smiths achieved spectacular results when simple motifs were repeated, inverted and arranged symmetrically using low and high relief repoussé techniques.

Articles such as decorated mirrors, torcs and brooches were made from a wide range of materials including gold, silver, bronze, iron, jet, coral, amber, baked clay and bone. Smiths embellished their wares with surface decoration, inscribing designs, modelling in the round and inserting inlays. Added colour was an innovation adopted in the first century AD by a few smiths who inlaid areas of the decoration with coloured glass, red being the most popular and widely used. Coloured glass would be fused onto the surface of copper alloys to produce enamelling. Glass beads were widely worn for decoration, protection and luck, and glass bangles were popular. In addition to the favourite red, the Celts found cobalt blue particularly appealing with yellow or white decoration.

Simple geometric elements such as chevrons, parallel lines and concentric circles decorated many objects. The artists and artisans were no doubt inspired by the classic Greek and Entruscan patterns such as the palmette, lotus bud and blossom, and acanthus tendrils. New motifs emerged; the trumpet void, a triangular shape with one side convex, the second concave and the third S shaped, showed the quality of inventiveness and technical skill achieved. Initially the background area of a tendril design, it developed a life of its own and features again and again in British art over the next 200 years. The vegetal style, or plant-derived patterning was a common mode of artistic expression across much of the Celtic world, and later developed into the distinctive La Tène style of art featuring distinctive sometimes asymmetrical patterns of twists and spirals, taking inspiration from nature. La Tène is named after an archaeological site in Switzerland.

Elaborate spiral constructions were incorporated into some fine works of Celtic art. The spiral itself can be found in its basic form as a decorative and symbolic ornament on very early times on carvings. Ancient spiral carvings almost certainly held symbolic and religious significance as they are often found at sacred sites and burial chambers. Throughout the Bronze and Iron Age, spirals were used in a simple but highly effective form to decorate many different forms of metalwork, from gold brooches to bronze sword scabbards.

The Celts used joined single spirals combined with bold, swirling curves to decorate fine metalwork. Elaborate geometric principles were developed and used to construct spiral artworks used on early religious stone slab carvings.

Human faces often distorted beyond recognition were a popular motif but not the full figure. There were however examples of anthropoid swords that had a tiny human head acting as a pommel. Animal representation was more common, particularly stylized figures like the boar that represented the god Celtic god Moccus who was equated with Mercury. Moccus was invoked as the protector of boar hunters and warriors, but boar meat was sacred and eaten mainly in ritual feasts. The flesh of the boar was often mixed with the seed corn or buried in the fields to promote fertility.[9]

A hoard found accidentally by labourers digging in a field near Hounslow, Middlesex around 1864 included both Bronze Age implements and Iron Age objects that may have been votive offerings at a shrine. This Iron Age hoard consists of three boar figurines and two other figurines that may represent dogs. The boars in particular may be the crests from sheet bronze helmets worn by cavalry men rather than free-standing figurines, but stylistically they are the earliest animal figurines found in Britain, and are now in the British Museum.[10]

Another example of the boar being used in ornamentation is evident on the Withan shield discovered in the River Witham in the vicinity of Washingborough and Fiskerton on the eastern edge of Brigante territory. Originally made of wood (now perished) and faced with decorative bronze, the shield is decorated with a long-legged wild boar. The shield also has a number of birds and animals incorporated into the design. The roundels at each end are inspired by the heads of birds, which are supported by horses with wings for ears, and birds similar to crested grebes are engraved on the central spine. The design later became known as Gaulish Shield.

The 3rd century saw the creation of British scabbard styles where sheet bronze scabbards were richly engraved with flowing scrolls. Examples from a burial at Bugthorpe in East Yorkshire show how engravers evolved strong regional identities.

The Celts developed a distinctive, highly stylized, curvilinear form of art that we now call the Celtic knot. The complex designs were probably traced out with a pair of compasses. In their art, the Celts reflected their ideas that spirit was an interconnected weaving of all things together in a tapestry of life. Nowhere is this more evident than in the art of Celtic knotwork. The triquetra, also known as the Trinity Knot is an ancient infinity symbol constructed of one continuous line interweaving around itself symbolizing no beginning or end, an eternal spiritual life. It overlies a circle that also has no beginning or end. In that respect, it resembles the Ouroboros, a circular symbol depicting a snake, or less commonly a dragon, swallowing its tail, as an emblem of wholeness or infinity.

Celtic knotwork is a symbol of the interconnection between destiny, the Three Worlds and the human soul. This belief in interconnection also shows up in the magical practices of 'taking a measure' and the tying of knots in cords and threads. There are also practices that centre around the 'cord of life' (which is the umbilical cord itself) and how it should be honoured and guarded.

From a peak of achievement in the third century BC, the art of later centuries declined in variety and originality with a limited range of reversed and repeated motifs used to make symmetrical patterns. Despite the centuries of Roman occupation, some elements survived and Celtic Art flowered again in the sixth century AD.

6

FROM WOMEN'S WORK TO LOCAL INDUSTRY

The central hole of this stone quern was filled with grain, then the top stone was ground against the bottom stone to produce flour.

From the archaeological evidence – grave-goods, etc – it seems that Celtic women were treated more as equals than in later periods. We can assume on the basis of parallels with the Classical World that they still had gender-based roles. Working in wood, metal and other such activities where sheer physical strength was necessary was probably largely a male preserve, yet for most early Celtic societies we do not have good evidence of this.

Domestic tasks were regarded as women's work, and it would have been the women's roles to produce the necessities to feed, clothe and keep their families healthy. Women were responsible for all the activities carried out in the home including grinding grain for flour, and making candles, reed lights and soap from tallow, a refined animal fat. To produce tallow, animal fat would be melted by simmering slowly for 30–60 minutes. It was then cooled and strained through a cloth. Half its volume of water was then added, brought to the boil then simmered again. After being allowed to cool undisturbed, all the impurities would be in the base of the pan and a disc of tallow would be sitting on top of the water. A wick would be inserted to make a basic, smelly candle, but for those who could afford it, the best scented candles were made from beeswax.

Soap was made in a similar way. First make your tallow, then boil wood ash (which is caustic) and water for two hours to make lye. This would be left overnight to cool, then strained through a cloth before mixing with the melted tallow. The mixture would be heated and allowed to simmer until milky, after which it would be allowed to cool and cut into blocks for use.

Cooking utensils, dishes and bowls would not be cleaned with soap but with salt, sand and/or wood ash. To keep away moths and mildew, dried wormwood, sweet gale and wild mountain thyme would be used.

Derbyshire has always been a sheep rearing area and wool was the fabric for most clothes in the late Iron Age Period. To make the wool useable, it first had to be carded and spun into thread so finding spindle whorls at many Derbyshire sites confirms that wool production took place. Spindle whorls (small fly-wheels), were used to weight spindles when spinning yarn. They were made in a variety of materials including stone, ceramic fragments, lead and fired clay. They could have been made of wood but these would not have survived.

Dyeing was considered to be a somewhat magical process, and dyers had a reputation for being herbal healers because many dyestuffs were also used in folk medicine. Dyeing was strictly a woman's craft. It was taboo to dye fabric in the presence of men. The Book of Lismore contains a passage in which St. Ciaran's mother tells him to leave the house as it is unlucky to have men in the house while dyeing cloth.

He curses and subsequently the cloth dyes unevenly. There were also rules about which days of the month or week were proper for dyeing although it does not state what days.[1]

Colour could be extracted from lichen and tree bark to produce a light and dark brown but the three main colours of the Iron Age period were blue, yellow and red. Blue came from Woad, a European cruciferous plant formerly cultivated for its leaves which yield a blue dye. This was also used for tattooing (see later section on Warrior Celts). Weld offered various yellows, chippings of Yew wood made a golden orange, and red could be extracted from the root of the madder plant. Elderberry gave a rich purple.

Once the wool had absorbed the colour it had to be fixed with a mordant that was a source of ammonia and alum, a naturally occurring mineral salt. To do this the wool was soaked in stale urine or ash, both sources of ammonia.

The wool was then ready to be woven into cloth on a loom that would be positioned just inside the doorway of the roundhouse where

Whet stones and stone whorls like these were used for weighting down wool while weaving, and were found in Old Woman's House Cave, Monsal Dale, near Bakewell. (British Museum)

the worker could benefit from the maximum light. Sewing would also be carried out here and it is not surprising that many small items like bronze needles and pins got lost in the gloom of the round house.

The loom would be made of two wooden posts 6feet high and set permanently in the ground but leaning slightly backwards and joined top and bottom with horizontal beams to form a large wooden frame. Vertical woollen thread called the warp were suspended from the top bar and weighted at the bottom with triangular-shaped stones or pottery weights, which kept the warp under tension.

About two-thirds of the way down the frame was a horizontal wooden rod called a heddle bar to which every alternate warp was attached. The heddle bar rested on wooden brackets fixed to each of the uprights. When the bar was drawn towards the weaver, it pulled open a gap between the alternative warp threads, called a shed. The weaver was then able to pass a horizontal thread called the weft from one side of the loom to the other. When the heddle bar was released, the weights on the warp pulled the alternate threads backwards, thereby opening up a new shed. The weaver then passed the weft back in the opposite direction and the whole process was repeated. To make a good quality, close textured and hard-wearing cloth, the weft had to be kept tight and the weaver used a flat board called a weaving sword which was inserted into the shed and used to hammer up the threads to keep the weft tightly woven. Using a warp-weighted loom to weave the cloth required needed great dexterity.

Colour and pattern in clothing was striking. Some of the most sophisticated looms could produce complex weaves such as herringbone, a dog-tooth check and a broken diamond pattern. The dyed wool would be richly woven to form bold checks, tartans and tweedy compositions, heavy weight for winter, light for summer. Ceramic and lead spindle whorls and loom weights, bone shuttles, antler combs and needles are often found at excavations but virtually nothing survives of the woollen textiles woven in the 1st century. Fragments are sometimes preserved on corroded iron artefacts because iron corrosion impregnates the threads before they disintegrate entirely, fixing an impression of the woven textile on the surface. Because of this, scientists have been able to reconstruct a fragment of a 2,000-year-old patterned stole, cloak or shroud found in 1978.

Curing

Clothing was also made from hides and skins that also provided the leather goods like sandals and belts, but unless they were treated immediately the skins deteriorated rapidly. First the skin was scraped free of any fat and flesh then sprinkled with salt, which was rubbed well into the skin. The salting was repeated after a few days if the first application became saturated with moisture.

The process of tanning turns a skin or hide into leather, either by soaking or rubbing with a tanning agent. A very old tanning technique was to soak the skin in a mixture of salt and alum to produce skins that were flexible and stretchable. Wood ash was used to remove the hair from the skin, which was then rubbed with the brains of the animal. It is said that every mammal has sufficient brain to use as a tanning agent to cure its own skin. (*See also* page 185.)

As with sewing fabric, the hides would be cut and sewn together using needles made with bone, bronze or iron, but seams on clothing made from leather or skins were on the outside to maintain the water-proof qualities of the hide.

Organic materials like fabric rarely survive after 2000 years in the ground except in exceptional conditions such as water-logged soil, so such artefacts from the Iron Age have virtually disappeared from the archaeological records. So the most frequent archaeological finds from earlier periods are objects such as spindle whorls and whetstones made from stone or pottery.

The Pottery Industry

Although shards of pottery are perhaps the most frequently found items in any archaeological dig, there was actually very little pottery during the Iron Age. The raw material, clay, was easily obtained but poor quality clay produced less resilient pots. The low success rate when firing or the fact that unlike wood or metal bowls and plates, they broke quite easily meant the people probably used wooden plates and bowls for eating, and articles made of clay were used for storage, preparation, cooking and transportation. Pottery had many regional styles often derived from the earlier grooved ware, and although coarse domestic wares continued in use, new forms of finer quality were introduced during the Iron Age.

Spinning, weaving, making pottery, baskets and leatherwork would have been carried out in the roundhouse, which would double as a home and workplace. These crafts would later qualify as specialist industries, not low technology domestic activities, so they were not necessarily gender-based roles at all, but may have been the responsibility of house-slaves of either sex.

Where the raw materials were easily obtained, hand-made wares were produced mainly to supply the local villages. On the continent high-quality vessels were produced on a potter's wheel from as early as the 5th century BC, but the wheel was not introduced to Britain until the end of the Iron Age, so British pots were hand made by coil or slab shaping. Without a wheel the finished article was much coarser. As techniques improved, clay was mixed with temper such as crushed flint or sand, which reduced shrinkage and cracking in the finished pot which would be left to dry out ready for firing for up to two weeks.

The most common type of Iron Age pottery is black. This was produced using a pit clamp, which is similar in principle to the charcoal clamp. A pit would be dug, then lined with hot embers, followed by two or three layers of green wood. Onto this would be placed the pots. More dry wood would be piled on top to make a mound, followed by damp straw or bracken. Finally the whole would be covered with soil. This would be left for 24 hours, making sure that the soil covering remained intact, and the reduced temperature in the damp would produce blackened pottery. This technique is notorious for its low success rate, with less than 20% of the pots coming out intact.

During the later Iron Age period, the up-draught kiln made from a framework of hazel branches covered with daub was introduced. The kiln was gently warmed, then the pots were placed in the far end of the kiln on earthen shelves situated below the chimney. For best results, the temperature was raised slowly to prevent the pots cracking, and could achieve temperatures of over 900°C, which would turn the clay into red oxidized earthen ware. There was no way of recording the temperature, but the Iron Age potters became skilful at controlling the colour of the finished article by varying the amount of oxygen in the firing. The Iron Age potters could change the colour of the finished pot from black through to grey or red, but the process would take a full day, and the kiln would then be left for a further two days to cool down.

Sadly, the coarse pottery finds at Iron Age sites in Brigante territory have been affected by the Derbyshire soil conditions, and as a result the surface is often missing and the fabric is softened. But even in tiny fragments, pottery gives the archaeologists evidence of occupation during specific periods. Coarse, heavily gritted wares are typical of the early Iron Age period with denser, thinner and better fired wares occurring in later phases. And even from a small piece of pot, it's possible to tell the size of the original piece from the curve of the shard.

During this period, a distinctive pottery known as Derbyshire Ware developed. Originally it would have been to serve a local market but developed to supply a wide circulation area including the northern Roman military garrisons. We know this because pieces have been found at many of the northern sites. Derbyshire ware doesn't appear to have been made in any specific place because new kiln sites are continually being discovered. However, Holbrook and Hazelwood near Belper were large production centres for pottery. (Denby pottery ware is still produced there.) Several kilns were found near the Derby Racecourse Playing Fields in 1967/8, manufacturing jars, bowls, flagons, beakers and mortaria.

Derbyshire Ware was orange to blue-grey in colour with abundant quartz, which created a pimply surface and made the pot extremely hard. Surface treatment included burnishing on the rim and shoulder, lattice patterns and linear rusticated decoration. The forms changed very little and the commonest vessel form was the lid-sealed jar, twenty five examples of which have been identified. Wide mouthed jars are comparatively rare.

Brigante Pottery

Mam Tor is one of the best known and most extensively excavated Celtic hillforts in Derbyshire, and pottery from these excavations has been found in large quantities. To calculate the amount of pottery found on a site, the different rims ranging from large jars to beakers are counted. Pottery finds there have been termed Brigantian ware. Dating from 1,000–800BC, this pottery is described as 'typically coarse and thick, heavy gritted and rough hand worked'.

All the grits used in Brigantian ware would have been available within a five-kilometre radius of its production, and the clay probably

Above: Pottery selection found at Little Chester. The lamp on the

Below: Lip of an early pouring vessel.

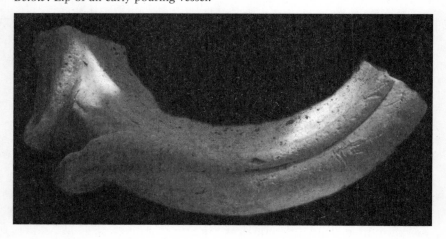

came from the banks of the River Derwent that runs through the county. Over the centuries the Derwent has had various names including the Darant and in Celtic/Roman times it was known as Deruentiu, latinised to Deruentio meaning belonging/pertaining to the forest of oak trees.

Above left: Derbyshire ware pottery selection on display at Little Chester Museum, Derby.

Above right: A clay oil lamp found at Pools Cavern, Buxton. It has no soot round the nozzle, which would indicate that it was unused and put into the grave for the deceased to use in the afterlife. (Courtesy Poole's Cavern)

A cinerary urn found at Bretton, near Eyam. (Courtesy of Western Park Museum, Sheffield)

The pottery can be divided according to eight criteria; colour, feel, hardness, fracture, frequency of inclusions, sorting of inclusions, average sizes of inclusions and petrology. This kind of analysis provides insight into the technological skills of the potters. Virtually all the pottery found at Mam Tor is coarse and poorly finished, which would indicate that it was manufactured by individual domestic groups. It doesn't appear likely that they would have produced the surplus necessary to support pottery specialists.

There is a common repertoire of vessel types. There are some bowls but it's mainly jars, many with a simple S-shaped profile.

There is evidence of a slip or slurred coating on the surface and there are traces of rough tooling and smearing. Although decoration is rare, there is some evidence of surface treatment using fingertip impressions below the rim or on the shoulder on some vessels. A few finer wares found on site could be the result of multi- phase development or a part time specialist, as again the grits used were available locally.

The most widespread more refined pottery was Samian ware, the bulk of which was from south and central Gaul. A terracotta piece could have been part of an amphora or storage jar, and would be proof that the Brigante tribe had access to luxury imports like wine and olive oil. Had the jar come up the river on a boat that had perhaps made contact with a Mediterranean vessel, or (more likely) come from a trader from France who had carried the amphora across the Channel?

Most of the Samian pottery shards found at Strutts Park, an early Roman camp at Derby, are very small, which makes it impossible to date some of them closely, but it should be noted that none have the very high gloss which is characteristic of the Neronian period, and where dating is certain it is Claudian. That means that none are likely to be later than 60AD.

The Samian ware found at Melandra, the Derbyshire Roman fort at Glossop, constructed *c.* AD80, is extremely badly preserved. The surface of both plain and decorated ware has largely disappeared making precise identification difficult, and the fabric has been altered in colour by soil action. The alkaline soil at Melandra has not only destroyed the surface on pottery, it has had a devastating effect on anything in bone, iron, or bronze. Objects in these materials survived only as stains in the soil.

7

DEATH, REINCARNATION
AND THE DIVINE

At the shrine of Coventina, the local goddess of springs in Carrawburgh, Northumberland, she is depicted in triadic form. (Courtesy Museum of Antiquaries, the University of Newcastle upon Tyne)

It is difficult to envisage Cartimandua's early years because, as we know, there is no mention of her until the time of the Roman invasion. But because the Celts were known for their outstanding riding ability she no doubt learnt to ride as soon as she could walk. She probably learnt to throw a spear, use a catapult and wield a small razor-sharp sword. It's doubtful that she would have been excluded from learning such things on the grounds of gender, particularly if it was known that she would one day be a tribal leader.

She may have possessed particular skills or knowledge that had passed to her along family lines in an almost instinctive manner. If Cartimandua had been destined to rule from birth she would have been trained in the ways of diplomacy and government. She may have been born into a long line of distinguished royal leaders, in which case she would have been taught by the Druids. According to Caesar, Druids were priests, wise counsellors and judges, Cartimandua's destiny could have been decided by the Druids who would consult the gods and look for signs. Those pre-historic people were influenced by pagan beliefs and a profound suspicion of the outside world.

The Druids believed in spirits, omens, and reincarnation. The word reincarnation derives from Latin, literally meaning, entering the flesh again. An alternate term is transmigration implying migration from one life/body to another. Reincarnation is the philosophical or religious concept that after each biological death, some aspect of a living being starts a new life in a different physical body or form. It's the doctrine of cyclic existence, a belief that some aspect of every human being continues to exist after death. This aspect may be the soul or mind or consciousness or something transcendent which is reborn in a cycle of existence.[1] The origins of the notion of reincarnation are obscure. An early Greek thinker known to have considered rebirth is Pherecydes of Syros. The dates of his life cannot be fixed exactly, but his birth is usually put around 570BC.[2] Reincarnation's most famous exponent is Pythagoras (570–495BC). He may have been Pherecydes' pupil. Authorities have not agreed on how the notion arose in Greece, but another Greek term sometimes used synonymously with reincarnation is palingenesis, meaning being born again.

We know that the Celtic Druids taught a doctrine of reincarnation, as did other early religions. The ideas associated with reincarnation may have arisen independently in different regions, or they might have spread as a result of cultural contact. Diodorus Siculus thought the Druids might have been influenced by the teachings of Pythagoras. In the 1st century BC the Greek scholar Alexander Polyhistor (Alexander of Miletus) wrote: 'The Pythagorean doctrine prevails among the (Celtic) Gauls' teaching that the souls of men are immortal, and that after a fixed number of years they will enter into another body.'[3]

Julius Caesar recorded that the Druids of Gaul, Britain and Ireland had metempsychosis as one of their core doctrines

> The principal point of their doctrine is that the soul does not die and that after death it passes from one body into another ... the main object of all education is, in their opinion, to imbue their scholars with a firm belief in the indestructibility of the human soul, which, according to their belief, merely passes at death from one tenement to another; for by such doctrine alone, they say, which robs death of all its terrors, can the highest form of human courage be developed.[4]

The Druids were philosophers, and other classical historians echoed Caesar's observation. The Celts apparently had no concept of heaven or hell as a reward or punishment for their conduct during life. There was no time factor involved. The soul could stay in the Otherworld for a number of years before entering another body. The life into which a person was reborn appeared to be tied to fate and the will of the gods. The Celts believed that reincarnation was the gift of the gods. Rebirth was thought to be automatic. A spirit could return in the same family, particularly exceptional people like tribal leaders. This could be the case with Cartimandua.

So strong was this belief that there is evidence that pre-Christian Celts thought that debts, honour, and obligations did not vanish at the end of a lifetime. One could be dishonoured but redeemed through actions and payments in the next life. According to Valerius Maximus, even the payment of debts could be deferred to the next incarnation: 'They lent sums of money to each other which are repayable in the next world, so firmly are they convinced that the souls of men are immortal.' Contracts were sometimes composed with provision for payment in future lives, and there was full expectation of payment, because such debts would have reflected on the honour of oneself and one's family. The obligation to repay them went beyond lives and lifetimes.

The belief that a family member was the reincarnation of a forebear seems to have been a strong Celtic belief that would strengthen family ties. Any grandchild could be the grandfather reborn, and they would pay back the neighbour's grandchildren at the completion of a contract's term of agreement. But as we all know, family ties do not always guarantee loyalty or repayments of debts of honour so most contracts were also prudently sealed with a material forfeiture in the event of failure to fulfil them.⁵

Such beliefs have not disappeared. Adherents of Tibetan Buddhism believe the Dalai Lama, the religion's highest spiritual authority, has been reincarnated in an unbroken line for centuries. He is believed to have the power to choose the body into which he is reincarnated, meaning that the current Dalai Lama, the 14th, is a reincarnation of the 13th. Tibetan Buddhists believe that not only is each Dalai Lama the reincarnation of his predecessors, but they are all the manifestations of Avalokiteshvara, or Chenrezi, the patron saint of Tibet and Bodhisattva of Compassion. The search for the reborn Dalai Lama is the responsibility of the High Lamas of the Gelgupa tradition and the Tibetan government.

Skeptic Carl Segan asked His Holiness, the 14th Dalai Lama, what he would do if reincarnation, which is a fundamental tenet of his religion, was definitively disproved by science. The Dalai Lama answered, 'If science can disprove reincarnation, Tibetan Buddhism would abandon reincarnation ... but it's going to be mighty hard to disprove reincarnation.'⁶

Was Cartimandua the Reincarnation of a Former Chief?

What if the Celts had a similar system to that followed by the Tibetan Buddhists? The Brigante tribe could have had an unbroken line of leaders, each being the reincarnation of the previous tribal chief going back in an uninterrupted lineage for generations. That could have been why Cartimandua was chosen to lead her people, not because she had been born into a line of 'royal' leaders but because she had another connection just as recognisable. She was the reincarnation of their former leader. If so, the Druids must have had strong reason to believe that she was the same soul reborn in a different, female body. The Druids would have consulted the oracle when deciding on a new leader. (*See* page 12).

Some believe that people that tribes such as the Brigante used a system of divination akin to lecanomancy. A bowl of water was placed by a deceased person's head and three days later, the Druids and the deceased's family would watch the bowl for ripples that would be interpreted to determine the whereabouts of the deceased's soul. This would lead them to the reincarnated body.[7]

The Celts also believed that certain knowledge and awareness came from the soul through heightened spiritual experiences, so Cartimandua may have appeared to have special abilities, such as psychic vision and healing powers. She may also have had one or more physical blemishes, like a prominent birthmark, moles or some other form of identity that linked her to her predecessor.

When looking for evidence of reincarnation, many people have believed that provide evidence of a previous incarnation. Throughout the ages, pretenders to various royal households and kingdoms used birthmarks or 'royal marks' to bolster the claim that they had royal blood. Some believed birthmarks from past life trauma appeared at the location of injuries from a previous incarnation. For example, some birthmarks or birth defects may show up at the same place as a fatal wound in a previous life.[8] There is also, even today, support for the theory that the power of the mind can leave physical marks on the body, so past life traumas may appear in the new life as unexpected scars.

Moles can occur on our bodies from birth and stay with us till our death, although they can also appear at any time in our lives. The Celts (and many people since) believed that moles happened because of the planetary influences during the time the foetus was forming in the mother's womb, and some planets influenced the foetus more than others. The planets regulated the colour, shape and size of the mole, and these factors and their placements represented the destiny of the person. Moles in red, honey or green were generally believed to bring good fortune. Black moles and moles in zigzag shapes represented bad outcomes. Long moles gave good results. Square shaped moles gave bad results in the beginning but produced good results in the end, and moles in the form of a triangle produced mixed results. These were all modified by their placement on the body. Moles were also grouped with other birthmarks that the Celts believed had special significance to produce a fuller account.

Evidence from the Grave

The Classical historians comment on transference of souls, rebirth and life after death, but Caesar also notes that special attention was paid to a good send-off:

> Funerals were splendid and costly. Everything the dead man is thought to have been fond of is put on the funeral pyre, including even animals. Not long ago, slaves and dependants known to have been their master's favourites were buried with them at the end of the funeral.[9]

Strange rituals were sometimes demonstrably carried out and this observation by Caesar, distressing as it might seem to us, can be endorsed archaeologically. Evidence has been found in archaeological digs from the first century and before. The Celts regarded death as merely a pause in a long life, as a bridge between one life and another and a person needed material things to help them on their way. The important items buried naturally mirrored a person's activities and needs in their life. Their afterlife was considered to be one where earthly status was recognised, something that could be prolonged to eternity. The burial of grave goods was not just a ritual, it was a positive approach to death. The burial of pots, toiletries and personal items indicated a belief in a tangible afterlife. Being well equipped for the Otherworld was of prime importance.

Hobnail boots were placed in about half the graves in the obvious belief that they would be needed for the journey. In some areas there are examples of infant burials in which shoes that were far too big for them, were placed beside the little bodies in the assumption that they would grow into them. Pipe clay 'Venus' figurines have been found at Verulamium, York and elsewhere signifying a special attempt to protect the dead in the afterlife.[10] While such pipeclay figurines are commonly found across Gaul, in Britain they are found specifically in the graves of high status infants.

The burials of the higher stratum of Celtic society were characterised by enclosure of the body in a plank-lined chamber, often with a four-wheeled chariot or cart. Chariot burials were not just reserved for men. A woman was interred with a dismantled vehicle at Wetwang Slack, East Yorkshire. This area between York and Bridlington would have been in Brigante territory, and has yielded literally thousands of Iron Age burials. The grave pit of this chariot burial would probably have been covered by a mound built from the spoil of the surrounding ditch to form a barrow or tumulus. Although some still survive, many of these mounds have been ploughed flat over the centuries, thus hiding their treasures.

This belief in the continuity of life could explain the many acts of bravery in battle for which the ancient Britons were famous. Soldiers would be buried with their swords, halberds, spear heads, quivers, bows and arrows. The burial of a soldier at Ebberston, Yorkshire, is a typical example. Ebberston is a small town due south of Whitby in the heart of Brigantine territory. It is recorded that this man was buried with his Hallstatt C sword, deliberately and evidently ritually broken into four pieces.

The more important warriors would often be buried with their complete battle equipment and other items considered appropriate to this world and the next. In death, they were equipped with the things necessary for the pleasures of fighting, feasting and indulging in other pastimes. They believed in some sort of Valhalla that in Norse mythology is the home of fallen warriors. Valhalla is a majestic place roofed with shields, and under the leadership of the god Odin. The slain warriors feast on the flesh of a boar slaughtered daily and made whole again each evening. The boar was of special significance as boar meat was sacred, and eaten only in ritual feasts. As mentioned earlier, the boar also represented the Celtic god Moccus invoked as the protector of boar hunters and warriors.[11]

The wealth of the grave is indicated not only by the accompanying weapons, but by jewellery and rich textiles. Burial rites differed from region to region and person to person. One interesting find revealed that spears had been hurled into a number of graves during the burial, often piercing the body. Pathologists could distinguish these spear thrusts from the ones that had apparently killed these men before burial.[12]

Life expectancy was very low. Provided they survived childhood most males died in their twenties, thirties or early forties. Women were more likely to die in their late teens or twenties largely due to the hazards of childbirth.

The Otherworld

If death is merely a pause between lives a bridge is needed to cross from one to another, and/or a safe haven to wait until we live again. According to the Celts, this was supplied by a place called the Otherworld (*orbis alias*). They believed that the soul must revisit the three sods (soils) before passing through the doorway to the Otherworld: the place of birth, the place of baptism and the 'sod of death'.

The Celts believed that everything important in the world came in threes; three stages of life, past, present and future, three elements, and three domains, land, sea and sky. The realm of the land was the centre of the three worlds and joined the realms of sea and sky at the shore and horizon. The realm of the land was the realm of the present where humankind lived out their countless lives alongside the spirits of nature and the gods and goddesses who were responsible for fertility of the land. The realm of the sea represented the Otherworld and was the realm of the ancestors. This was where

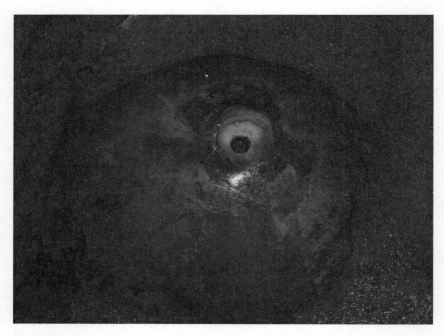

Is this the eye of a menacing subterranean creature breaking through the potholed floor of Poole's Cavern? It has been formed by nature and the constant drip of water that in neighbouring caves form stalactites and stalagmites.

the cycle of life, death and rebirth was granted. The realm of the sky was where the deities were believed to dwell and represented the future. This was the realm of the spiritual where the realization of goals and dreams existed.

Folklore depicts the Otherworld as existing over the western sea, a realm layered like a transparency over the world of the living. It's debateable whether there is one layer or three layers creating the Elemental and Faerie Realm, the Realm of Deities, and the land of the dead. This Otherworld is invisible to our sight most of the time, but at certain times, such at Samhain, the Celts believed that the veil between the worlds was lifted.

The realm of the sea represented the Otherworld and was the realm of the ancestors, or alternatively the Otherworld could be underground. In the depth of the underworld anything could happen. It was a place of change and unpredictability, presided over by Arawn, the Lord of the Underworld. This horned and glowing figure rode a wild, white horse. White hounds followed him and he blew a great horn summoning all who would follow him.

By entering into a trance, a shaman could enter that Otherworld, make contact with the ancestors and consult them on a wide variety of problems and issues. The ancestors were the keepers of the knowledge of the old ways. They had lived and learned and crossed the veil, and they had much wisdom and guidance to share. The Celts considered that the communication between the present and the past was vital. Being able to bridge the two worlds, the world of the everyday and the world of the ancestors, was an essential skill possessed by the wise man.[13]

The Otherworld could be perceived in different ways. It could be a happy place, free from care, disease, old age and ugliness with an abundance of music, magic and birdsong dominating the scene. On the other hand, here could have been unpleasant elements, hazards and fighting in a world presided over by the god Donn, the dark one, the god of the dead. No one was sure because information on the Otherworld and the afterlife was, as always, elusive. What little there was, is both confused and confusing but has survived in folklore to today. There are tales of various mythical heroes who visit the Otherworld either through chance or after being invited by one of its residents. Natural features like springs and rivers were seen as entrances, and the Otherworld could also be entered via ancient burial mounds or caves, or by going underwater or across the western sea.[14] Sometimes, the Otherworld intrudes into this one; signalled by phenomena such as magic mist, sudden changes in the weather, or the appearance of divine beings or unusual animals.[15]

The sombre other world reflects a dark aspect of the afterlife, and it is this lugubrious image that dominates the Festival of Samhain when the spirits of the dead move freely among the living. For the Celts, the barriers between the worlds were ill-defined and apparently disappeared entirely at the great festival of Samhain. Like our modern Hallowe'en, Samhain marked the passing of summer, the end of the harvest season and the beginning of winter or the darker half of the year. Traditionally, it is celebrated from 31 October to 1 November, as the Celtic day began and ended at sunset. At this junction between summer and winter, the barriers between the natural and supernatural world were temporarily broken down and the normal laws of creation were temporarily thrown into chaos. The souls of the dead were thought to revisit their homes seeking hospitality, and the souls of dead kin were beckoned to attend feasts held in their honour where a place was set at the table for them.

Transmigration from Human to Animal

The Celts believed that spirits didn't always necessarily enter the Otherworld, they could exist in this world by inhabiting other living things. This belief in spiritual migration and transmigration takes many forms. One of these is a belief in the transmigration of the soul from human to animal form. Romanian historian of religion Mircea Eliade (1907–1986) observed that beliefs regarding transformation into animals are widespread. An animal counterpart to a person is corporeal, can understand human speech, and shares the same soul. It also shares many characteristics, like birthmarks and blemishes from the person's former life.[16]

In their animal forms the ones who had been transformed were able to learn something about the natural world not easily accessible to humans. Their perspective is broadened to a more intimate knowledge of the wild, natural world which they are then able to impart to the human family.

Shape-Shifting Deities

Amongst Iron Age finds are stone carvings and statuettes of figures sitting cross-legged and showing that their feet are hooves. One particular small stone figure wears a torc and shows a boar figure on his chest. It's been suggested that these figures represent shape-shifting deities, the latter representing a deity capable of shifting between human and boar form. It was believed that the shapeshifting gods and goddesses moved between the realms of the Otherworld and this world, bridging the two for the earthborn.[17]

Some gods and goddesses were able to adopt various animal guises at will. Aine, summer goddess of love, light and fertility, took the form of Lair Derg, a red mare that no one could outrun. In her horse form she offered guidance to the people through her ability to access the heights, and to express freedom, strength, and endurance. Epona, the Celtic/Romano horse goddess is even now commemorated in white horses etched on chalk hills in England. The Celtic tribes of the Peak District worshipped Epona who is still retained as guardian of the High Peak moorlands, and is said to haunt the mountain edges above Hayfield.

Artio, Celtic goddess of wildlife, transformation and abundance, sometimes appeared as a bear who itself was associated with transformation. In this form she journeyed in the darkness and emerged to the light returning with new wisdom and insights to share with the world.

The Morrigan, Celtic goddess of war, sovereignty and fertility was a shapeshifter in the realm of life and death. In her raven/crow form she was seen as the harbinger of death to the warrior who saw her. She also appeared as a cow, a wolf and an eel.

The flower goddess, Bloedwedd was created by the magician Gwydion from flowers. After her betrayal and murder of her husband Llew, who transformed into an eagle, Gwydion changed Bloedwedd into an owl. She remained in this form as a Goddess of Life and Death and keeper of deep wisdom. Shape-shifting Hecate, the Greek goddess of crossroads and the wilderness, was believed to take the form of a wolf.

After Gwydion helped his brother, Gilfaethwy commit rape, as punishment, King Math changed them both into three different animals for one year each. In these forms they learned the ways of the animals and gained humility and greater understanding of their place in the natural world.

Birds play an important role in Celtic mythology. Throughout time birds have been symbols of birth, death, healing and as messengers between the mundane world and the Otherworld. Fand the Celtic sea goddess regularly took the shape of a sea bird. Together with her sister, Li Ban, they travelled with their flock of enchanted birds. Each pair of birds was joined by a silver chain, but Fand and Li Ban were linked by a golden chain. Even today, many coats of arms depict stags, rams and other animals wearing golden chains, which symbolise their ability to shape shift between animal and god. Swans appear frequently in Celtic mythology, often connected with a goddess. They are associated with love, purity, the soul, and music. Like Fand in seabird form, swans linked with a goddess can always be recognised by the gold or silver chain hanging around their necks. Caer Ibormeith, Celtic Goddess of Dreams and Prophecy, was a shapeshifting goddess who spent one year as a beautiful woman and then the next year as a swan. Accompanied by one hundred and fifty swans, she underwent this transformation every year on Samhain, a liminal time when swans were seen as guides to the Otherworld.

Some accounts of Boann, Celtic goddess of inspiration and creativity, say she was transformed into a salmon after the water sprang up from the sacred well which created the River Boyne. It was believed that the salmon possessed all the wisdom of the worlds.

Etain, the shining one, or sun goddess, was transformed by her husband's jealous first wife into a butterfly, a worldwide symbol of transformation. After thousands of years she fell into a glass of wine, was consumed by a lady and was reborn again as the beautiful Etain. She later transformed into a swan, symbol of love and purity, and flew off with her original lover.[18]

The great Welsh poet Taliesen began life as Gwion Bach but to escape the wrath of the goddess Cerridwen, whose brew of wisdom he had accidentally tasted, he transformed himself into various animal shapes – a hare, a fish, then a bird. In an attempt to catch him, Cerridwen also transforms herself. When Gwion was a hare, Cerridwen became a greyhound. When he was a fish she became an otter, and when he was a bird she became a falcon. Each time he managed to escape and finally he became a grain of wheat. Cerridwen transformed herself into a hen and ate the grain of wheat. Supposedly this grain of wheat germinated in a rather mystifying way. Cerridwen became pregnant and gave birth to Taliesin.

There's the Irish story of Tuan Mac Cairill, the great-grandson of Partholon who was the leader of one of the five invading races of Ireland. Tuan was the lone survivor of this race and lived out many lives on the island as a stag, a boar, a hawk and finally as a salmon. It was as a salmon that he was caught by a fisherman and served to the wife of Cairill. The lady became pregnant by eating the salmon, and gave birth to Tuan.

There is a striking similarity in these two myths, as in both cases, the men's second lives as humans were brought about by women unknowingly consuming them and becoming pregnant. Baffling and impossible as this is to us, this theme is echoed throughout Celtic myths. I was stumped for an answer until I realised that the Celts believed that everything was possessed of a spirit that could be reborn, even a grain of wheat. Taking care not to partake of certain foods or plants for fear of becoming pregnant must have given many Celtic women eating disorders.

The Horned Gods and Goddesses

Elen of the Ways, in her most ancient guise as the horned goddess, shifted form into that of a reindeer. Flidais, earth goddess and lady of the forest was another shapeshifting goddess who was associated with and could become a deer or a cow. She might also be a later incarnation of the paleolithic reindeer goddess. In ancient times in Northern Europe the reindeer, like the cow, was the source of food, shelter, and clothing, and held the key to prosperity for our Northern European ancestors. The female principles embodied in the horned goddesses was balanced by the horned god, a potent virility symbol associated with the sun, hunting, forests and animals. Dagda the bull god had a magic bowl which was never empty no matter how much was consumed from it. The Celtic version was known as Esus – god of the chase. Hunting deities were venerated among the Celts, and like Diana and Artemis in classic mythology, they often seem to have had an ambivalent role as protector both of the hunter and the prey. In mythology the hunting of a sacred stag often leads the hunters into

Naked horned warrior god of the Celts with spear and shield, Maryport Cumbria. (Courtesy trustees of Senhouse Roman Museum)

the Otherworld. The Greek author Arrian, writing in the 2nd century, said that the Celts never went hunting without the gods' blessing and that they made payment of domestic animals to the supernatural powers in reparation for their theft of wild creatures from the landscape. Hunting itself may have been perceived as a symbolic, as well as a practical activity in which the spilling of blood led not only to the death of the beast but also to the earth's nourishment and replenishment.[19]

An artefact of the horned god was found at Isurium Brigantium (Aldborough) in Brigante territory. It is made from a copper alloy, possibly originally colourfully enamelled. The horned god like the triple goddess was a common representation of a local deity in pagan tribal worship. Whether with stag antlers or the horns of a bull or ram, fertility and strength is implied. It was only in the Middle Ages that the horned deities became associated with the devil.

Polytheism

The Celts were beholden to their gods, the spirits and the Druid priests. Like their Greek and Roman counterparts, the Celts were polytheistic, they believed in a multiplicity of deities, spirits and supernatural forces that could be appeased by the correct propitiation rites and sacrifices at the appropriate time and place. Perhaps because of the diverse histories and origins of the Celtic peoples there were no definite universally worshipped Celtic deities. Celtic gods and goddesses seem to have fluctuated according to location and tribe. Caesar speaks about the Celtic deities as if they were identical to those of Rome, and gave them Roman names, but research has revealed that the Celtic pantheon had over 1,200 named deities with many regional variations and additions. It's impossible to give a comprehensive list, but we can be selective.

Some Celtic tribes could have adopted and absorbed the gods from neighbouring tribes with whom they fought or traded or intermarried. This meant that alongside their main gods, tribes would incorporate the local gods of other tribes, then after the Romans arrived, there would be an interaction between the more formal Roman pantheon and the shadowy, multifunctional, localised gods of the Celts. Added to this hybrid, religious culture were any deities belonging to the auxiliaries who would worship their own gods, so the union of so many gods and goddesses is as fascinating as it is full of problems of interpretation. But occasionally there is a breakthrough.

Binchester is one of thirteen permanent forts on Hadrian's Wall near Bishop Auckland, County Durham on the edge of Brigante territory. At the vicus (civilian settlement) outside Benwell (Condercum) Fort, there is a small temple with an altar stone dedicated to Antenociticus, and as this is the only site in Britain where the god Antenociticus is mentioned it would signify that he was a local deity. However, Benwell was occupied by an auxiliary regiment, so the god may have been transferred there as their patron deity to be worshipped as a source of inspiration and intercession in military matters. It was on this temple site in 2013 where a sandstone head 20 cm high was found and as a similar head was found in 1862 with an inscription identifying it as Antenociticus. This second find would also appear to be the god. Parts of the lower leg and forearm of the statue were discovered indicating that this was a life-sized statue of the god that once stood in the temple.[20]

8

ANIMISM AND LEY LINES

According to anthropologists and archaeologists as long as there have been humans there has been religion, yet religion is hard to define. It's been called the glue that holds together society, but it's also the biggest cause for war. Anthropologists believed that religion evolved from magic, yet magic is even more difficult to define than religion. A loose definition would be a social paradigm encompassing beliefs and practices which enable people individually and collectively to make some sense of life and death. As to why or how religion originated and how it developed in pre-history is pure guesswork gleaned from the earliest burials that show evidence of ritual association with the dead continuing in another life. The Celts left no record but the Classic writers offer fascinating, sometimes wildly

Eldon Hole, a sinister slit in the earth that the Celts would have perceived as an entry to the Otherworld.

exaggerated glimpses of Celtic religion, their beliefs, their gods, burial rites, symbolism, taboos and sacrifices. To modern observers, Celtic religion seems deeply exotic and alien, its mystery compounded by blood-curdling tales of human sacrifices and the shadowy figures of the Druid priests, the authority figures who constrained the people to accept what they were told, but seeing the past as the Pagan Celts would have done is impossible – we have our own set of beliefs, biases and baggage.

The word pagan came to be used synonymously with non-Christian, but not in a disparaging way. The word comes from the Latin 'paganus', which originally meant a country dweller or rustic. As Christianity spread through the Roman Empire, rather than embracing the new belief of Christianity, people in the rural communities tended to hold on to the traditional earth- and season-centred spiritual practices that had made up the old religion. They believed in living in harmony with the earth, observing and celebrating its cycles, and honouring the changes in the seasons.

According to Classical sources, the ancient Celts were great believers in animism, the belief in the spirit of nature and the physical environment. Animism as practised by the early Celts is considered to be the basic form of primitive religion. They believed that spirit didn't just exist in gods and humans, spirits and divine beings could manifest in every aspect of the world around them – plants, trees, wells, caves, stones, rivers, ponds, and fields. The list would appear to be unlimited. This migration of spirit between worlds, places, animals and people was a reflection of the communal nature of Celtic life. The ancient Celts venerated these spirits, and in tribal territory, the ground and water that received the dead were imbued with sanctity and revered by their living relatives. The Celts believed that humans could establish a rapport with these beings so offerings of jewelry, weapons or foodstuffs were placed in offering pits and bodies of water, linking the donor to the place and spirits in a concrete way. The Celts believed in the the soul's journeys through many forms and bodies, its connection to the land and the various shapes and forms of reincarnation available.[1]

Archaeological and literary records indicate that ritual practice in Celtic societies lacked a clear distinction between the sacred and profane, maintaining a hazy balance between gods, spirits and humans. In contrast to the Classic World, the Celts had nothing that compared with the major Graeco/Roman gods such as Zeus/Jupiter, Aphrodite/Venus or Ares/Mars. They did not envisage their deities in human form and could not comprehend how men could believe that gods resembled humans. The Celtic leader Brennus is said to have mocked statues of the gods at Delphi. According to Diodorus Siculus, 'When he came only upon images of stone and wood he laughed at them, to think that men, believing that gods had human form, should set up their images in wood and stone.'[2]

The Celts perceived the presence of the supernatural as integral to, and interwoven with, the natural world. Everything was inspirited, and the close link with the natural world is reflected in what we know of the religious systems during the 1st millennium. Many topographical features were honored as the abodes of powerful spirits or deities, and were named for tutelary deities. The local deities were the spirits of a particular feature of the landscape, such as mountains, trees, or rivers, and thus were generally only known by the locals in the surrounding areas.

These beliefs were at one time so widely acknowledged that the Council of Tours in 567 declared that those who worshipped trees, stones or fountains should be excommunicated, but the pagan animistic tradition of worshipping natural deities continued despite all attempts by the early church to stop it and, knowingly or otherwise, we still practise some of these traditions today.

One example is the making of corn dollies. The Celts believed that a nature spirit resided in each field of corn, so at harvest time, the last sheaf was cut with great care in order to preserve the spirit of the corn. This was then made into a corn dolly – the word dolly is derived from the word idol. The spirit was preserved in the dolly during the winter, then in the spring, the dolly was broken up and mixed with the seed corn in order to transfer the spirit back to the soil to ensure a good harvest. This form of animistic rituals is still practised today in many rural communities.

Earth Energy

The old Celtic word *wouivre* referred to sinuous, telluric energies, some of which spring from the movement of subterranean waters, others from faults that are a manifestation of a life that goes on deep inside the earth itself. The Celts would walk barefoot so that they could feel these energies. The great chasms or fissures in the earth were sacred places believed to link the two worlds and from them came fumes that caused the people to act strangely. They would enter a trance-like condition in which they claimed to be able to see visions of the future, and such places became sacred.

Nowhere are there more great chasms in the earth than in the Brigante territory of what we now call the Peak District. Sir Arthur Conan Doyle stayed near Castleton and described it thus:

All this country is hollow. Could you strike it with some gigantic hammer it would boom like a drum, or possibly cave in altogether and expose some huge subterranean sea. A great sea there must surely be for on all sides the streams run into the mountain itself never to re-appear. There are gaps everywhere amid the rocks, and when you pass through them, you find yourself in great caverns which wind down into the bowels of the earth.

Eldon Hole near Peak Forest is one such place that would have been viewed with awe by the Celts. This fearsome chasm plunges 245 feet into the bowels of Eldon Hill and has always been considered a place of wonder. Fascinated visitors multiplied when in 1622 Michael Drayton listed it as one of the region's great natural phenomena in his book *Poly-Olbion*. Eldon Hole was seen as a curiosity and a worthy contender for a place in 'The Seven Wonders of the Peak'. The phrase was coined by Drayton, the Tudor poet who devised a sort of Grand Tour for intrepid travellers who viewed this mountainous wilderness as a strange, mysterious and even threatening place.[3]

In 1761 John Lloyd carried out a careful exploration of Eldon hole and having been lowered down 'forty fathoms', he reached the floor of the first cave but discovered another lower cave and the mouth of a shaft with water at the bottom. When dye was put in the water at Eldon Hole, forty-eight hours later the water at Peak Cavern, Castleton, was coloured. This would indicate that there are underground streams running all through this area, or perhaps Sir Arthur Conan Doyle was correct, there is some huge form of subterranean sea. At 470 m (1543 ft), Eldon Hill is one of the highest hills in the Peak District and dominates the landscape. The name comes from an early period when it was believed to be the hill of the elves. It has a number of tumuli dotted around its slopes and was worked for lead from very early days.

In June 1921 amateur archaeologist Alfred Watkins 'rediscovered' leys. Many people said he actually 'discovered' them, but that is not so. In 1904, Dr Moeller, Director of the Royal Museum in Copenhagen, had made the same observations that ley lines are hypothetical alignments of a number of places of geographical interest, such as ancient monuments and megaliths. Watkin's book *The Old Straight Track* brought the alignments to the attention of the wider public when he wrote that 'leys are the remains of old trading tracks laid down in Britain in the neolithic period roughly 5000–2000 BC'(which, if nothing else, is certainly 'roughly'). Using ranging rods and beacon fires, he saw the lines as being sighted from one hilltop to the next in alignment, linking significant Celtic or druidic points of interest. He observed that in the Iron Age climate there would have been no difficulty in sighting from one eminence to another forty miles away, and between the two points the line was marked by features such as mounds, henges, waterflashes, stone circles, tumuli, escarpment notches, menhirs, and marker stones.

He was ridiculed by most of the professional archaeologists although later Col. Kitson Clark, a prominent Leeds industrialist and archaeologist, applied this theory to the enormous number of cairns, tumuli and stone circles in east Yorkshire and found them to be in alignment.

It used to be thought that place names ending in ly or ley were derived from leah meaning a wood or clearing in a wood, but now there is a strong belief that the ley suffix denotes a place that has ley lines or where ley lines cross. Leys are well submerged both actually beneath accretions of buildings and earth, and metaphorically beneath layers of time. Later writers took up Watkins' findings and suggested that that these leys were not merely pathways but in fact energy channels, and where they cross, powerful forces are concentrated. This theory implies that ancient man didn't just erect monuments on any old hill, he knew how to tap and utilise these earth energies. The tribal shaman experienced visions and used intuition and if he recognized some location as special, a place where the energy was at its strongest, the whole tribe would take note and the ancient markers such as stone circles and megaliths would be focused there so that as they worshipped, the people could benefit from the earth's power.

Peak District Henges

I applied the theory of ley lines to the Derbyshire Peak District that formed the western side of Brigantia. With fallen stones and modern obstructions the lines that Watkins recognised are now impaired, but you'll find that Arbor Low, Stanton Moor and the Fabric, once a Druid temple site 980 feet above the village of Ashover, all sit on the same line. Though it must be said that linking such sites in a straight line is made easier by their sheer number in certain areas.

Arbor Low near Monyash in the former Brigante territory is now the region's most important prehistoric site and has become known as the Stonehenge of Derbyshire. Low comes from the old English word hlaw meaning high hill and usually refers to a site of prehistoric significance. This egg-shaped henge consists of about fifty large limestone blocks and is one of the finest examples left by early man. It's part of a larger complex, and is linked by an earth ridge to the earlier Neolithic oval barrow of Gib Hill 320 m away. Stanton Moor is situated on elevated ground to the west of the River Derwent, near Bakewell in the Peak District. It is littered with archaeological remains, most of which are thought to date from the Bronze Age. It contains the remains of two definite stone circles, three other possible circles or ring cairns, and an estimated 120 additional cairns as well as several natural standing stones and rock outcrops.

These were sacred sites for early man where the milestones of a person's life would have been celebrated – religious ceremonies, rites of passage, rites connected to childbirth, puberty and marriage as well as death. Stone circles acted as mystical walls to contain the magic of the occasion while excluding everyday life. A core element of many sacred henges and monuments was the astronomical aspects that were built into their structure. These orientations linked them with the heavens and surrounding landscape so that the midwinter sun would shine directly down the entrance passage or along the main axis. Some central gap usually framed the midsummer sun rise or other significant lunar events. This association with ancient astrology is one of the reasons why traditional festivals that reach back to pre-Celtic times took place there. Such festivals relate to the astrological divisions of the solar year, the solstices, equinoxes and the cross-quarter days between. These are Imbolc (February) Beltane (May) Lughnassadh (August) and Samhain (November)

The most evocative and well-known of the stone circles on Stanton Moor is the Nine Ladies Stone Circle, a name that comes from the local legend that is attached. The devil played his fiddle while nine ladies danced, but because it was the Sabbath, god was furious and turned them to stone for disregarding his holy day. The nine ladies form a circle (although recently a tenth was discovered lying flat and half submerged) while the fiddler, now turned into what is known as the King stone, is set 40 m (131 ft) to the west-south-west of the circle. Similar folk lores are attached to many stone circles up and down the country but instead of calling them ladies, the term maiden is used. Maiden is believed to be a corruption of meyn meaning stone, so there is every possibility that this is an inchoate folk memory and over time the name meyn was changed to maiden.

Places like Arbor Low and Stanton Moor remained sanctified pagan sites but many others were later Christianised by having a church or cross superimposed on them. The leys were often called Holy lines or archaic tracks. In Ireland these invisible lines were known as fairy paths and it was considered unwise to build on them.

Many people have experienced a sense of languor at these ancient sites and it has been suggested that perhaps it's the heightened natural radiation that can engender this feeling. If this is so, it is possible that this factor was used by our Celtic ancestors to help promote ritual sleep at these sites. It's been claimed that these unusual energies leak from the earth at suitable release points to be seen like a transparent heat haze that sprays into the air before dispersing and disappearing. At its most powerful, this energy leaks out into the atmosphere creating visual changes in the air, which creates radio and TV interference, power overloads, and temporary disruptions to street lighting. Sometimes this causes particles to be charged and transformed into glowing effects in the atmosphere.

People who are particularly sensitive to changes in atmospheric pressure report hearing faint sounds like whining, humming or buzzing, much like those emitted from transformers and power lines. All the stones at these sites are believed to hold electrical energy which can be harnessed. Some people who touch the stones claim to feel the energy and some even claim that it is possible to get a mild electric shock. These geophysical conditions might also affect the subconscious mind, which may account for the idea that these stones can aid conception and act as a powerful healing element.

Even though the Celts thought there was an energy force that surrounded and permeated everything, we have difficulty accepting that any inanimate object can pick up and store the energies of a person or event that has been associated with it. Psychometry is the technique of tuning into these energies, and a psychometrist claims to be able to deduce facts about events by touching objects related to them. They can tune into the vibrations of an item and detect the circumstances surrounding the individuals who have had immediate contact with it. When this same technique is applied to buildings or other structures like ancient standing stones, it is called psychic archaeology. While touching ancient stones it is possible for a psychometrist to be taken back to the times when these places were inhabited. Sceptics will point out that such material can't be checked, and in the cases where it can, its highly possible that the psychometrist has actually obtained the information by normal means, so it's a no-win situation. Despite this, psychometry remains popular and explanations as to how it works keep being offered, although none give a fool-proof answer.

When applying the ley line theory to Brigantia, it has been found that not only are hundreds of cairns, tumuli and stone circles in alignment, so are scores of churches and Norman castles built on the remains of Roman camps that are commonly suspected of standing on pre-Roman cultural centres. In Brigantia there are many centres, or nodes, where alignments cross that appear to have been pivotal to prehistoric development. Such incidents can't be haphazard accidents but must be the result of deliberate planning. One such example is at Clifton on the north/west outskirts of York. Here scores of alignments converge on the village green in what may well be one of the biggest nodes in Britain. The spot may have been of such overwhelming importance thousands of years ago that it may have retained sufficient status to be Cartimandua's capital. Some historians say that before the Romans arrived in Brigantia, her headquarters were unquestionably at York, yet no evidence has been found to support this theory. York's history begins with the Romans who founded Eboracum in 71AD. However, it's interesting to find that the Romans built their main cemetery on what is now the village green at Clifton. They were no doubt following the example of the Celts who also buried their dead in the cairns and henges at these places that appear to benefit from the alignment of leys.[4]

9

THE SPIRIT IN THE STONE

Stone heads were revered by the Celts. Until they were removed for safekeeping, this fine selection were on display in Bakewell church porch.

Because the Brigante territory was a very stony region, it is no surprise to find that the Celts believed that spirits inhabited stones. This is just part of the folklore of prehistoric sites, the stone lore. Our ancestors believed that the spirits that resided in rocks had special powers to grant wishes, a conviction that is so old and so universal that it can't be dismissed simply as ignorant superstition. There is a stone at Lumsdale near Matlock where it was believed that the spirits that lived in the stone could grant wishes. It's a universal and time-honoured tradition for lovers to carve their initials within the shape of a heart on a tree trunk or rock. They are following an ancient custom, and knowingly or otherwise asking for the blessing of the nature spirit that resides within.

According to legend, young men would climb a suitably difficult rock face to demonstrate their manhood and receive the blessing of the spirit that resided within the rock. There is one such stone at Baslow Edge. Known as the Eagle Stone, this is probably a corruption of Aigle, the Saxon god who could throw stones that no mortal could move. Presumably it was hoped that in exchange for this show of bravado, the nature spirit would reward the young men with some of Aigle's strength.

Other stones would supposedly turn, rock or move at certain times of the day or year. A stone with a natural hole eroded by the elements was considered particularly potent for warding off evil. Often called a hag-stone, it was prized for its intrinsic powers. People used a holed stone for luck and to protect their home, family, trade or stock. It was believed that if they held the stone up to the full moon and peered through the natural opening, they would be granted visions of future events. A number of larger holed stones around the county have local traditions which claim that they were useful for healing various ailments. Where the hole is large enough to crawl through or pass a child through, this action was reputed to effect the cure of such ailments as scrofula, rickets, whooping cough and epilepsy.

Stones also had a part to play in divination arts. Pessomancy is divination by drawing or casting specially marked stones – known as wise stones – to foretell the future. They are now known as rune stones, a term that can also be applied to runic inscriptions on boulders and on bedrock. Rune stones for divination purposes come in a set of 24 ancient alphabetic symbols and ideally are cast on an east-west axis or facing the sun.

Like the story of the nine ladies, the stone circle on Stanton Moor, many upright stones are said to be Druids or others who have been changed to that state by magic or the will of the gods. There's a stone called the Warren stone in the River Wye at Monsal Dale, just below the Brigante Celtic hillfort of Fin Cop. According to a local legend, a giant named Huluc Warren lusted after a young shepherdess named Hedessa. She resisted his advances until one day he saw his opportunity and grabbed her. She called to the gods for help, they heard her plea and momentarily stunned Huluc, allowing Hedessa to escape, but ahead of her was a rocky precipice and she threw herself to her death. Almost instantly, a spring of pure water said to be as pure as Hedessa's soul sprang from the ground. Furious at being robbed of his opportunity to possess Hedessa, Warren cursed the gods who sent a mighty gale to blow him off the rock into the river, where his petrified state still stands paying an eternal penance.

There are similar stories of how certain aspects of the land contain the spirit of people or deities. There are legends about night prowling people who were turned to stone after unexpectedly being exposed to daylight. In the Catholic hagiography of Saint Barbara, she was pursued by her sword-wielding father Dioscorus after he learned of his daughter's acceptance of the new faith. Her location was given away by a shepherd who was punished for this deed by being turned into stone, and his flock were turned into locusts. The best known story of petrification is of course that of the powers of Medusa. North of Whitby, on the edge of Brigante territory is the story of Saint Hilda (614-680) who was credited with having miraculously turned snakes into stone. The ammonite fossils that are found in large numbers at Sandsend, north of Whitby are said to be the remains. The coat of arms of nearby Whitby includes three such 'snakestones'.

There are widespread examples of stories of sleeping kings and famous warriors who will awake from their petrified states in the hour of need. Cailleach in partnership with the goddess Brigid were seasonal deities or spirits (see earlier section). Cailleach ruled the winter months then at Beltain, the first day of summer, she turned to stone. Brigid ruled the summer months then Cailleach reverted to human form on Samhain in time to rule over the winter months.

Gargoyles, Sheela Na Gig and Stone Heads

Stone was also carved into shapes that had meaning and many grotesques in local churches and cathedrals have their origin here. Legends tell of Satan sending creatures to do harm, only to be turned into stone by the gods. More prosaically it was the task of the early stone sculptors to portray fantastic or mythical figures who populated the folk lore of the times, and many of these were grotesques and

Sheela Na Gig. A crude distortion of the female figure believed to represent the pagan goddess of fertility and creation, this at Kilpeck Church, Herefordshire.

chimerae. They could also serve an instructional purpose for an illiterate population.

One such creature was the Sheila (or Sheela) na gig. She is represented as an overtly sexual image, a crude distortions of the nude, female figure displaying an exaggerated vulva. Also known as the divine hag, she's been described as pornographic. Most of these figures are so weathered it's hard to make sense of the pose which has been described as both acrobatic and pugilistic, but in order to qualify as a Sheela the knees are hunched, the arms folded and the hands are pulling apart an overstretched vulva. The Sheela na gigs are stone representations of a very explicit sexual nature, and the figure was thought to have served as an ecclesiastic warning against the sins of the flesh.

There are many known examples of Sheela na gig in Ireland and some forty-five in Britain and they are nearly all in ecclesiastic establishments. However there is one at Haddon Hall on the outskirts of Bakewell that was in the centre of Brigante territory. Its precise origins are unknown but it was found in a nearby field and very probably came from some early religious establishment, a theory that is reinforced by the fact that a round barrow was found on the nearby Haddon Fields.

Gargoyles adorn countless churches and other buildings to drain rain water from the gutters. They tend to sit on their haunches on the parapet of buildings projecting out several feet so that the water is spouted out well clear of the base of the building. Perched up there, they seem quite harmless, and after the introduction of the lead water pipe in the 16th century, quite useless.

Grotesque stone heads are a common sight in the Pennines, incorporated into the fabric of churches, farmhouses and walls. Although they would have come from earlier structures, churches from the 11th and 12th centuries have an abundance of them with their staring, bulging eyes: horned men, mouth pullers, tongue stickers and strange animals. Many are representations of forgotten gods and goddesses, which is why some historians claim that some of these stone heads with expressionless faces that gaze out from buildings could be 2,000 years old.

That means that a number of these stone heads were the handiwork of the indigenous Celtic tribes and may have been of cult significance because the Celts venerated the human head. Archaeological excavations of numerous pagan, Celtic and Saxon burial sites reveal that the interred corpses had their heads placed between their knees or feet. In later periods there is recorded evidence that the human skull was particularly valued in the belief that it cured all ills, and this may have been true of the Celts. Powdered or grated skull bone has been mixed into food and eaten to cure epilepsy, headaches and plague. Moss scraped from an old skull was said to staunch bleeding of a wound or a nose bleed. If dried, powdered and taken as snuff, it was believed to cure a headache or act as protection against the plague. A person bitten by a mad dog was advised to take pills made from the powdered skull of a hanged man. Water drunk from a skull was believed to be beneficial for numerous medical problem.

The Celtic tribes followed a tradition of preserving human heads to act as magical talismans to be used and feared. Their original function was to bring luck and avert evil, and according to the Greek writer Diodorus Siculus, the Celts cut off their enemies' heads and hung them above the doors of their huts, displayed them on poles, or hung them around their horses necks as grisly trophies of war. They preserved the heads of their most high ranking victims in cedar oil and kept them carefully in wooden boxes. The Celts believed that the human spirit lived in the head and by displaying the heads they could prove that they had not only captured their enemy's body but also his spirit. At Beltane or Hallowe'en, the spirits become free, so to entice them back, a lighted taper or candle was put inside the skull. This is the derivation of the Hallowe'en pumpkin, hollowed out and cut to represent a skull with a candle burning inside.

A whole package of folklore and superstitions have become woven around the human head. The annual Royal Shrove Tuesday Football game played at Ashbourne near Derby is so old there is the macabre theory that the ball was originally a severed head tossed into the waiting crowd following an execution.

After the arrival of the Romans, the taking of real human heads was outlawed, so the Celts carved stone heads with expressionless faces to gaze out from buildings or act as key-stones on a bridge, over an entrance or window, weak spots which required protection from the attentions of witches, evil spirits and ghosts. For many centuries, the human head sculpted in stone continued to act as a magical talisman used to avert evil, and act as a guardian spirit. Some marked graves or sacred burial grounds.

Around 1967, Sydney Jackson, the then keeper of the Cartwright Museum, Bradford, collected together an assortment of carved stone heads from all over Brigantian territory. In total there were 110 heads, all carved in Yorkshire stone and ranging in size from 5 to 15 inches (12–37 cm). The heads formed an interesting exhibition but there was some doubt about their authenticity. Dr Anne Ross who around this time was compiling her book *Pagan Celtic Britain*, visited the collection and was struck by the extraordinary continuity of culture shown by the collection that was of mixed ages, the earliest dating from the first century. Anne Ross thought it possible some were Celtic, in part because of their heavy moustaches.

Apotropaic is an adjective that means warding off evil or deflecting misfortune and although that was probably the main purpose of stone heads, as well as imbuing them with positive attributes it is not so unlikely that the native Celts could have

Above left: A Celtic head set into the stonework of St Michael and All Angels Church, Birchover.

Above right: A face-pulling gargoyle on Hope Church.

also considered them as conduits of misfortune too. Cursed stone heads were a means of promoting fear in their enemies. A man who unearthed one at Marple gave it to a friend who suffered a number of heart attacks. He returned the head, which was then taken to the owner's workplace. Its arrival coincided with illness and misfortune, and left his staff in a state of terror. Eventually it was taken to a museum. Little Manny is the name given to a vile-looking stone carving unearthed during the 1960s. The figurine had large lentoid eyes. People didn't want to handle it. The museum's curator Dr John Prag said it brought mischief and bad luck. His car window was smashed, his trouser zip broke, he scratched the side of his car after 17 years of accident-free motoring, then the following day scraped the other side, and the baby buggy collapsed. Not exactly pertifying but certainly bad luck!

The Mouselow Stones and the Hexham Heads

A collection of stones that included stone heads, fertility symbols, strange 'shadow figures' and a crude representation of the horned god Cernunnos were found by a Wesleyan Minister, the Reverend George

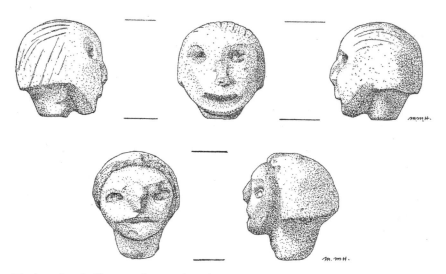

Hexham heads illustrated in *Archaeologia Aeliana*.

Marsden, near a Bronze Age barrow at Little Hadfield, on what is known as Castle Hill near Glossop in 1846. It is less than a mile from the Roman fort of Melandra and almost on the route of the Roman Road between Glossop and Hope. The stone heads were subsequently built into the gable end of a house in the village.

There were about ten carved stone heads, some with typically Celtic, bulging eyes, strange shadow figures and a crude representation of the horned god. They were carved with a number of symbols and letters. Some of the symbols have been recognised as representing the river of life, the wind blowing from the four quarters of the earth, the god Thoth, and other objects that they worshipped. Historians claim they could be 2,000 years old, carved by the native Celts who occupied this area, and may have been of cult significance, used to mark graves or sacred burial grounds with the symbols denoting rank and gender in the tribe.

Early in the 20th century, the stones were removed from the house wall and taken to Buxton Museum for safekeeping. A number of other stones, including Celtic style stone heads, were subsequently added to the group and in 1985 the stones were returned to Glossop to coincide with a three-year archaeological excavation on Mouselow Hill, near the site where they had first been found. A local woman called Glynis Reeve who was in charge of the dig decided to display the stones in Glossop Heritage Centre in order to gather information about them. She was unprepared for the feelings of fear and dread they aroused amongst local people, who considered them to be evil. There were numerous anonymous phone calls warning of curses, and there were so many unexplained accidents and injuries that the site excavation was temporarily halted.

When it was time to move the stones again, they had to be stored overnight in a room containing a number of computers, which suddenly stopped working. Checks with the electricity supply found there was not a power cut as originally suspected. Technicians who checked the computers could find no reason for the failure. Electrical equipment refused to work when placed in the same room as the Celtic stones that were believed to have powerful magnetic properties. When the carvings were finally returned to the museum, the computers began working again. Make of this what you will.

In 1971, two children found two small stone heads in their garden in Rede Avenue, Hexham, Co Durham, deep in Brigante territory. The heads were passed over to the Newcastle Museum of Antiquities, where they were formally drawn to scale in a conventional archaeological style. Archaeologists and curators Roger Miket and David Smith, who handled or knew of the heads, were non-committal about what these strange objects actually were. They travelled the length and breadth of Britain and the heads became even more famous when Anne Ross showed an interest in these strange little objects. She had long had a research interest in 'the cult of the head' across Celtic Europe, writing in 1967 that 'the human head was regarded by the Celts as being symbolic of divinity and otherworld powers.' Ross tried to give the heads an archaeological credibility by including them in an article with other heads with a better provenance and stronger claims to be authentic, but she acknowledged the difficulties in dating and lack of context. Anne Ross gave them to a colleague, Professor Frank Hodson, at the University of Southampton for analysis. Hodson concluded that they were both made from coarse sandstone with rounded quartz grains, hints of a lime coating and some applied colour pigments. He suggested local sources for this but could give no hint of their age or purpose. His analysis seems to have been based on microscope work and limited visual analysis, but later, a second analysis, based on the invasive removal of a sample, came up with a very different conclusion. Undertaken by Dr Douglas Robson of Newcastle University his report concludes that the material from which the heads had been formed was an artificial cement and 'the material [was] unlike any natural sandstone.' His report is published in Paul Screeton's 2010 book, *Quest for the Hexham Heads*.

Meanwhile, in 1977, the heads passed into the care of Don Robins, a controversial chemist whose most famous work is probably the book *The Secret Language of Stone*. Robins dabbled in a range of 'earth mysteries' related to things like the magnetic properties of stones and megaliths. He also collaborated with Anne Ross on their book *The Life and Death of a Druid Prince* about the Lindow Man bog body (see page 175). He became convinced that the Hexham Heads could help prove his stone-tape theory, that stone could 'record' events and human emotions and then could play them back, so he removed them from a box in Hodson's office at Southampton University. He kept them for analysis until February 1978 when he passed them onto a dowser called Frank Hyde for further experimentation. They have never been seen since. Then the bombshell was dropped by local man Des Craigie, who claimed to have made them as playthings for his children in the 1950s![1]

10

GODS AND SPIRITS OF THE NATURAL WORLD

Statue of the
Celtic Goddess
Arnemetiae, the
goddess beside
the sacred spring.
(Courtesy Buxton
Museum)

To early man, a rainbow was an inexplicable phenomenon. He would have viewed a rainbow, lightning, a mysterious cloud formation or a meteor as awesome, mysterious signs from the gods. He would have read and interpreted the shapes formed by clouds, listened to the sound of the wind, marvelled at the ferocity of storms. Sky watching now comes under the general heading of aeromancy which is subdivided into austromancy – divination by the study of winds; ceraunoscopy – divination by the study of thunder and lightning; chaomancy – divination from aerial visions, and meteormancy – divination from meteors and shooting stars. Early man acknowledged that these meteorological patterns and phenomena were inspirited and these deities needed propitiating. The Celts believed that within the shifting landscape of clouds and shimmering stars dwelled the gods and goddesses who were responsible for the weather, the sun, the moon and the winds. The ancients looked to the heavenly bodies to help them reckon the proper times to plant and harvest. They watched and celebrated as the sun and moon grew in strength and prayed for the return of the light and warmth when the sun seemed to be weakening.

Many gods are known to us by name through texts and inscriptions from the Roman period or from recorded place names. Lugh's name is enshrined in town names including Luguvalium (Carlisle) meaning walled town of Lugh, and Lugdunum (Lyon, France) meaning stronghold of Lugh. He also gave his name to Lugnasadh, the Celtic festival of 1 August, the summer festival. In the insular Celtic lands, Lugh meaning shining light was known as a sun god and a fierce warrior. He is also known as a god of storms, particularly thunderstorms. Lugh was associated with the raven, crow, and lynx, and had a magic hound. He also possessed several magical weapons, including a spear that never missed its target. It was so bloodthirsty the spear would often try to fight without anyone wielding it.

There were a vast number of solar deities, gods and goddesses who represents the sun or an aspect of it. Solar deities and sun worship can be found throughout most of recorded history in various forms. To name but a few, Aine goddess of love, summer, wealth and sovereignty is associated with the sun and midsummer; Alaunus was a Gaulish god of the sun, healing and prophecy; Belanos was another Gaulish god of the sun; Etain was an Irish sun goddess and Olwen was a Welsh sun goddess.

In addition to light, sky and sun aspects of a celestial cult, the Celts revered Manannan, god of the sea. He controlled sea mists and fogs with his magic cloak or mantle. It was believed that it was the goddess Cailleach, a word that literally means old woman or hag, who brought the first winter snows by washing her great plaid, a process that took three days. When she had finished, her plaid was pure white and snow covered the land. Although this was a Scottish belief, there would have been similar legends elsewhere.[1]

In Scotland where she is also known as Beira, Queen of Winter, Cailleach is credited with making numerous mountains and large hills, which are said to have been formed when she was striding across the land and accidentally dropped rocks from her creel or wicker basket. In other cases, she is said to have built the mountains intentionally, to serve as her stepping stones.

In partnership with the goddess Brigid (Brighde, Brigit) the Cailleach is seen as a seasonal deity or spirit. St Brigid was allegedly born at sunrise on Imbolc, 1 February. Brigid is of special interest to us as the goddess of the Brigante tribe. Her name means The High One, and is cognate with the name of the Celtic British goddess Brigantia. Cailleach rules the winter months between Samhain (1 November or first day of winter) and Beltain (1 May or first day of summer), while Brigid is associated with the spring season and rules the summer months between Beltain and Samhain. Brigid is the goddess of fertility, healing, poetry and smithery. Some interpretations have the Cailleach and Brigid as two faces of the same goddess, while others describe the Cailleach as turning to stone on Beltain and reverting to humanoid form on Samhain in time to rule over the winter months. (*See also* page 15.)

The Celts had a thunder god named Taranis. In his epic poem *Pharsalia*, an account of the Civil War between Pompey and Caesar, the Roman poet Marcus Annaeus Lucanus, more usually referred to as Lucan, mentioned three Celtic divinities encountered by Caesar's army – Taranis, Teutates and Esus.

Taranis was the thunderer, the noisy god of thunder, weather and storms. Taranis embodied a power struggle in the sky with overtones of battle. There are many representations of a bearded god with a thunderbolt in one hand and a wheel in the other representing Taranis, who came to be syncretised with the Roman god Jupiter.

The Romans imported their own celestial god, Jupiter, to continental Celtic lands by *interpretatio romana*. His imagery was merged with that of a native deity to produce a hybrid sky-deity who resembled the Roman god but who had additional solar attributes. Altars decorated with wheels were set up by Roman soldiers stationed at Hadrian's Wall. This would indicate that in some things they were not only tolerant of the native's beliefs, they supplemented them.[2]

Teutates was the second of the three Celtic gods mentioned by Lucan. Many deities were venerated in triads, or were three aspects of the one god, sometimes depicted as three-faced. The name Teutates means god of the tribe and was perhaps a common title for many different gods rather than the name of just one. The association with the Roman god Mars suggests Teutates was connected with fighting and battle. He was identified with Mercury as well as Mars; however, another commentator identifies Esus, the third member of the trio, with Mars. Esus means the good master, the respected one, or lord, yet Lucan refers to Esus as a barbarous Celtic god.

Lucan also described the cruel rites associated with each god who all needed appeasing with human sacrifices. Victims sacrificed to Taranis were burnt, victims sacrificed to Teutates were killed by being plunged headfirst into a vat filled with an unspecified liquid. Victims sacrificed to Esus were hanged from a tree, stabbed and left to bleed to death while incantations were said. Their blood was used in auguries. Perhaps the elements of fire, water and air are represented here.[3] Caesar writes:

> The whole nation is greatly devoted to ritual observances and for that reason those who are smitten with the more grievous maladies and who are engaged in the perils of battle either sacrifice human victims or vow to do so, employing the Druids as ministers for such sacrifices. They believe in effect that unless for a man's life a life is paid, the majesty of the immortal gods may not be appeased.[4]

The Sacred Trees and Groves

The association of trees with wisdom and knowledge goes back into antiquity and has always been part of religion. We featured this earlier in the section on ogham. The image of white-clad Druids performing their rituals deep within a forest glade is not entirely unfounded, for the Druids worshipped the spirits of the trees; their temples were the sacred oak groves. Lucan the Roman poet wrote that the people worshipped in sacred, open-air enclosures rather than roofed structures. Trees and clumps of trees were revered and the Celtic name Nemeton, synonymous with sanctuary, also correlates to the goddess of a sacred grove.[5] However, other evidence suggests that the word Nemeton implied a wider variety of ritual spaces, such as shrines and temples.[6] In his *Pharsalia,* Lucan described such a grove, probably to entertain and shock his Roman readers:

> No bird nested in the nemeton, nor did any animal lurk nearby; the leaves constantly shivered though no breeze stirred. Altars stood in its midst, and the images of the gods. Every tree was stained with sacrificial blood. the very earth groaned, dead yews revived; unconsumed trees were surrounded with flame, and huge serpents twined round the oaks. The people feared to approach the grove, and even the priest would not walk there at midday or midnight lest he should then meet its divine guardian.

Classical writers made much of the gruesome Celtic sacrifices in dark woodland clearings, perhaps because worship in such places was so alien to them compared to the town and city temples and enclosures that they frequented for worship. Dio Cassius refers to a sacred grove where sacrifices to the war goddess Andraste were carried out. Lucan refers to the grim practice of sprinkling human blood in sacred woods. Tacitus describes Mona (Anglesey) as a centre of Druidical learning at the time of the Roman conquest and speaks of the forest clearings in Anglesey as the last Druid strongholds.

The tree of life is a widespread myth. Various trees of life are recounted in folklore, culture and fiction, and are connected to heaven, the underworld and the tree of knowledge.[7] From the early Druids onwards, wise men would sit under specific trees and interpret the rustling of the leaves and other subtle signs as oracular messages. It was an ancient belief that trees were inhabited by the gods and spirits who gave them powers to foretell many things. Silvanus from the Latin meaning 'of the woods' was the woodland god, protector of forests and plantations. The Celts revered certain trees, the most sacred being the old, hallowed trees that stood in a central area and were often the social and ceremonial meeting place for a tribe.[8]

One of the longest-lived species are yew trees. These are frequently associated with churchyards but before any form of church was built, these old trees marked significant pagan meeting places and grew on sites that had been considered sacred for centuries. Evergreen, the yew was seen as a symbol of immortality, and has long been revered for its ability to protect against evil. Sprigs of yew were once put into a dead person's shroud, and branches were carried by mourners before being put into the grave to keep the devil out and to prevent the soul of the dead from escaping. Branches have been found in ancient burial mounds. Early betrothals were conducted under a yew tree.

The Celts made wooden statues and votive offerings usually of oak that have been found at river sources. One of the most familiar trees in the British Isles is the mountain ash, or rowan. It has also acquired numerous English folk names like Quickbane, Rune tree, Thor's helper, whispering tree, Wicken tree, Wiggin, Witch wood, and Witchbane. Some of these names may date back to the early Celtic period. The protective property of the mountain ash was acknowledged way back. People took branches into their homes in the belief that it would protect them from lightning. It was used for broom handles, and the fire was poked with a length. Carters made whips from the wood to protect them and their horses on journeys, and it was carried on sea-going vessels in the belief that it would guard against storms. The old Derbyshire lead miners had great faith in the protective power of the mountain ash and took branches down the mines. Being a very dense wood, the mountain ash was used for carving and turning such things as tool handles and walking sticks. It was also made into Druids' staffs, dowsing rods, rune staves, divining rods and magic wands.

The association of trees with wisdom and knowledge is recognised in the age-old tradition of divining. A forked branch from a tree used as a divining rod is mysteriously able to summon up the secrets of the earth, including predicting the presence of hidden water or buried treasure. Although most people now only associated divining with discovering the presence of water, the original uses of the divining rods were many. According to ancient belief, for a divining rod to have maximum potency, it should be cut between sunset and sunrise, ideally on a holy day or new moon. Some say it should be cut on the first new moon after the winter solstice.

Tree branches are also fashioned into wands, which by tradition are agents of intense psychic energy. The cutting and shaping was usually carried out in great secrecy, with prayers offered to give the rod power and authority. Hazel was a favourite wood, and a branch would be cut at sunrise to endow it with maximum solar energy. The effectiveness of a wand and its specific power depended upon the wood used. Traditional attributes include ash for reverence; hickory for endurance and firmness of belief; maple for kinship, energy, healing and enthusiasm; oak for increased awareness and heightened consciousness; poplar for protection and resolution; beech for achievement of goals; pine for new beginnings; and willow to deter evil.

People had faith that trees could remedy all ills, but they had positive and negative attributes. A laurel wreath hung on the door was believed to prevent disease entering the house, and wearing laurel leaves would supposedly avert the plague. This evergreen bush is traditionally linked with Greek mythology. The god Apollo was besotted by the nymph Daphne but she did not return his affections. Fleeing from his attentions, she prayed to the gods for assistance, and they answered her supplications by turning her into a laurel (bay) tree. Apollo crowned his head with the leaves and the tree became sacred to him. He is usually depicted wearing a laurel wreath on his head because of his love for Daphne, and in ancient Greece, it was given to special people such as winners of competitions in poetry or sports, especially the ancient Olympic Games. The Romans carried on the tradition.

Similarly, the beautiful nymph Pitys was loved by both Boreas, the mighty Greek god of the north wind, and Pan, god of nature, shepherds and flocks. When she chose Pan, Boreas blew her off a cliff, but Gaia the earth goddess took pity on her and turned her into a pine tree. When the north wind blows through the trees it is said that you can hear her weeping.

There is archaeological evidence to suggest that a half-man, half-animal horned deity was present in European cultures spanning thousands of years. Three of the later notable examples are Pan, the

Greek god of the woodlands, Herne the Hunter, and Cernunnos the Celtic God of fertility, of whom it has been suggested that the Cerne Abbas Giant is a representation. The Cerne Abbas Giant is a hill figure near the village of Cerne Abbas in Dorset. It's 55 metres (180 ft) high, and like many other hill figures, it is outlined by shallow trenches cut in the turf and backfilled with chalk rubble.

As we have seen in the previous chapter, the Celts believed in deities capable of shifting between human and animal form and Pan has the hindquarters, legs, and horns of a goat, in the same manner as a faun or satyr. In Greek mythology, he is often represented playing panpipes, whence the instrument derives its name. According to another Geek myth, this time Pan was in love with the nymph Syrinx, daughter of Ladon the river god, but Syrinx did not return his affection. Pan was just on the point of capturing Syrinx but she begged Zeus to save her. He heard her plea and turned her into reeds. Pan was mortified but as he kissed the reeds, he discovered that his breath could create sounds from them, so he made them into a musical instrument. First used by the ancient Greeks, they are known as the panpipes but the official name is the syrinx, named after the lost nymph.

Although the wood of the apple tree was used to make Druids' wands, it's the fruit of the tree that is usually featured in mythology, legend, and folklore. In the body of medieval Celtic myths and sagas, the apple is featured as an emblem of fruitfulness and sometimes a means to immortality. In mythology, the soul of Cu Roi was confined in an apple that lay in the stomach of a salmon which appeared once every seven years. Cuhullin, the reincarnation of his father Lugh, once escaped by following the path of a rolled apple. The Breton pseudo-saint Konorin was reborn by means of an apple; and Conle the son of Conn, High King of Ireland, was fed an apple by a fairy lover that sustained him for a month. The story of Baile and Aillinn is about two tragic lovers who died and were buried side by side. On Baile's grave grew a yew tree and on Aillinn's grave grew an apple tree. Their spirits entered the trees which became intertwined until one day they were chopped down. Eventually Ogham staves (see earlier section) were made from their woods and when the staves were presented to the King at Tara, they sprang together.

Traditional Practices

The Celts believed in the nature spirits that lived in trees although they couldn't be seen because like all nature spirits they blended into their surroundings. The closest representation that we now have could be the Green Man. This icon usually takes the form of a man's head surrounded by sprouting living foliage, a pagan symbol of a vegetation spirit representing the raw, primal force of nature. As an embodiment of the life force which renews the world in spring, he is still associated with spring festivals today.

Every year, the remote Derbyshire village of Castleton that lies at the foot of Mam Tor holds a special celebration, the Castleton Garland Ceremony. This annual celebration absorbed some of the customs normally associated with May Day, which in the old Celtic calendar was the start of one of the most important festivals of the year – Beltane. Yet opinions about the origin of the Castleton Garland Ceremony in its present form are mixed and it appears to be a fusion of May Day and Oak Apple Day. In 1660 after years of bitter conflict and strict puritan rule, Charles II was welcomed back to take his place on the throne of England. After hiding out in an oak tree (thus the name) the Stuart restoration was met with a great surge of national enthusiasm and 29 May 29 became the first anniversary appointed by Act of Parliament to be observed as a day of general thanksgiving.

At Castleton, the main event is a dancing procession through the streets led by the king and his lady on horseback, although the king is actually hidden by a huge floral garland. It's large enough to fit over his head and cover him to the waist, then on his shoulders rests a separate, smaller bunch of flowers that covers his head making the complete garland over a metre high.

It's this garland that is the real centre of attention and takes the custom much further back into history because using flowers and greenery in abundance is more in keeping with the earlier pagan fertility rites which have their roots in the worship of the earth. The king looks remarkably like that May Day character 'Jack in the Green'. This was a man who danced inside a wood or basketwork frame that covered him from head to ankles. An abundance of greenery and flowers was fixed on this framework until the visual effect was of a conical bush on feet. There's a distinct link between

Above and right: Over Haddon's unusual and very striking well-dressing depicting the Green Man, a Celtic icon representing the raw, primal force of nature.

Jack in the Green and the Green Man and both are said to be pre-Christian spirits of nature and fertility.

Primitive people regarded the alder with awe because when cut the wood turns from white to red. The alder was thought to have power of divination, especially in the diagnosing of diseases, and in pre-Christian Ireland, an alder rod was used for measuring corpses and graves. The alder tree was sacred to the Druids. The pith could easily be pushed out of green shoots to make whistles or pipes. Several shoots bound together by cordage were trimmed to the desired length for producing the notes used to entice air elementals or the spirits that lived in the sky. The old superstition of whistling up the wind began with this custom.

The elder tree has clusters of white flowers in spring and red or blackish berry-like fruit in late summer, and was commonly thought of as a fairy tree. Where the elder grew abundantly it had many associations with the fairy world and was thought to be haunted by fairies or demons. Another fairy tree is the hazel, and both the wood and the edible nuts of the hazel have played important roles in early traditions. Wood from the hazel was sacred to poets and heralds carried hazel wands as badges of office. A twig of hazel would be given to a rejected lover but the wood was a taboo fuel on many hearths. More esteemed than the hazel's wood were its nuts, often described as the nuts of wisdom. Hazel leaves and nuts have been found in early British burial mounds, shafts and pits.

Cedar wood is aromatic because it produces thujaplicin, a natural antibacterial and antifungal agent that has insect-repellent qualities. It's also naturally rot-resistant. The Celts had a special use for cedar oil – to preserve the heads of enemies taken in battle. We now know that cedar wood oil is a sedative. It can relieve tension and has a soothing and calming effect on the mind. It also reduces inflammation and muscle pain, and minimises skin irritation or itchiness. Whether the ancient Celts were aware of this is unknown, but they must have had some reason for being so selective about the use of cedar oil for preserving their enemies' heads.

The Celts believe that trees had special powers of healing. Hawthorn, or trees that were associated with protection, were reported as being used as votive trees as early as the 4th century. In exchange for an offering, usually a strip of cloth or item of clothing, there is still a belief that the tree itself bears the weight of the problem, and by the time the offering rots off the branch, the request will be granted. One such specimen can be found on Stanton Moor near Bakewell, a place that has other evidence of early man's occupation.

Farmers would cut corn with a flail that had a handle of holly or hawthorn. Holly wood is white with an almost invisible grain and looks like ivory. It was one of the three timbers used in the construction of chariot wheel shafts, and was used to make spear shafts that needed balance when thrown. But holly is more closely associated with the death and rebirth symbolism of winter in both pagan and Christian lore and is important to the Winter Solstice. Pagan peoples took evergreens indoors during their winter festival. To them the spirits had departed from the deciduous trees, yet these evergreen branches signified life. The Celts believed that holly kept its leaves throughout the winter months to offer protection for the spirits in the woods. The origin of decorating the house at Christmas can be traced to this earlier festival. The temples and houses were decorated with foliage and flowers, and on the bay trees and branches of laurel they hung trinkets and masks of the god Bacchus – the god of wine and giver of ecstasy. On these decorated trees were secured twelve candles, one for each month, and on the top they placed an image of Apollo, the god of light.

Another plant associated with Christmas decoration is the hemiparasitic mistletoe. The mistletoe had special significance and was venerated by the Druids. Pliny tells us of a feast prepared on the 6th day of the moon involving the Druids, who

> ... having made preparation for sacrifice, and a banquet beneath the trees, they bring thither two white bulls... Clad in a white robe, the priest ascends the tree and cuts the mistletoe with a golden sickle and it is received by others in a white cloak. They then kill the victims praying that the god will render this gift of his propitious to those to whom he has granted it... They believe that the mistletoe taken in drink imparts fertility to barren animals and that it is an antidote for all poisons.[9]

The Celts dedicated people and animals to the gods, but it was the human sacrifices that had a particular morbid fascination for the

Greeks and Romans. The fact that they were using gladiators and animals to spill human blood simply for the amusement of the crowd doesn't get a similar reaction from them.

Mistletoe gets another mention when the waterlogged mummified body of an ancient Briton was discovered in 1984 during peat cutting at Lindow Moss, 10 miles, (15 km) south of Manchester. Known as the Lindow Man, the body was so well preserved that it was transferred to a hospital mortuary for radiocarbon dating. Only then did they realise that the corpse was 2,000 years old. Scientists subjected the body to numerous tests and found a few grains of pollen from the mistletoe plant in the stomach. The mistletoe suggests that this was a human sacrifice. (*See* the full story on pages 175–78.)[10]

When the hierarchy of Celtic society disintegrated under the Romans, the Druids seemed to lose their national influence. Druidism was tolerated in Augustinian times as long as Roman citizens were not involved, but with the advent of Christianity, mistletoe was banned. This was not necessarily because of its pagan association but because mistletoe wood was purportedly used to make the cross on which Christ died. It is still not allowed to be used in church. Yet these early people believed that mistletoe was the plant of friendship. If enemies met under a tree on which mistletoe grew, they would lay down their arms and call a truce. If friends met under a tree bearing mistletoe, they would consider their friendship blessed with good luck, and we are all aware of the custom of kissing under the mistletoe.

Water Worship – Gifts to the Gods

Natural water features were considered sacred in Bronze and Iron Age Britain because they were links between the physical realm and the Otherworld. Early man believed that water spirits or undines lived in all bodies of water from wells to oceans, but like all nature spirits they blended into their surroundings. All the numerous spirits and deities that resided at watery places were honoured as givers and takers of life, so water rituals were ubiquitous. Our ancestors believed that if the water spirits were appeased by the correct propitiatory rites and sacrifices at the appropriate time and place, the water would continue to flow, and that was vital. Early hill settlements were sited where one or more springs emerged, but if the spring failed so did the village economy, and life itself was in jeopardy.

The spring at Buxton so sacred to the Celts is still producing fresh water, available to everyone from this fountain.

There is abundant evidence for the veneration of water by the Celts and by their Bronze Age forebears. Lakes, rivers, fresh water springs and murky peat bogs were all considered sacred places where the deities were acknowledged and venerated both by means of appropriate imagery and of votive offerings. A votive offering is given as a gift to the gods literally in fulfilment of a vow. Special significance was given to a confluence where two or more rivers meet and merge, and to bridges or fords which symbolise boundaries of life and death. As much as 50 tons of gold and a similar amount of silver looted from sacred water sources in Britain alone cleared the Caesar's vast debts and financed his career.

Few of us can resist the urge to throw a few coins in a wishing well, but how many of us realise we are actually following the ancient rite of making an offering to the water spirit? It may not be a conscious ritual, but it's based on the same principle – we are asking the water spirit in return for our offerings to implement our wish. It wasn't just coins, jewellery and metalwork that were offered by the early Britons. Goods, animals and people were sacrificed in bogs and pools until the early centuries AD.

Rivers were considered to be divine and several have been named after Celtic gods, like the Seine in France, the Boyne in Ireland, and the Danube in Eastern Europe. Britain's longest river, the River Severn that flows for 220 miles from its source in the Welsh Cambrian Mountains until reaching the sea in the Bristol Channel was originally called Sabrina (or Hafren in Welsh). Some believe the name is based on the mythical story of a river nymph, and there's a statue of the reclining figure of Sabrina in Dingle Gardens in the Quarry in Shrewsbury.

Supernatural water powers included the Celtic Saint Elian or Saint Helen, believed to be a descendant of Ella the water sprite, and Anu, a water sprite that ate children. There are many folk traditions associating female spirits with rivers, often at potentially dangerous spots like the Strid near Bolton Abbey in Yorkshire, where the waters change orientation creating a deep and deceptively powerful current. It is said that sometimes the goddess of the river appears here as a white horse and claims a victim. Such folk tales commonly surround British rivers, particularly those that have been claiming lives for centuries.[11]

The names of some water deities were recorded on inscriptions. The River Wharfe flows through the heart of Brigantia from the north-west dales through Ilkley and east to Wetherby, Tadcaster, and the Humber estuary. The spirit of the River Wharfe was Verbeia and at Ilkley we find evidence of her, sometimes referred to as the goddess of Wharfedale. Just south of where the River Wharfe passes through Ilkley is All Saints Parish Church. It stands on the site of the old Roman fort that once occupied an area about three times the area of the present church grounds. Although the fort had been given the Roman name Olicana, current opinion now favours Verbeia as the name of the Ilkley fort, associating the name with both the fort and the Romano/Celtic goddess. In the 16th century, William Camden (1551–1623) one of the founding fathers of English local history and author of *Britannia* (1586), the first comprehensive topographical survey of England, found an altar stone being used to support some stairs in a house in Ilkley. The carving and inscription were almost illegible due to earlier exposure, but a copy was made and the inscription reads VERBEIAE SACRVM CLODIVS FRONTO PRAEF COH II LINGON – 'To holy Verbeia, Clodius Fronto, prefect of the Second Cohort of Lingones'.[12]

So there was a link between the goddess Verbeia and the fort (manned by the Second Cohort of Lingones), and indirectly to the warrior aspect of Brigantia, tutelary goddess of the Brigantes tribe. The altar stone shows a female figure wearing a long pleated robe and what looks like a shaped head dress. She also holds two long wavy objects, described by historian Anne Ross as serpents. The depiction of Verbeia holding a serpent in each hand is thought to be a representation of the fort with the two streams which once flowed down from the moors to the south, either side of the fort, into the River Wharfe. The carving can now be found behind a large Anglo-Saxon cross inside the All Saints Parish Church, Ilkley.[13]

It may not be a coincidence that the name Verbeia is similar to verbena, the herb commonly known as vervain. In fact, Verbena was the generic name in ancient Rome for herbs that were considered especially potent and used in sacrifices. It is said to have been extensively used by the Druids, for healing and divination.

Water Rituals

The name Latis, which occurs at times in northern Britain, is probably derived from the proto-Celtic word lati meaning liquor. In ancient Celtic polytheism, Latis is the name of two Celtic deities; one is a goddess (Dea Latis), the other a god (Deus Latis). A dedication to Dea Latis who may have been associated with the nearby rivers, was found at Birdoswald Roman Fort in Cumbria in 1873. It reads simply: DIE LATI, 'For the goddess Latis'. The dedication stone is now in the Carlisle Museum. The dedication to Deus Latis, recovered on an altar stone at the Roman fort of Aballava, Burgh-by-Sands, also in Cumbria, was found near an image of a horned god named Belatucadros. It reads: DEO LATI LVCIVS VRSEI, 'To the god Latis, Lucius Ursei [dedicates this]'.[14]

Coventina was a Romano-British goddess of wells and springs. Dedications to Coventina and votive offerings were found in a walled area which had been built to contain the outflow from a spring now called Coventina's Well near Carrawburgh, a Roman settlement previously called Procolita, and sometimes called Brocolitia, on Hadrian's Wall near Haydon Bridge. Begun in AD122 in the reign of Emperor Hadrian, the wall runs across the whole country from the banks of the River Tyne at Newcastle on the North Sea to Carlisle on the Solway Firth. Along the length, small fortlets were built every 1,500 metres, a Roman mile. (*See also* page 186.)

The site near Coventina's Well was excavated by British archaeologist John Clayton in 1876. John Clayton was an antiquarian and town clerk of Newcastle Upon Tyne, where Clayton Street is named after him. The well itself is of great interest. The spring, in a rectangular basin 2.6 m x 2.4 m, is in the centre of a walled enclosure 11.6 m x 12.2 m within a wall 0.9 m thick. Coventina must have had a temple built in her honour as two dedication slabs and ten altars dedicated to the goddess have been found. The assortment of objects found in the well included 13,487 coins dating from Mark Anthony to Gratian (emperor AD367–383), the head of a male statue, a relief of three water nymphs believed to be Coventina, two clay incense burners, and a wide range of votive objects.[15]

When the Romans conquered, water worship was strictly forbidden, but people still wanted to give thanks for the precious gift. Human sacrifice was no longer permitted but votive offerings such as garlands of flowers were used to dress the wells and the practice was absorbed into Christianity with a few adaptations. Water worship survived as well-dressing, under the patronage of the church. (Well-dressing customs take place in Derbyshire and the Peak District, but on Ascension Day every year the pupils of Bisley Blue Coat School dress the wells in Bisley, Gloucestershire, just a few miles from the offices of the publishers of this book.)

Wells, particularly 'miracle' and curative wells in many places in Britain and abroad are still decked with flowers and greenery on ceremonial occasions, but nowhere does it quite like Derbyshire. Well-dressing, or as it was once known 'well-flowering', is a custom that surely developed from the age-old fear and worship of water-gods and spirits. Well-dressing in the White Peak village of Tissington can be traced back to 1350, when neighbouring villages were devastated by the plague. Tissington alone remained immune and this was credited to the purity of their water, so the village wells were dressed in thanksgiving. Other white peak villages followed suit and continued this beautiful old custom. Throughout the summer months, more than fifty villages and towns throughout Derbyshire dress their wells, springs and more recently taps using flowers and other natural objects to form pictures.

Often, natural locations such as lakes, rivers or where springs were located would be turned into sacred groves. These were sanctuaries, sacred spaces separated from the ordinary world and often ruled over by their own deity. Grannus was a god associated with the sun, spas, healing, and thermal and mineral springs.

Thermal Springs

The solar deity of the Celts was Sulis and by adding the prefix aquae that in Latin means waters, the Romans denoted natural spas or springs. Aquae Sulis is now the spa-town of Bath in Somerset. There's a legend that Bladud, the eldest son of the Celtic King Lud, was banished from his father's court when he contracted leprosy. He was sent to Swainswick where, in order to survive, he became a swineherd. He watched as his pigs wallowed in a particular muddy spot fed by a hot spring, and noticed that the pig's scurvy had cleared up. Because the mud had the miraculous effect of improving the condition of their skin, Bladud decided to give it a try and after wallowing in the mud, he was amazed to find his leprosy cured. Bladud returned to court and succeeded his father as king. In gratitude he built a temple at the hot spring in honour of the goddess Sulis (sometimes Sul) the Celtic goddess associated with medicine, fertility and healing. This place became sacred to the Celts and developed into the Roman spa-town.

Prior to the Roman occupation, there was a religious centre of some significance used by many generations of native Britons at Buxton in the middle of Brigante territory. This sacred grove was made special by the thermal springs that arise there. It was an important shrine where the Celts worshipped a water-goddess called Arnemetiae, 'the goddess beside the sacred grove'.

We have no idea what area was covered by the sacred grove but it's been estimated that nine thermal springs emerged from the ground in the heart of Buxton – the Crescent, Pavilion Gardens and the surrounding low-lying area. There would undoubtedly have been a temple dedicated to Arnemetiae but no one is sure where. It may have stood in the grove near the current St Anne's well, or in a more commanding position further up the slopes looking down on the sacred grove. The base of what could have been a temple was found by archaeologist Major Rooke in 1787. It was fully described at the time and is now included in the 1994 review of Roman finds in Buxton Museum.

The Pavilion gardens, previously known as the Bath Garden, are sited in the area that would have encompassed the sacred grove. In the 19th century, when Miller remodelled the gardens, a Celtic temple that had stood for 2,000 years was demolished. It was said that in 1755 almost all the lettering could still be read, but decoding proved problematic. The name Aeona was deciphered with a spot of guesswork, and unless she was a local deity of which we now have no trace, it was decided that this temple was dedicated to either Epona, horse goddess, or Apona, healing water goddess. Considering its location, the latter would be more likely. The temple's octagonal base was retained and still exists in surprisingly good condition near the footbridge over the River Wye. Circular discs cover indents in the stone where columns would have been inserted.

When the Romans arrived, they did as they had done at Bath; they added the prefix Aquae and gave the sacred grove the name Aquae Arnemetiae to honour the Celtic deity. In Roman times Aquae Arnemetiae became second only in importance to Aquae Sulis for the curative quality of its water and in order to bend the rules to suit the Romans, the goddess Arnemetiae became Saint Anne.

11

CARTIMANDUA'S RULE BEFORE THE ROMAN INVASION

Perhaps Cartimandua's power, privilege and influence were only guaranteed provided she remained chaste. Although Cartimandua married, it was probably more along the lines of a partnership because there is no mention of Cartimandua having children, and any grown-up children would surely have been mentioned.

It is likely that as a child Cartimandua was sent as a fosterling to another tribal group to broaden her horizons, form friendships and find a husband to expand and ensure a dynasty. Such arrangements were usual and she in turn would have sent her own children to other tribal groups or perhaps even to Rome to learn the ways of the Romans. This is something that the Roman historians would most definitely have recorded, but they didn't.

In describing the events of the AD50s, Tacitus refers to Cartimandua as the Queen of the Brigantine tribe with her consort Venutius. He was described as a Brigantian, but prior to his marriage to the Brigantian Queen, it has been suggested that Venutius was a prince of the Corvetti tribe, which would account for why they seemed to be particularly prominent amongst the Brigantine splinter tribes or subdivisions. The territory of the Corvetti was what is today Cumbria, and incorporates the area around the Lake District along the northern edge of Brigante territory in the region of Carlisle. This is the area which would later be bordered in the north by Hadrian's Wall, named after the

Emperor Hadrian whose rule began in 170 AD. The Corvetti are a poorly known group as there is very little archaeological evidence of the people who lived in this area before the Roman conquest. The tribe's name is cognate with the Latin name 'cervus' meaning a deer, so it could be speculated that they may have been followers of the deer-antlered god Cernunnos. Around 79AD, Luguvalium, located within present-day Carlisle, was constructed and may later have become a centre.[1]

There is no evidence to support this, but it would seem that Venutius was not the leader of the Corvetti tribe, or the Brigantes and the Corvettis would have merged into one group. He may have been a younger son or the chief of a splinter group that amalgamated with the Brigante tribe but kept their name and independence within the large kingdom or federation of the Brigantes.

Venutius was no doubt of noble birth but inferior in rank to his wife. Cartimandua was the rightful queen of the Brigantes but shared power with Venutius while he supported her. It could be that Venutius was a Roman citizen or had been sent to Rome to learn the ways of the Romans. According to Tacitus, Venutius had a long standing loyalty to Rome. His name sounds Roman, but names could be Romanised. Perhaps the marriage was arranged to secure a Roman presence in Brigantia, or perhaps Cartimandua considered marriage to a candidate acceptable to Rome to be beneficial in such troubled times. As with any major decision, she would no doubt have looked for signs and asked the gods for guidance, and initially Venutius would appear to have been the perfect consort and entirely happy to support his wife.

Marriage seems to have been more of a partnership for the Celts than it was in the Roman world. According to Caesar, the practice amongst the Celts was for the husband and wife to pool resources. At death, the surviving partner inherited everything.

The men after due reckoning, take from their own goods a sum of money equal to the dowry they have received from their wives and place it with the dowry. Of each sum account is kept between them and the profits saved; whichever of the two survives, receives the pool of both together with the profits of past years.[2]

The Brigantine empire covered a huge area but unfortunately there is no mention of a tribal headquarters or a specific area where Cartimandua and the ruling elite lived. This could mean that they moved on a regular basis, perhaps because the Brigante territory covered such a large area. We have no firm guidelines as to the size, but the Brigante kingdom in pre-Roman times controlled the largest section of what would become northern England, and in particular Yorkshire and Derbyshire. The name *Brigante* shares the same proto/Celtic root as the goddess Brigantia meaning high or elevated, and as I was looking for the most worthy contender as the home of our Celtic Queen, the most obvious name to look for was Brigantium.

Isurium Brigantum (Aldborough)

Mosaic floor from Aldborough; Romulus and Remus being rescued by the wolf. Drawn by Jacqui Taylor. (From *Roman Britain*, Patricia Southern)

Although it is not well documented, I was delighted to find *Isurium Brigantum* in the very heart of Brigante territory. The name is derived from the Latin name of the river *Iseur*, now the River Ure, and the name of the Brigante tribe, which would indicate that this was their tribal centre. Isurium Brigantum is now the Yorkshire village of Aldborough in the civil parish of Boroughbridge in the Borough of Harrogate in North Yorkshire. Traces of early housing have been found, with many potshards, coins, bronze, iron and other objects, but there is nothing to identify Isurium Brigantum with Cartimandua or the Brigante elite. However, this could have been the administrative centre or civit of the Brigantes in the period when Queen Cartimandua collaborated with the Romans. Sadly we know nothing about the Brigante settlement of Isurium Brigantum because any early building was totally destroyed when the Romans built a town on the site. Tacitus reports that the Roman town of Isurium Brigantum was the work of Julius Agricola in 79 AD.[3]

Isurium Brigantum may have been the base of the Roman Legio VIII Hispana. It was obviously of major importance to the Romans and it's rather surprising to find that in this early period, Isurium Brigantum had the same status as Chichester, Canterbury, Exeter and Leicester. While they have remained major towns and expanded into cities, Isurium Brigantium fell out of favour and into ruins. Later development virtually destroyed all the Roman town but a large part of the town walls can still be seen. The population of Aldborough is now 1,300 compared to Chichester – 23,731, Canterbury – 43,432, Exeter – 127,300 and Leicester – 443,760. The Roman Site museum, run by English Heritage, contains relics of the Roman town, including mosaic pavements. (*See* page 139).[4]

The High Ones
Brigante could have referred to the high ones meaning the tribal chiefs, or the high ones meaning highlanders who lived in the hilly region later known as the Pennines. This range of hills formed the spine of the Brigante territory and is sometimes called the backbone of England. Sadly there was no elevated fortification or settlement called Brigantium, but I started my search at the base of the Pennines in what is now the northern Derbyshire Peak District. Evidence from excavations and aerial photography has revealed many

ritual earthwork complexes that were the cemeteries and religious establishments of the Stone, Bronze and Iron Age people. Within the territory of the Brigante tribe alone, it is estimated that there are 10,000 earthworks, cairns and barrows, and hundreds, possibly thousands of hillforts where the Celtic people would have lived. It is no thanks to our cannibal builders who devoured their stones that our landscape it still dotted with them, and only a handful have been excavated and evaluated. I was on a mission, a quest to find evidence of Queen Cartimandua and her tribal headquarters somewhere in the middle to north of England, so I began with the remarkable Mam Tor. That surely is one of the most worthy contenders as the home of our Celtic Queen.

Mam Tor

Hillforts by definition topped hills and the Peak District's most spectacular hillfort was the one that topped Mam Tor; the Mother Mountain. At 1,695 ft (517 m) above sea level, Mam Tor is the highest and largest of the Derbyshire hill forts perched at the south-west end of the ridge that separates the Castleton and Edale Valleys. It lies in the heart of Brigante territory.

Mam Tor, a Celtic hillfort that may have been inhabited by Cartimandua.

It would have commanded an important position on the east-west trade routes between the valleys of the Rivers Don and Rother, and the Cheshire Plain, so it could have been a significant political as well as military centre. The larger, more important hillforts were often placed at the boundaries between areas with different topographies and resources, and although the precise significance of the name is now lost, there is no doubt that Mam Tor translates as 'Heights of the Mother' or 'Mother Mountain', and that was a very important Iron Age Hillfort.

Mam Tor must have been a significant place for people long before the Bronze Age, because a polished stone axe and flints from the Neolithic age have been found there. Excavations have also revealed much broken pottery as well as whetstones and shale beads. During the later Bronze Age and into the Iron Age, the hill was occupied as a slight univallate hillfort, which is defined as a hilltop enclosure consisting of a single line of defences. Mam Tor's earthwork was a single rampart, a bern or flat terrace, then a U shaped ditch which is now silted up but which could have been up to 2 metres deep and about 2.5 metres wide. The spoil from the ditch would have been used to build a smaller outer bank around I metre high and 2 metres wide, enclosing an area of 5–6 hectares or 12–15 acres.

Mam Tor was not ideally suited for occupation; the hog-backed nature of the ridge means that the ground drops away quite steeply from the maximum height of nearly 1,700 feet on the narrow crest to the rampart on the west and east. Nevertheless, there are clear indications that it held quite numerous hut-platforms cut into these internal slopes on both the sheltered eastern and exposed western sides. It held up to one hundred circular stone and timber huts.

It's very likely that Mam Tor was built in its highly prominent location as an impressive display of prestige and community identity as much as for defence. It is thought that the original rampart round Mam Tor was a wooden palisade cut into the hillside, but these turf and timber forts needed extensive refurbishment and rebuilding every thirty or so years. When the wooden palisade was replaced by a more sturdy stone defence, it could have been as much as 10 ft (3 metres) high and 5.5 metres wide, except in the south-east corner where the sheer cliff face of the tor provided a natural defence. Earth ramparts were often topped with timber stockades, complicated wooden structures often with wooden palisades or revetments – wooden posts to strengthen or heighten the walls.[5]

Thanks to aerial photography, we can see the ramparts marked out on Mam Tor's summit. Its stone and timber walls now show as grassed-over banks and ditches. Surface evidence of gatehouses and timber structures in the interior is rarely visible, but we can see entrances to the north and south west. There are clear remains of the two gateways on the paths leading from Mam Nick and from Hollins Cross. Of these, the south-west entrance is better preserved. Entrances were placed at key locations and the south-west entrance would have given access to The Portway, the ancient, prehistoric track that led south from Mam Tor to the River Erewash at Stapleford on what is now the Derbyshire/Nottinghamshire border. (*See* page 289). The northern entrance would have connected Mam Tor with the small inlet upstream of the River Noe. There may even have been a small quay or port here.

Near the summit of Mam Tor are two barrows or tumuli, round mounds over burial chambers. The barrows within the area enclosed by the defences are evidence of the continual use of the hillside. A trig point that records the height as 517 metres above sea level has been placed on one barrow. Now owned by the National Trust, this area has been paved to prevent further erosion and to protect it from wear and tear, so the barrow is hard to make out, but the other barrow to the southwest is quite well preserved despite having a crater-like hole in its top. In recent excavation work, a bronze axe and cremation urn were found in one of these barrows producing radio carbon dates of around 1,200BC.

When the drier climate of the Bronze Age changed to today's Atlantic period, Mam Tor began to slip. The fact that it is still active and is seen to be moving has gained it the local name the Shivering Mountain as it slowly engulfs the flat fields at its toe, and creeps towards Castleton at a rate of 1 inch per year. Geologists think it will only stop when the face of the hill reaches an angle of 30 degrees – probably in another 1,500 years.

The rock falls and landslides are due to its unstable rock structure, a peculiar composition of shale and grit in alternate layers. After heavy rainfall, water seeps between the rock layers, lubricating the joints and enabling the different layers to slip over each other. In 1819, the Sheffield Turnpike Co constructed the A625 Manchester to Sheffield road using spoil from the nearby Odin mine. It followed the hairpin bend route in front of the face but over the next 160 years it needed constant repairs and reconstruction. In 1977 the landscape moved again and the road was restricted to a single lane, then two years later, it was permanently closed to traffic. Layers of tarmac and gravel up to 2 metres thick in places show the effort taken to keep the road open, but nature has almost re-claimed it, and it's now a track for walkers and cyclists. Access to Mam Tor is via a short, steep walk from Mam Nick car park on the Chapel en le Frith to Castleton Road.

Legend has it that although the surface constantly crumbles and slides downwards, the shadow of the hill never grows any smaller. For this reason, Mam Tor is seen as a wonder and a worthy contender for a place in 'The Seven Wonders of the Peak'.[6]

Burr Tor Hillfort, Great Hucklow

You will find many places with a 'low' suffix around the Peak District: Grindlow – Tideslow – Hucklow – Wardlow – Foolow etc. 'Low' is derived from the Old English *hlaw* meaning hill, particularly one that was noticeably higher than others nearby. These high places were frequently used by early man as burial mounds, but I was searching for a prominent tribal hillfort, that iconic symbol of the Iron Age Celts, that could have been Cartimandua's headquarters. Sadly, most of these prominent hilltops have been extensively disturbed and plundered over the centuries. At Great Hucklow, I found not only an ancestral burial mound but a tribal hillfort.

Burr Mount or Burr Tor near Great Hucklow overlooks the limestone plateau between Eyam and Hazelbridge. It is one of the largest hillfort sites in the region enclosing an area of eight acres and standing at 396 m (1300 ft). Although that is 121 m lower than Mam Tor, it's still an impressive height. The name tor would indicate an exposed rock mass, and the name Burh means fortification or fortified place, as in Harbour or Harborough at Harborough Rocks further south. Harbour or Harborough derives from *here-beorge* and may mean camp/shelter. So would the name Burr indicate that there was a dwelling or fort here, and could that have been Cartimandua's headquarters?

Also known as Camp Hill, it is very broad or deep. On the west side, the enclosure is defined by a bank and berm, or terrace, which lies just below the crest of the steep face of Burr Tor. At some time prior to 1824, a carved stone of Bronze Age date was found in the vicinity there's the remains of an oval enclosure measuring 400 m (north to south) x 170 m (east to west). In 1789, Creswell described these earthworks as comprising a double ditch. The stone is finely carved with spiral designs on both sides and is now on display at Sheffield City Museum.

Later fieldwork, included a survey by Preston in 1954 and another carried out by Hart in 1978, confirmed that the material from these ditches had been used to construct low banks in between. These banks are no longer visible because in 1978 the ditches were infilled and the earthworks flattened to provide a level field for the Derbyshire and Lancashire Gliding Club. Burr Tor is now the landing ground of the club, founded in 1934.

Also in 1978, the interior of the enclosure was ploughed to bedrock but the area still retains deep-cut archaeological features such as post-holes, drains and trenches. The line of the earthworks is still visible from the air, although there is not a great deal to see apart from faint traces of a bank and ditch towards the eastern edge of the fort.

Sadly, Burr Tor has not revealed any of its secrets, but from the little that we do know, it certainly would not have been a suitable abode for our Celtic Queen. It's even been suggested that although it is similar in area and appearance to a promontory hillfort, due to the limited scale of the earthworks that formerly defined its east and south edges, it may not have been a hillfort at all. Burr Tor is now believed to have been a late Bronze Age or Early Iron Age stock enclosure.

Fin Cop

Another prominent summit suitable for a royal residence, Fin Cop is approximately 12 miles from Mam Tor. This elevated site stands on the western end of a limestone hill at 1,025 feet above sea level, and commands magnificent views over the River Wye and Monsal Dale. It's a unique and beautiful landscape which has been left largely untouched by post-Iron Age and Roman influences. There are five Iron Age hillforts within five miles of Bakewell, is a well-known market town in the Peak District.

Fin Cop is one of the largest enclosures within the Peak District, originally encircling four hectares. The name Fin Cop is Old English

Above: Fin Cop, a dramatic headland that was once a Celtic hillfort.

Left: Digging at Fin Cop, near Bakewell, the team found skeletons of women, children and babies (courtesy of Archaeological Research Services Ltd, Bakewell)

and means 'Head of the Heap'. The track leading to the ancient Celtic fort is called Pennyunk Lane. The University of Wales studies the ancient Celtic language and has suggested that this is phonetically derived from Pen-y-uwch meaning 'Higher Head'. Hierarchically as well as geographically, this could make Fin Cop a possible contender for Cartimandua's headquarters.

It was known from excavations carried out in the 18th and 19th centuries that Fin Cop was an Iron Age hill fort, and that

Bronze Age farmers living in the area around 2,000 BC buried their dead on the crest of the hill in rock-cut graves covered in stone. Although a number of rapid surveys have been undertaken over the years, Fin Cop had never been subjected to an all-encompassing study until 2009. A series of test pits produced over 1,700 stone artefacts made from chert, also called hornstone, an impure black or grey microcrystalline variety of quartz rock that is chemically similar to flint. Used in pottery and as a primitive tool, early man would have been familiar with its magical quality. When struck with steel, chert, like flint, produces a spark.

The main focus of the 2009 dig was to discover how the ramparts that enclose the ten-acre hillfort were built and when they were erected. The architectural jigsaw revealed that the ramparts had been breached and destroyed during a devastating attack on the fort around the 4th century BC. The skeleton of a woman found amongst the jumbled stone of a collapsed rampart was thought at first to be a foundation sacrifice. Female skeletons have been found under the gate area of other fortified sites, and it's been suggested these are human sacrifices made to protect the gates. Tests carried out on the skeleton showed that it was a pregnant woman between twenty to thirty years old when she died. But a trench next to the southern rampart of the hillfort contained the skeletons of people who had been thrown from the battlements and buried beneath stone blocks that had been pushed onto them from the ramparts. Almost all the skeletons were the remains of women and children, and two of the women appear to have been pregnant. So numerous women and children were victims during the sacking of the Fin Cop hill fort. The absence of male skeletons could indicate that the men were spared in this massacre so that they could be put to work or sold as slaves. Jim Brighton, one of the project managers said; 'Quite a lot of very important finds don't look like much on site, but when you get back to the lab and throw the scientific techniques and analysis at them, that's when you start to get the story out.'

The investigation at Fin Cop was named Britain's Best Community Archaeological Project in 2010. Under the leadership of Dr Clive Waddington, the dig involved 120 volunteers, lots of visitors and 450 schoolchildren. The Longstone Local History Group and

Archaeological Research Services Ltd have now been awarded a grant of nearly £50,000 and extra lottery funding to enable them to make a second dig at the Fin Cop hillfort site to find out more about the people of Iron Age Britain. If this fort was sacked and abandoned around the 4th century BC it can't be an obvious contender to be Cartimandua's headquarters.

Ingleborough Celtic Hillfort

Moving north to the other end of what would have been Brigante territor y, there is Ingleborough. Situated in the south-west corner of the Yorkshire Dales, Ingleborough is the second highest mountain in the Dales, being at the highest point of a large triangle of land with corners at Ingleton, Ribblehead, and Settle. The second part of the name Ingleborough, as in Burr Mount or Burr Tor, is derived from the Old English word *burh*, meaning a fortified place. The Celtic hillfort sits atop the imposing hill of Ingleborough at an altitude of 723 m or 2,372 feet, 206 m or 677 ft higher than Mam Tor. The furthest important mountain peak visible from Ingleborough is Manod Mawr in Snowdonia, North Wales, 103 miles (166 km) away, and on a clear day it's possible to see the Irish Sea and the Isle of Man in the west. Unsurprisingly, it's one of the highest Iron Age forts in Britain. Ingleborough would certainly qualify on altitude alone to be the headquarters of Cartimandua.[7]

The striking appearance of Ingleborough from all directions and from a great distance is due to the unusual geology of the underlying rocks. Topped with a cap of Millstone grit there are layers of limestone sandwiched between softer rocks. The base is composed of ancient Silurian and Ordovician rocks on top of which lies a 600 ft (180 m) thick coat of Carboniferous limestone, the Great Scar Limestone. Due to the limestone's permeability, all the streams flowing down from the mountain disappear into numerous pot holes, with names like Fluted Hole, Pillar Hole and Meregill Hole. Also, there is Juniper Gulf which descends 420 ft (130 m) underground through an impressive rift. Like Mam Tor, Ingleborough sits on a hill that seems to be hollow.

The fort on this relatively flat, fifteen-acre plateau was believed to have been built by the Brigantes in the first century BC. The remains of an old walled enclosure have been discovered, containing the foundations of Iron Age huts. Its position was no doubt chosen for defensive purposes and it was an extensive fortified settlement. But unlike other hillforts in North Yorkshire which showed evidence that they were under attack from the invading Roman army, this hillfort is unique in that it wasn't constructed purely for military use. It's the only one of its type in Yorkshire.

A rampart of rubble and millstone grit 13 feet wide and 3,000 feet long encircled the relatively plateau at the summit, and although this was well built, the massive dry stone walls below the north and west sides of the fort were crudely constructed and incorporated large boulders. The reason for this is unknown. The position of the original entrances is uncertain, but the most likely spots are on the north-east and south-western sides. There is no evidence that it was ever besieged, but because it had no water supply, it was certainly vulnerable to siege. This would tie in with the fact that the Romans never attacked Cartimandua and her people, so this could easily have been one of her strongholds, if not *the* one.

Within the protective walls of Ingleborough are the remains of at least twenty circular stone hut foundations, usually with south-facing entrances. The hut circles lie mostly to the relatively sheltered eastern side of the fort and tend to be in clusters or groups. All are between 5.5 metres and 8.0 metres in diameter within rubble walls. Some of them have external drainage gullies.

According to Bowden, the site is so exposed it's unlikely that people lived there all year round, others disagree. Seasonal occupation as part of a transhumance cycle, grazing stock on higher pastures in the summer and returning to the valleys in the winter, may be a possibility. It may also have served as a place for ritual and the expression of power. It seems to have continued as a tribal centre right through until the Roman occupation.

Although it's unusual for such a location, other sources have confirmed that it was used all year round, but we must take into account that at the time of the Romans the climate was much milder. They cultivated grapes in Newcastle during the Roman occupation, for example. The Romans called it the King's Fort. It may be that this was not Cartimandua's headquarters but was occupied by her husband Venutius, possibly after their acrimonious split.[8]

Almondbury Fort

The site of Almondbury near Huddersfield, Yorkshire, dominates the Holme Valley just south of its confluence with the River Colne. The river valleys have been a key artery of trade and communication since prehistoric times and connected Almondbury to the Peak District, Lancashire, the Yorkshire Wolds, the Mersey and Ribble estuaries.

The site was occupied for thousands of years with the earliest Neolithic settlers probably dating back to 2100BC. Occupation continued during the Bronze Age and Iron Age, and there is evidence that the site was occupied during the early part of Cartimandua's reign. But could this have been Cartimandua's tribal headquarters?

This prominent hill, now known as Castle Hill, owes its shape to an outlying cap of hard Grenoside sandstone that has protected the softer stone beneath from erosion. Today it's a striking natural landmark nearly 1,000 ft (300 m) high, covering some eight acres (3.2 ha) and surrounded by very steep slopes. The site is dominated by a nineteenth-century folly but underneath the earthworks is a series of earlier defences which date back to the early Iron Age. It is regarded as one of Yorkshire's most important early Iron Age hill forts, and given the lack of similar hill forts in the region, could have been a tribal capital of some significance.

The earthworks encircling the hill were constructed in stages over a period of roughly two hundred years. The earliest enclosure, dated by radiocarbon and thermoluminescence techniques to the late seventh century BC, consisted of an area of 2 ha at the south-west end of the hill enclosed by a single bank measuring 3 m in width. This first enclosure did not have an external ditch but the bank would have been surmounted by a wooden palisade topped with sharpened stakes. One simple inturned entrance bisected the bank that crossed the hill and had a small guard room with a hearth to one side.

This univallate (single rampart) hillfort was upgraded in the sixth century BC into a multivallate (multiple rampart) configuration when a ditch was dug external to the existing defences and the spoil used to create a new rampart to give multiple lines of defence. Inside this area would have been a number a circular huts forming a permanent village. Further upgrades were made in the late sixth century BC with the addition of another ditch and the defences were also extended to the north-east, effectively doubling the size of the original enclosure to around five acres. This hillfort would have been full of noise and bustle and vigorous life. Inside the fort would have been the huts of farmers who tilled the fields and pastured cattle and sheep. Alongside the farmsteads would be sheds and cattle pens, storage pits for grain, and rubbish pits.

By the fifth century BC the hillfort would have been occupied by the Brigantes tribe and the substantial and significant upgrades made to the hillfort's defences would indicate that this was undoubtedly an important site. The main rampart was revetted in stone that was held in place with timber frames. An outwork, one of the earliest examples of its kind, replaced a simple inturned entrance. The outer ditch was also enhanced and converted into a deep V-shaped trench.

Some sources claim it was named Camulodunon, meaning the stronghold of Camulos, but Camulodunon was the name of Colchester in Essex, capital of the Trinovantes and later the Catuvellauni tribes.[9] The confusion may be due to the site of the nearby Slack Roman fort named Camulodunum or Cambodunum mentioned as a station on the route alongside the Pennine section of the Roman road from Deva Victrix (Chester) to Eboracum (York) in the Antonine Itinerary.[10]

During a series of excavations, a variety of Iron Age pottery was found in the shelters behind the inner rampart. The finds represent jars which could have come to the fort by trade or barter and are an important aid in dating the site. It's not clear what the inhabitants of Castle Hill had to offer in return, but it may have been skins, as post holes were found which may have been drying frames to stretch and cure the skins.

In a series of digs stretching from the late 1930s to the early 1970s, however, Dr William Varley dispelled these previously held views. He believed that the early timber settlement was destroyed by fire *c.* 430BC and remained unoccupied for the next 1,500 years. The date was arrived at after excavations carried out in 1972 analysed the burnt clay from the ramparts. It was found that the burning varied in intensity within the ramparts. Some parts were hardly affected, while other sections only a few centimetres away were burnt to a cinder. To support Varley's theory, officials of the Yorkshire Division of the National Coal Board who examined the sections in the field were of the opinion that these effects resembled those they were familiar in coal waste-tip fires attributed to spontaneous combustion.

The fact that five coal seams lie within the shales of the lower slopes of Castle Hill corroborates this theory. Over the centuries, some of these shallower seams have been worked along the hillside by adits and shafts, the workings of which are still visible in several places.

If Varley's theory is correct, Almondsbury would not have been occupied again until the 2nd century AD so could not have been Cartimandua's tribal headquarters. New research and finds could one day show that this is not so and the first-century Celts did inhabit the fortress. However, following the Norman Conquest of 1066 and the subsequent rush of castle building, the materials and earth works of Castle Hill were re-used to build a motte and bailey castle. This effectively obliterated any evidence of earlier buildings. The Norman castle was abandoned in the late thirteenth century, probably owing to its exposed and impractical location, and today the site is dominated by the Victorian Tower, a large folly built in 1897 to celebrate Queen Victoria's Silver Jubilee. It's very likely that once again the building materials were salvaged and reused, and now the only recognisable masonry of the medieval castle is the well, no doubt the same source that supplied water to the Iron Age hillfort too.

Stanwick

The next most logical site for the Brigante queen's tribal headquarters is the remarkable Iron Age fortress at Stanwick, north of Richmond. This was a prime location in the Tees valley west of Darlington commanding the route north through the Vale of York to Northumberland, as well as being strategically placed to control east-west movement over the Pennines via the key pass into Cumbria at Stainmore. Sir Mortimer Wheeler's excavations suggested a positive link with the royal house of the Brigantes. Was this the royal headquarters of Cartimandua?

Stanwick is the largest hillfort in Britain. Colin Haselgrove, Professor of Archaeology at the University of Leicester and editor of an excavation report on Stanwick, wrote:

Prior to 1977, there were only two Iron Age sites of any note that had been excavated south of the Tyne until you got down into Yorkshire. It was just a blank. You could almost see why some Roman archaeologists thought that the army had moved into an empty, disorganised landscape. Yet there has been a growth in evidence over recent decades, especially in an industrialised landscape like the northeast of England.

The name Stanwick is believed to be derived from the Old Norse word 'steinvegges' meaning stone walls. It could also have been known as Rigodonum, a Brigantian fort of unknown location mentioned by Tacitus. Stanwick Iron Age Fort comprises over six miles (9 kilometres) of ditches and ramparts rising to a height of almost 16 ft (5 m) in places, and completely surrounding the village of Stanwick St John. In its final stage the massive earthworks enclosed an area of 740–850 acres and it's often referred to as the royal centre of Stanwick. So have we found what we are looking for?

This area was considered of outstanding significance by Sir Mortimer Wheeler when he carried out his last major archaeological excavation in 1951–1952. Wheeler announced that Stanwick had been constructed in three separate phases, starting with a modest seventeen-acre earth work enclosure on a low hill known as The Tofts. He dates this first phase to around AD40. According to his report, around AD50–60 the site was extended with a new 130-acre enclosure to the north, then around 72AD the whole was extended by another 600 acres to the south. Wheeler's theory is that the Brigantes fortified the site when the Romans invaded.

During the course of his excavations, Wheeler cleared a 50 ft (15 m) section of ditch that the Brigantes had cut from the underlying limestone rock. He partially reconstructed a 10 ft (3 m) length of dry-stone revetment wall from the fallen stones found in the ditch. This was constructed to a height of approximately 2 feet above the existing ramparts, although Wheeler estimated that the original wall height would have been nearer 15 ft (4.6 m) above the ramparts. This small section known as Wheeler's wall close to the hamlet of Forcett, 2 miles south-west of Piercebridge and about 5 miles north-west of Scotch Corner is under the guardianship of English Heritage and open to the public.

Wheeler calculated that a typical occupied hillfort, one where people lived, could hold up to 100 people per acre. This indicates that Stanwick could have had 85,000 inhabitants, although allowance must be made for utilities, animal enclosures etc. There was metal working on site in copper-alloy, as well as a thriving pottery industry and other necessary trades. Some of the vessels which the Iron Age potters produced would have had a ritual function, and it's likely that Stanwick was also a ceremonial site, drawing in celebrants from a wide area. The presence of two Roman coins of the Augustan period and one Iron Age coin from the East Midlands suggests a trading link with the wider world.

Amongst Wheeler's most famous finds at Stanwick were an Iron Age sword, unusually still in its well-preserved ash-wood scabbard, and a severed head showing considerable damage from wounds inflicted by an axe or sword. These were found in a ditch terminal next to the location of the main north-western gate, and Wheeler believed the severed head may have been hanging from the gate structure itself as a trophy or warning to enemies.

Percival Turnbull and Colin Haselgrove disagreed with some of Wheeler's theories although later archaeologists have said that Wheeler was 90% correct. From 1981–89, an area of 1200m² was excavated in the northern part of the area known as The Tofts as part of a wider research project exploring Stanwick and its environs. The archaeologists also reinvestigated some of the earth works and sampled nearby sites at Rock Castle and Melsonby using radiocarbon dating. At Stanwick they found traces of building dating from 30–20BC, seventy years earlier than Wheeler had predicted. Radiocarbon dating and Bayesian analysis showed that during this period occupation took the form of a series of short-lived compounds, circular buildings, gullies and a midden. Major changes occurred AD30–40 with the creation of an oval ditched enclosure, followed shortly afterwards by the building of the Tofts rampart and two huge successive timber circular structures over the former midden. Later, the former circular structures were rebuilt in stone together with two further circular buildings. During this period, the 6.8-km long perimeter earth work was built, an expansion which put Stanwick on a par with major late Iron Age centres in southern England. This Iron Age earth work complex is among the largest late prehistoric oppida in Europe, and comparisons can be made with southern sites like Colchester, St Albans, and Chichester. These complexes were vast, featuring living, industrial, and burial spaces as well as areas used for agriculture and ritual gatherings.

Stanwick is unlike anything else in the Iron Age north. Instead of clinging to a hilltop, the ramparts were raised in gently undulating farmland. The outer earthworks girding the Stanwick complex were stone-faced and ran for 6.8 km, enclosing a staggering 270 ha of farmland. It's generally believed that the name Stanwick means 'stone dwellings'. The area is noted for its quarries.

Turnbull and Haselgrove showed that Stanwick wasn't somewhere that had only been occupied for a short period as Wheeler had originally suggested, nor were the origins of Stanwick in the mid-1st century. There were a number of structural phases present and the origins were found to be from 80–70BC. The earliest structure on the site based on the very small quantities of pottery finds from that period suggest that it was just another Late Iron Age farmstead, but by 20–10BC the site had undergone a dozen structural phases. During this time, a huge rampart was erected at the Tofts, enclosing the hillside overlooking the Mary Wild valley, an area of about 6.25 ha. Within the interior, a range of pens were constructed. One of these compounds had an oval footprint and survived in various forms right down to Stanwick's abandonment almost a century later. Its retention indicated a new stability to the layout of the site. A substantial circular structure incorporated timbers up to 0.6 m thick was erected just north of the oval compound. Whatever its role, the structure was sufficiently important that after 20 or 30 years it was replaced by a second building, which stood until about AD40.

The radical revamping in the mid-1st century AD when the outer stone-faced ramparts were added transformed Stanwick into 'one of the most grandiose sites in Iron Age Europe' (Professor Colin Haselgrove). Despite the scale of the new fortification, it was defensively flawed, with a perimeter that was too long to defend effectively and a course that did not always use the terrain to maximum tactical advantage. The size of the enclosure was not commensurate with the accompanying signs of habitation; which raises the question, what purpose did this place serve? Was it a venue for seasonal gatherings?

An earlier trickle of imported Roman goods became a flood *c.*AD 40–70. About 200 ceramic and glass vessels were found in the limited area explored during the 1980s excavations, as well as small quantities of Roman window glass and tiles. This spans the period when Cartimandua was Queen of the Brigante tribe, a period when she was a Roman ally and Brigantia was a client kingdom. Here is evidence that Stanwick was Cartimandua's capital. Colin Haselgrove:

> If Stanwick was the seat of power of someone who achieved exceptional status, people would have been drawn there in large numbers; other members of the Brigantian elite and their entourages, craft workers dependent on wealthy patronage who fashioned prestige metalwork like that in the Stanwick hoard, ambassadors and traders, or those who owed services and tributes... If we look around for sites that fit the bill for a royal seat of power in Northern England, Stanwick is the outstanding candidate.[11]

In 1843, a hoard of 140 metal artefacts acknowledged as the Stanwick hoard was found half a mile away from Stanwick at Melsonby. These were believed to have been buried as a ritual hoard just outside the royal centre. They include four sets of horse harness for chariots, and a bronze horse head bucket attachment. Known as the Stanwick Horse Mask, this is a 10 cm bronze model of a horse's head. It's made from a thin sheet of bronze and the doleful looking horse appears to be flaring its right nostril. The head was made to be nailed or riveted to a wooden object, but because wood rots archaeologists have no idea what the object might have been. There's a theory that it could have been attached to a miniature wooden bucket possibly used as a drinking vessel for mead or beer.

12

THE ROMAN ATTACK

In 59 BC Gaius Julius Caesar achieved the position of Consul. He was appointed Governor of Gaul in 58 BC, and the whole of modern France and Belgium became part of the Roman Empire, ensuring Rome's safety from Gallic invasions. While there Caesar won great devotion from his troops. He stayed in Gaul for eight years and during this time led two expeditions to Britain, in 55 and 54 BC. Accounts

Bust of Caesar.

of the invasion are recorded by Caesar himself in his *Commentaries on the Gallic Wars,* and also briefly in *Agricola*, a biography of a Governor of Britain by the contemporary historian Tacitus.

The first expedition was apparently aborted because having crossed the Straits of Dover with 12,000 troops, the Roman legions refused to leave their ships at the sight of the naked blue savages massed on the shore. The Celts probably looked extremely savage but they were not savages. They believed that if the gods decided that they should die fighting, no amount of armour would save them and they went into battle naked. They would paint themselves with intricate and stylised magical designs using a dye from the plant *isatis tinctorial*, better known as woad, which produced a blue dye. They believed that this would deflect enemy blows and missiles. Caesar remarked that before going into battle 'all the Britons stain themselves with woad which gives a blue colour and imparts a ferocious aspect in battle.' This is why the Romans referred to the Ancient Britons as Picts, meaning painted or tattooed.

Caesar landed in England at Cantium (possibly Deal), accompanied by five legions and 2000 Gallic cavalry. This area of Kent and east Sussex was the territory of the Cantiaci tribe and like other people in southern Britain at the time of the Roman conquest, this group had very strong links with France and was open to influences from France and the Mediterranean World. They and the neighbouring tribes were early adopters of coins and French styles of cremating the dead. Caesar approved:

Ex his omnibus longe sunt humanissimi qui Cantium incolunt, quae regio est maritima omnis, neque multum a Gallica differunt consuetudine.

Of all these (British tribes), by far the most civilised are they who dwell in Kent, which is entirely a maritime region, and who differ but little from the Gauls in their customs.

After the Roman conquest the Cantiaci became a civitas, an administrative unit within a Roman province, based on their principal settlement at Canterbury known as Durovernum Cantiacorum.

Caesar fought his way across country, closely pursued by British tribes. The Cantiaci tribe was bordered by the Regni or Regnenses to the west, and the Catuvellauni to the north. It's been suggested that the Regnenses or Regni tribe was unknown at the time, and the Romans created this civitas for administration purposes within the newly formed Roman province. Or it was a smaller tribal subgroup of the Atrebates. There seems to have been some doubt about the neighbouring Belgae tribe too. Both the civitas of Regni and Belgae were most probably artificial creations of the Roman administration. Its administrative capital at Winchester was known as Venta Belgarum, which was an important settlement before the Roman conquest. The whole of the territory between what is today West Sussex, Hampshire and Berkshire was the territory of the Atrebates. This important kingdom had two major centres at Calleva, now the site of Silchester near Reading, and Chichester (West Sussex) on the south coast.

The River Thames Boundary

The River Thames, known to the Celts as Tamesis or Tamesa, acted as a boundary and frontier between the tribes, separating, for example, the Antrebates and the Catuvallauni, and the Regnenses and Catuvellauni. When Caesar arrived during his 54BC invasion he encountered Cassivellaunus, King of the Catuvellauni tribe, and his forces drawn up along the northern bank of the Thames. Julius Caesar translated it as *Thamesis* in his own report:

> The river was passable on foot only at one place and that with difficulty ... the bank moreover was planted with sharp stakes and others of the same kind were fixed in the bend of the river, beneath the water.[1]

We know that the crucial battle took place on the banks of the Thames but primary sources are too sketchy to locate the exact location. The site of Caesar's crossing point has been endlessly disputed, but apparently in that period, between Shepperton and Walton on Thames, along with Brentford in Greater London, were the only two places where the Thames could be forded. Legend insists that Caesar crossed the Thames at the former site, now named Cowey Sale, just upstream from where Walton Bridge now stands. He made camp on the high ground at the Iron Age Fort on St. George's Hill, now known as Caesar's Camp. Roman objects have been found in the neighbourhood and woad can still be found growing in profusion here.

Presumably the 'sharp stakes' recorded by Caesar were erected by Cassivellaunus, King of the Catuvellauni tribe, to stop Caesar's progress. In the 8th century AD, the Anglo-Saxon historian the Venerable Bede referred to these stakes and described them as

> ... formed of the entire bodies of young oak trees ... wood so hardened as to resemble ebony ... each about six foot long and as big as a man's thigh stood in two rows as if going across river. 9 feet apart as water runs, 4 feet apart crossing the river.[2]

A 'Cowey stake' was deposited in the British Museum in the 18th century and described thus:

> This stake was on 16 October 1777 drawn out of the bottom of the river Thames in which at least five sixths of its length was embedded; it stood with several others which (the water being uncommonly low) were then easily to be seen about one third of the river's breadth from its south bank and a quarter of a mile above Walton Bridge.[3]

William Camden wrote about the Cowey stakes in his *History of Britain*. Daniel Defoe also mentioned them in his *Tour Through England and Wales*. Geologists calculate that the river bed here at Walton has moved steadily north into Shepperton over the years, so it does not reflect the river path as it was in Roman times. It's also believed that the stakes were moved from their original positions and re-arranged to form an early bridge or passageway for cattle to walk over or swim through, which would explain the origin of the name Cowey as 'Cow Way'. The area is now known as Cowey Sale.[4]

Caesar didn't stay long in Britain, but long enough to realise that the Celts had for centuries been making offerings to the gods and spirits that lived in lakes, rivers and other water sources. These offerings were often quite substantial, a fact that wasn't lost on the Romans. They were not averse to pillaging the sacred water sources, and as stated earlier, as much as fifty tons of gold and a similar amount of silver, looted from hallowed water in Britain cleared Caesar's vast debts and financed his career.

At the end of his Governorship, Caesar feared prosecution by the Senate and refused to disarm. Instead he crossed the Rubicon (the stream marking the boundary of his province), invaded Rome and declared war on the Senate. Caesar made himself both consul and dictator of Rome, and this great power allowed him to carry out greatly needed reform, build the Forum Iulium, enlarge the senate, relieve debt, and revise the calendar. However his dictatorship didn't last long. On the 15th (Ides) of March 44BC, Caesar was assassinated on the steps of Pompey's Theatre in Rome. Fourteen years of civil war followed that eventually ended the Republic and established Caesar's nephew, Octavian, as 'Augustus', the first emperor of the Roman Empire.

Between 55BC and the 40s AD, in common with other regions on the edge of the empire, Britain enjoyed diplomatic and trading links with the Romans. The *status quo* of tribute, hostages, and client states remained largely intact without direct military occupation. Strabo's *Geography*, written during this period and first published around 7BC, says Britain paid more in customs and duties than could be raised by taxation if the island were conquered.[5]

Roman economic and cultural influence was a significant part of the British pre-Roman Iron Age, especially in the south, but that did not put Britain beyond invasion. The Emperor Augustus prepared for invasion three times, in 34BC, 27BC and 25BC, but each time it was called off.[6]

Caligula may have planned a campaign against the Britons in AD40, and if so this readied the troops and logistics that would make Claudius's invasion possible three years later. For example, Caligula built a lighthouse at *Bononia* (modern Boulogne sur mer), that provided a model for the one built soon after at Dubris (Dover). The Roman conquest of Britain was a gradual process, beginning effectively in AD43 under Emperor Claudius and his general Aulus Plautius.

The Second Roman Attack, Ad43

In AD 43, nearly a century after Julius Caesar invaded Britain in 54/55BC, the Romans made a second attempt. This was all to do with propaganda and the new emperor, Tiberius Claudius Drusus Nero Germanicus, better known as Claudius. Physically infirm and accused

Tattooed natives went into battle naked.

of imbecility, he was the only adult male of the royal family left when the emperor Caligula was killed. Despite objections from the Senate, in AD41 Claudius succeeded to the imperial throne but he had very little support in Rome. He needed something to give him prestige and as the conquest of Britain was unfinished business, in 43 he sent off a Roman fleet to invade further north than they had ever gone before. This time Rome spared no expense. The invasion of Britain had to succeed and 40,000 soldiers made up the invasion force, including men from Spain, North Africa, and Gaul as well as Romans.

The Roman invasion of Britain is an event which, perhaps rather strangely, has not been featured much in either TV or film until January 2018 when Sky Atlantic produced a new British historical drama called *Britannia*, written by playwright Jez Butterworth. It follows ancient Rome's conquest of the Celts in the British Isles, described as a mysterious land ruled by wild warrior women and Druids who can channel the powerful forces of the underworld. General Aulus Plautius is the only character from the series who existed.

For the real story, the only detailed account of the invasion comes from Cassius Dio's *Roman History* written in the early 3rd century. Dio describes how the troops saw a shooting star whilst at sea and were cheered by this omen. It travelled from east to west and as this was the direction the Romans were sailing in, which made made it more propitious. This would indicate that they were travelling from somewhere around Dunkirk in France, which is almost due east of the Kent shore where they allegedly landed. It would seem the most obvious route, yet others have questioned this.

Dio states that the main invasion force under Aulus Plautius sailed under the overall command of Plautius. The Legio II Augusta was under the leadership of Vaspasian, the legion XX Valeria Victrix was under an unknown commander, while the legions IX Hispana and XIV Gemina were under Plautius. Once ashore, the three forces advanced from the coast and met at the River Medway.

British resistance was led by Togodumnus and Caratacus, sons of Cunobeline, the late king of the Catuvellauni. A substantial British force met the Romans at a river crossing thought to be near Rochester on the River Medway where the battle raged for two days. The British, pursued by the Romans, were pushed back to the Thames where both sides suffered considerable losses in the Essex marshes. The Celtic leader Togodumnus died shortly after. (*See also* page 205.)

At this time, there were thirty three known British tribes, although this number is often debated. Each tribe had its own leaders that probably came together from time to time to form alliances and trade, and although a common enemy could have bound a large number of these previously disunited people together, animosity existed between many of the tribes and they remained divided. The tribes in the south did not unite to fight alongside the Catuvellaunis who suffered substantial losses. Many were killed or taken as slaves. Their tribal lands were torched, making them unfit for habitation.

At this stage, Plautius halted and sent word for Claudius to join him. Cassius Dio presents this as Plautius needing the emperor's assistance to defeat the resurgent British, who were determined to avenge Togodumnus, but Claudius was not a military man. His presence on a battlefield would have been more of a hindrance than a help. It's more likely that Plautius was an astute politician and was keen to retain the Emperor's gratitude. Knowing that the Catuvellauni were already as good as beaten, this allowed the Emperor to appear as conqueror on the final march on Camulodunum (Colchester in Essex). Undoubtedly this move advanced Plautius' career, as he served as the first governor of Roman Britain.

Cassius Dio relates that Claudius arrived with war elephants and heavy armaments, a sight guaranteed to strike fear in the natives. Overawed, the remaining British resistance caved in and Claudius was paraded through Camulodunum (Colchester) in triumph. Tribes of south-east Britain began to surrender and Claudius's triumphal arch recorrded he received the surrender of eleven kings without any loss. In his book *The Twelve Caesars,* Suetonius says that Claudius received the surrender of the Britons without battle or bloodshed. The Romans established their new capital at Camulodunum and as the Roman armies prepared to move further west and north, Claudius returned to Rome to celebrate his victory. Only a few weeks after landing, the invaders had control of much of the south and east of the Pretannic Isles.

The next stage took rather longer, years rather than weeks. The tribal leaders chose their path, twenty to famous defeat, thirteen to unacknowledged surrender. We don't even know the names of those thirteen tribes or the leaders because history recorded the deeds of the stubborn and glossed over the acquiescence of those who volunteered

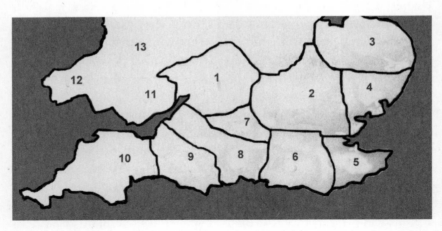

A map showing the southern tribes that were defeated or surrendered to Caesar.

1 Dubunni	6 Regni	11 Silures
2 Catuvellauni	7 Antrebates	12 Demetae
3 Iceni	8 Belgae	13 Ordovices
4 Trinovantes	9 Durotriges	
5 Cantiaci	10 Dumnonii	

allegiance. The pre-Roman tribal organisation was not obliterated by the invaders, although the boundaries were modified and towns were founded either on or close to Iron Age Centres of power, to serve as the new market and administrative focus of each civitas. The Romans were first to build towns in Britain, and in most cases the sites chosen had started as military forts in the conquest period. Most of the sites are still today thriving cities.

Client Kings

The area around Chichester in west Sussex was pro-Roman and served as one of the bases for the Roman Conquest of Britain. The ruler of the area was King Togidubnus (sometimes Cogidubnus or similar) who became a client king, and took the Roman name Tiberius Claudius Togidubnus. In Tacitus's *Agricola* published *c.* 98AD, his name appears as Cogidumnus. He is said to have governed several civitates as a client ruler after the Roman conquest, and to have been 'loyal down to our own times'. He is credited with building the great palace at Fishbourne outside Chichester for his own use but modern methods of archaeology have shown that the first buildings on the site were granaries. Over 33 metres long, they were constructed in the early part of the conquest as a supply base for the Roman army. Later, two residential timber-frame buildings were constructed. One had clay and mortar floors and plaster walls, a more than comfortable abode. This could have been the home of Togidubnus. These buildings were demolished in the AD60s and the materials used to build a substantial replacement villa nearby, now referred to as Fishbourne Royal Palace.

The Roman villa at Fishbourne was not unique in the area as another large Roman villa from the same period has been found at Augmering between Littlehampton and Worthing in West Sussex. It was part-excavated in the 1930s. Another villa from the same period known as Lullington Roman Villa was discovered near the village of Eynsford in north Kent in 1939. There must have been many more Roman villas built during the early years of the Roman occupation, and as they showed a distinct similarity, they were no doubt built and decorated by the same Italian craftsmen. If they, and no doubt others, were built for the British ruling elite, then an elaborate and substantial stone-walled villa, or proto-palace, including a courtyard garden with colonnades and a bath suite was quite a perk that client kings loyal to Rome could expect. Chichester remained a client kingdom and was not part of the new Roman province until Togidubnus' death in about AD80.[7]

The Romans Advance

Not everyone was happy to bow the knee and accept the palace. The main resistance was led by Caratacus, son of Cunobeline of the Catuvellauni. Caratacus and his brother Togodumnus had fought the Romans from the very beginning, but with his brother dead, Caratacus escaped and fled west into Wales. He was to become a central figure in our story from this point on.

Campaigns under Aulus Plautius had focused on the commercially valuable south-east of Britain. Vespasian took a force westwards subduing tribes and capturing oppida as he went. He reached as far as Exeter, which would appear to have become an early base for Leg. II Augusta while Legio IX Hispana was sent north towards Lincoln (Lindum Colonia).

Within four years of the Roman invasion it is likely that an area south of a line from the Humber to the Severn Estuary was under Roman control. That this line is followed by the Roman road known as the Fosse Way has led many historians to consider the route's role as not only a road but as a frontier during the early occupation. It's probable.

The Fosse Way ran from the mouth of the River Axe in Devon linking Exeter (Isca Dumnoniorum) in south-west England to Lincoln (Lindum Colonia) in Lincolnshire. It travelled in a north-eastern direction across the country through Ilchester (Lindinae) in Somerset to Bath (Aquae Sulis) and Cirencester (Corinium), then straight for 60 miles (100 km) to High Cross (Venonae), where it intersected Watling Street, and on to Leicester (Ratae Corieltauvorum). From there it continued to Lincoln on a line that is now the A46 trunk road.

By the late 50s the Roman legionary bases were at Gloucester, Lincoln and Wroxeter (Viroconium Cornoviorum) near Shrewsbury on the upper Severn in the territory of the Cornovii in Shropshire, paralleled in the east by the sister fortress of Lincoln (Lindum Colonia).

Agricola was poised ready to bring the weight of the Roman armies north into what is now Derbyshire

This was Brigante territory, and Queen Cartimandua was a strong, practical leader. She saw the future security of her realm ensured by diplomacy, not warfare. She wanted her people to prosper, she didn't want to see her territory torn apart by the ferocity of the Roman army, but she couldn't stand alone to face such a daunting opponent. Others had tried and failed. The Belgae, Atrebates, Regni, Cantiaci, Trinovantes, Corieltauvi and Catuvallauni tribes were all now under Roman authority.

Cartimandua called together other tribal leaders and they debated whether to unite and go south to fight, or wait. Having defeated the Cantiaci and the Catuvellauni, would the Romans be content with the richer land and the wealth of the more compliant southern kingdoms, or would they turn their attention further north? By joining together a federation of smaller tribes like the Setanti in Lancashire, the Lopocares, the Corionototae and the Tectoverdi from around the Tyne valley, they could form a formidable group. The Brigantes were bordered by other major Celtic tribes. In the northwest were the Carvetti to whom they may have been linked through Venutius, Cartimandua's husband. To the east were the Parisii, and to the south were the Corieltauvi and the Cornovii, while to the north was the territory of the Votadini that straddled the present-day border between England and Scotland.

There were pockets of resistance in the south and west where fighting continued and messengers kept them informed of progress. Cartimandua looked for signs from the gods, but the gods did not stop the Roman armies advancing north. She saw that the portents were not favourable. The eagles were circling over the fells and that was a bad sign. The lives of the men and women for generations to come depended on Cartimandua's decision. She had to do what was best for her people.

13

OMENS AND ORACLES

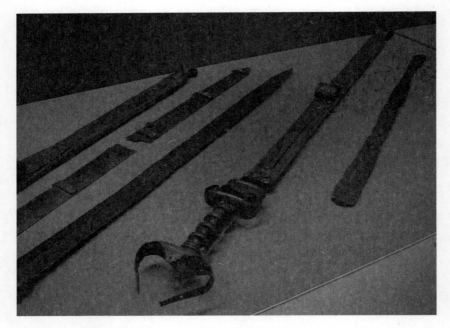

Broken swords retrieved from sacred waters.

When making life-changing decisions, Cartimandua would have looked for omens and consulted the oracle to come into contact with sources of wisdom beyond her own. Throughout the history of the human race, trust has been placed in portents and omens, and belief in their validity has played a prominent part in public and private life. The folklore of practically every race and nation offers numerous incidents of man's instinctive faith in omens. The Celts were no exception. They held the belief that 'coming events cast their shadow before' and future happenings can be foretold by signs actuated by some form of supernatural power. Cartimandua would have known the importance of omens, drawn mainly from nature. She would have known how to interpret signs and whether they presaged good or evil.

At this distance in time it's impossible to know how Cartimandua interrogated the future but she would have used methods handed down from earlier generations of Celts. Looking at historical events in general, there are numerous incidents where omens have played an important part. In fact, it could be said that omens have played as big a part as any other single factor in moulding men's actions throughout history. Looking for omens and consulting the oracle was undertaken for many purposes: to ascertain the nature of the season ahead, to find what was lost, or to ask a question and receive an answer about a planned enterprise. In this instance, Cartimandua was looking for guidance about the Roman menace. Should she fight or volunteer allegiance?

What was actually involved in the oracular process is unclear although there are various accounts by Roman writers, not be taken at face value. Shakespeare's *Julius Caesar* has a well-known reference to an evil portent disclosed by the Roman haruspices: – 'plucking the entails of an offering forth; they could not find a heart within the beast.' This truly monstrous omen which almost immediately was met with tragic fulfilment was supported by those described by Caesar's wife:

> *... There is one within*
> *Besides the things that we have heard and seen*
> *Recounts most horrid sights seen by the watch.*
> *A lioness hath whelped in the streets*
> *And graves have yawn'd and yielded up their dead.*
> *Fierce fiery warriors fight upon the clouds,*
> *In ranks and squadrons and right form of war*
> *Which drizzled blood upon the capital,*
> *The noise of battle hurtled in the air.*

> *Horses did neigh and dying men did groan*
> *And ghosts did shriek and squeal about the streets.*
> *O Caesar, these things are beyond all use*
> *And I do fear them.*

But the great dictator had more faith in his own destiny than the portents of his wife and the other soothsayers and rejecting their warnings, went to his death. Sadly, we do not know what portents the soothsayers gave Cartimandua.

There are a vast amount of portents around birds because birds were seen as messengers of the spirits or gods. The word auspice meaning an omen, is derived from the Latin meaning an observer of birds. Augury relies on subjectively interpreting observable objects or events such as the sight, sound and movement of birds. If a bird flies from left to right across the path of the observer it's a good sign; flying right to left is not so good. The flying height is important; the greater the height, the more favourable the indication. Bird song is a good sign, the quacking of a duck is a fortunate omen but not the croaking or screaming of birds such as crows, ravens, jackdaws or rooks. Like birds, animals were seen as the messengers of the spirits or gods, so to encounter an animal that was not in its usual environment or behaving in an uncharacteristic manner was of special significance, like the lioness whelping in the street, according to Caesar's wife. The interpretations were laid down by the Roman augurs, no doubt adapting those of the ancients. Great significance was placed on these omens but there was nevertheless a distinct lack of consistency in the interpretations.

Cartimandua would have been taught how to use Ogham as a means of writing, signing and as a divination tool. To endow them with special power, she would most probably have made her own Ogham sticks from a tree that had particular spiritual significance. She probably would have had several sets for different divination purposes. Ogham was a tool of the guardians of the oral Celtic wisdom, the druids, bards and oracle poets (*see also* pages 30–2).

To make wooden Ogham sticks, the bark would be stripped on two sides then etched with the ancient Ogham alphabet with their Ogham title inscribed against the bare edge. The top of the stick would be blacked to indicate which way up the Ogham symbol was to be read. That seems straightforward but the modern reader would read them from top to bottom whereas when they were used in ancient inscriptions, Ogham sticks were read from the bottom up.

An extra indicator stick was stripped of its bark on all sides, and the cardinal directions inscribed around it to help determine the appropriate oracle for each Ogham letter. Each of the twenty sticks has a possible four oracles attached to it and using the indicator stick provided a possible eighty answers.

A form of poetic prophecy was called *teinm laegada*, literally stripping the bark or pith. Poets would peel back poetic layers of meaning in an incantatory trance to solve problems and discover answers. The same image is used in the story of the mariner Maelduin where he was assured that Christ, like a master poet in search of prophetic resolution, had successfully stripped the bark of revelation.[1]

Divination by Dice and Consulting the Oracle

What is extraordinary, they play at dice, when sober, as a serious business: and that with such a desperate venture of gain or loss, that, when everything else is gone, they set their liberties and persons on the last throw. (Tacitus, *Germania* 24)

The use of dice for all kinds of games of chance dates from time immemorial. The oldest known dice date from 5000 years ago in the area of modern-day Iran. Dice originated from astralagi or knuckle bones, or other small four-sided bones. Knucklebones in Roman times were called *tali*. They were numbered I, III, IV and VI. Four *tali* were thrown at a time. In China knucklebones developed into dominoes. In ancient Egypt, classic Greece and countries of the Far East, cubes of wood, metal, ivory or glass with their sides numbered from 1 to 6 were created not only for gaming, but also as a means of consultation about future events, known as astragalomancy or astragyromancy, The ordinary Celtic people used dice made of bone, stone or antler but the wealthier possessed sets made of more exotic materials.

Modern methods require a circle to be drawn in white chalk on a board or table on which the throws are made. Three dice are shaken by the left hand then thrown within the confines of the circle. Any dice that fall or roll outside the circle predict difficulties, problems or an upset. If one dice lands on top of another, this predicts that the player will soon receive a gift of some significance. The numbers that fall uppermost are added together and the sum of the numbers is read. The meanings have almost certainly changed over the centuries but here are a few.

ONE Family difficulties are coming.

TWO Look closely at situations, things may not be quite what they seem.

THREE Expect pleasant surprises in the very near future. Your circumstances will change without warning and very soon.

FOUR A setback or some unpleasantness will disappoint you. Expect arguments or a disagreement. An unpleasant surprise.

FIVE A stranger or a surprise brings you happiness. Plans come to fruition. Unexpected information or assistance. A new friendship.

SIX Misfortune and loss. A friend may ask a favour of you.

Cartimandua would have been taught how to use the oracle at a place where the gods gave an answer to the anxious questions of the devotees through the mouths of the attendant Druid priests. The priest or diviner usually appeared to enter a trance-like state, which perhaps could have been achieved if the process took place at a point where the earth energy was considered to be strong, or somewhere where toxic fumes leaked into the atmosphere. Presumably the diviner became quite frenzied, and uttered mumblings or ravings interpreted and converted into intelligible language, sometimes in verse or riddle form, by the attendant priest or Druid. The importance of such interpretations is shown by the fact that the Druids had the power to delay certain actions in order to await an auspicious day.

It was considered more effective to consult the oracle at specific times or on specific days, probably on the quarter days of the Celtic year: Samhain, Imbolc, Beltane and Lughnasa. Not only would the date play an important part, so would the time, and sunrise had special significance. If the augury waited with closed eyes and chanted a special invocation, when opening his eyes, whatever he saw first gave the augury or divinatory the necessary signs. From the nature and position of these signs, the augury would draw conclusions. For example, when observing celestial omens, the auger would sit on a hill from where he had an uninterrupted view. Having offered up a sacrifice and invoked the guidance of heaven, he would then turn towards the south and wait for the answer from the gods. If, for example, lightning flickered in the west or on his right-hand side it was regarded as an auspicious omen, if it was seen in the east or his left side, it was unfortunate. In many other examples, the right was considered fortunate or positive; the left was unfortunate or negative.

According to Caitlin Matthews in her book *Celtic Visions: Seership, Dreams and Omens of the Otherworld*, these natural portents were dependent upon the formation of a question. Once the search for an answer had begun, nature became charged with meaning.[2]

Scrying

There seems no limit to the means and methods of divining. Oneiromancy depends on the interpretation of dreams and is a practice as old as time. Scrying is the practice of looking into a reflective, refractive, translucent, or luminescent surface in the hope of detecting significant messages or visions for personal guidance, prophecy, revelation or inspiration. It is an ancient method of divination and the Celts would have used water surfaces, fire, smoke, clouds or other natural items to read such signs. Anthrocomancy involves interpreting the images in glowing coals, turifumy involves scrying into smoke, and hydromancy involves scrying into water, and interpreting the colour, ebb and flow, or ripples produced by dropping in pebbles.

Some practitioners assert that when you stare into your chosen media, these visions come from the subconscious, or the psychic mind, or from the gods or spirits. Scrying is neither a single, clearly-defined, nor formal discipline yet it has been widely used over the centuries. It has a number of divisions and names including common terms like crystal gazing, crystallomancy, spheromancy, and catoptromancy. Catoptromancy is divination using a mirror suspended over water.

It is often used as a presage of death or recovery, depending upon whether the reflection in the mirror appeared fresh and healthy, or of a ghastly aspect. Lecanomancy is a form of divination using a dish, usually of water, onto which oil is poured. Flour was sometimes substituted for the oil. The scryer would then observe the patterns formed by the oil to predict the future. There is no clear limit to the coining and application of such terms and media.[3]

A place of special significance like the sacred grove dedicated to Arnemetia at Buxton would have had a pool to reflect the moon for scrying. The area was probably consecrated not just to allow the people to express their devotion, but to give the augers and auspices powerful visions. There could have been several types of seers, but the Druids were the most important, probably an itinerant class who would have had the freedom to move around between the various tribal groups. They were esteemed councillors and gave advice to the tribal leaders. If they decided something, people took note. Their word was law.

Human and Animal Sacrifices

There would have been other rituals like fasting, going barefoot and bare-headed to appeal to the all-seeing gods to seek an answer. Some divination was practised alone, but others were in a communal setting, especially where the Druids were concerned. They were great believers in divination in many forms including animal sacrifice.

The druids would throw cold water on a tethered or caged animal and the shivers were 'read'. It was a relatively common practice to make an animal sacrifice. Methods ranged from interpreting the way the blood spurted or by studying the entrails of a dead animal.[4]

But it wasn't just animal sacrifices, the sacrificing of humans is a ritual that has both appalled and fascinated people ever since. As far as the Druids were concerned, the main aim of human sacrifice was not so much to propitiate or appease the gods but for divination purposes. Diodorus and Strabo describe the custom of stabbing victims and foretelling the future by observing the death-throes, and Lucan wrote that the Druids claimed to understand the secrets of the gods and 'resumed the barbarous rites of their wicked religion'.

It is hard for us to understand the significance of human sacrifice as practiced by the Druids. It was not to torture or inflict maximum

Lindow Man, a sacrifice to the gods thrown into a bog at Lindow Moss, Cheshire. (British Museum)

pain to evil-doers or prisoners of war. Evil-doers were imprisoned for five years, then killed by impaling. Prisoners of war were sometimes herded together with their animals, incarcerated in wicker man-shaped images, shot with arrows, then burnt alive.

Perhaps one of the most evocative examples of human sacrifice is the 1984 discovery of a peat bog burial mentioned earlier at Lindow Moss, near Wilmslow, Cheshire, deep in Brigantian territory. Now known as Lindow Man, his discovery triggered an unprecedented scientific investigation. Scientists discovered many facts about Lindow Man. He was naked except for a fox-fur armband, which would indicate that he could have been conferring potency and prosperity on his people.[5]

He was 1.73 m tall, weighed 64 kg (10 stone), and was around 25 years old. His natural coffin had preserved the soft tissues remarkably well including not only skin but hair and even fingernails, enabling scientists to work on every minute trace of evidence. Analysis of the skeleton and teeth proved that this was the body of a healthy, well-fed young man with no signs of earlier injuries or disease. Electron microscopy of his fingernails has shown that he'd had a fine manicure, he was well groomed, with trimmed beard and neatly clipped moustache worn in the style of Celtic portrayals in literature and iconography. His good health and physical condition clearly indicate that he was not a labourer or agricultural slave but was of high status. It would seem that he was one of the finest male examples of his race.

Just before he died, he ate a flat, unleavened griddle cake baked over an open fire. Several grains of mistletoe pollen were also found in his stomach, so Lindow Man had drunk the pollen of a potent and sacred plant. It is not certain whether he swallowed these deliberately or accidentally but it's quite possible that a sprig of mistletoe had been dipped in his drink or brushed onto his food in a ceremony surrounding his last meal. As the mistletoe plant is strongly associated with the Druids, this would strengthen the belief that he was a Druidical sacrifice, but why was he offered as a sacrifice? Did he willingly offer to be slaughtered in order to enter the realm of the divine?

The word 'slaughter' accurately describes his death. He was first poleaxed, hit two or three times on the head with a narrow-bladed axe. He did not die instantly but lost consciousness, so this was not designed to inflict maximum suffering. There is evidence that the wound swelled so at that point the heart was still beating but death would have followed within hours. But there was more to do in that time. While he was still alive, a cord was tied round his neck and this is still in place today. A stick was inserted in the cord at the back, then twisted to tighten what was in effect a garrotte. This strangulation was done with such violence it broke his neck, and this was the actual cause and moment of clinical death. There was more. His throat was then cut.

If, as suspected, this was a ritual killing to appease the gods, it is known that the Druids who officiated at such events despatched their victim and observed their dying struggles for divinity purposes. They watched and analysed the victim in the throes of death looking for signs that they could interpret to show the best course of action to take. The way the blood squirted would be of special significance and the blood would be collected in cauldrons where it was also examined.[6]

After this elaborate execution, the body was pitched face down in a pool in the peat bog where it remained for 2,000 years. Bogs are cold, acidic places lacking in oxygen, which makes then hostile environments for micro-organisms that break bodies down. It's the sphagnum mosses that grow in bogs that preserve bog bodies. When the mosses die, they release a sugary substance that acts as a tanning agent. This turns skin, tendons, ligaments and muscles into leather. It also turns skin brown and hair red.

Lindow Man's nakedness, the complexity of his death and the final act of being buried in a watery bog would definitely indicate a ritual killing. The ancient Britons believed that such places were gateways between the worlds and because the peat bogs provided iron and fuel, the people threw offerings into the bogs in thanksgiving to the gods. Lindow Man was a chosen sacrifice who would have been unafraid of dying because it was strongly believed that his soul would go to the otherworld. Being chosen or volunteering to die in such a fashion would indicate that a major misfortune had befallen the people who needed the ultimate sacrifice of a human being to appease their gods. A man of wealth and influence would have been the tribe's most precious offering if the people thought their gods had deserted them and some terrible ill was about to befall them.[7]

Radiocarbon dating indicates that Lindow Man was killed sometime between 2BC and AD119. This is the period we are looking at, the first century when Cartimandua ruled the Brigante. The body was found in Brigante territory, so it is possible that Cartimandua was aware of this sacrifice. She may even have instigated it and been present at its implementation. If the gods needed to be propitiated because the country was suffering famine or war, such a sacrifice was deemed necessary, and this was the time when the Roman armies were advancing north, destroying all in their path. It's an interesting theory that Lindow Man could have been selected as a sacrifice to stop the Roman invasion destroying more Celtic territories. It is possible, but of course the variables are so great that we can make no firm argument for it.

Scientists at the British Museum had to find a suitable way of preserving Lindow Man as they wanted to prevent his remains decaying after he had been removed from the bog. The body was first immersed in a solution of polyethylene glycol, a chemical that prevented the body shrinking when it dried out. He was then wrapped in cling film and frozen, after which he was freeze-dried to remove water. This treatment successfully preserved his body and meant that it could ultimately be displayed at the British Museum.

Lindow Man is not the only bog-body that has been investigated. Another preserved body was elaborately dressed – he wore a blue checked cloak and linen undergarments, a blouse or tunic made of plant fibre, and a woollen shawl – and was shackled with withies. Torrent Man was found in Denmark in 1950. He had apparently been hanged yet he didn't show the signs of hanging. There was a rope round his neck but it is now believed that he could have been a ritual hanging as an offering to the god Odin who hanged himself to get more power.

In 1952, peat diggers found Vinderby Girl near Swarski in Germany. She was perfectly preserved as once again the peat had acted like an antiseptic to preserve her body and the cow hide cloak that she was wearing. Unlike the others, historians have said it's doubtful that she was a sacrifice because her head had been shaved. This would indicate that she was a sinner, perhaps an adulteress.

14

THE COMBATANTS

Above left and above right: Late 16th-century fanciful prints of a male and female Celtic warrior.

Cartimandua, Queen of the Brigante tribe and her elders watched and waited as the Roman legions invaded the south. Messengers would have carried the news but the native Britons would also have used fire for signalling, lighting bonfires on prominent hills, a practice followed ever since. The Celtic fire signalling was usually controlled by the Druid elite.

The Romans signalled with flags to a specific code. The Roman alphabet was split into five groups A-E; F-J; K-O; P-T; U-Z. Using five torches, each letter was sent with two signals. The first signal would show which group, so to send the letter C, which is in the first group A-E, one flag would be raised, followed by three to indicate the third letter in that group. They used a water clock to time the signals. The length of time the torch was raised was timed and the message read from a list of possible messages. The water clock was something like a modern egg timer – a steady trickle of water through a hole.

The Roman army was an impressive sight simply by the sheer numbers, as well as the splendour of the arms and armour. Thousands of men marching across the countryside in orderly columns – the infantrymen in their gleaming metal armour, auxiliaries perhaps in chain mail, signallers carrying their exotic looking horns and trumpets, standard bearers identifying each unit.

The alternative to chain mail or scale armour was a solid metal or leather breastplate that protected the upper body but was inflexible. By the 1st century AD the working alternative was the first articulated plate armour made of a series of overlapping iron plates joined by leather straps, known to modern archaeologists as *lorica segmentata*. The legionary added a helmet, a pair of greaves to protect the legs and hobnailed leather sandals for the feet. For extra protection the legionary carried a shield, which before the 1st century was oval. Around the time the Romans invaded England the fashion charged and legionaries began to carry rectangular shields that were much more effective when drawn together to form a solid wall of shields in battle.

One of the legionary's most important weapons was a javelin called the pilum. Around 2.25 metres long, the pilum had a wooden shaft tipped with a sharp metal shank. The tip was hardened iron, but the rest of the shank was a softer metal which bent on impact making it impossible for the pilum to be thrown back. When General Marius noticed that some of the pila were not bending on impact so were able to be thrown back, he had one of the two iron nails that held the

Above left: 1st-century AD standard bearer (vexillarius). (Artwork by John R. Travis from *Roman Shields* by Hilary and John Travis)

Above right: Legionary from a marine unit of the 1st century wearing padded linen armour and carrying a transitional semi-rectangular scutum with curved sides. (Artwork by John R. Travis)

metal shank to the wood replaced with a wooden peg. This shattered on impact, the shank swung free and the pilum was useless. The Romans followed up the shower of pila with hand-to-hand sword fighting. The legionary's swords had short, broad blades and were used for stabbing.

The trained foot-soldiers of the legions were the heart of the army. Each legion was divided into ten groups called cohorts, each of which was divided into six centuries. A century was made up of 80 men. This made the theoretical force of a legion 4,800 men, although this varied considerably. In addition to the legions, there was a similar number of auxiliary troops. They included cavalrymen, archers, slingers and troops. Auxiliaries were men from countries previously conquered and subjugated by the Roman armies. Vegetius in *The Military Institution of the Romans* described the auxiliaries as

> ... a hired corps of foreigners assembled from different parts of the Empire, made up of different numbers, without knowledge of one another or any other tie of affection. Each nation has its own peculiar discipline, customs and manner of fighting... And although the legions do not place their principal dependence on them, yet they look on them as a very considerable addition to their strength.[1]

Auxiliaries often had specialist rather than fighting skills that helped the army function. But corruption was rife amongst some unscrupulous officials. They would choose the sons of wealthy families who would be willing to pay to avoid their sons being shipped abroad as auxiliaries. Bribes for their release became quite a profitable little side line.[2]

The Romans had catapults. The name comes from the Greek *katapaltes*, which means to hurl down. There was a type of catapult the Romans called the onager. The name means wild-ass and comes from the way asses will kick backwards, sending stones flying. They had developed the cross bow and discovered that they could make it larger, thus the ballista, an overgrown cross bow mounted on a stand that could shoot large bolts and arrow heads.

They had battering rams and used a shelter, a wooden structure covered in hides or iron plate to make it fireproof. This enabled them to get close to the walls of a fort. From there, if they couldn't use the battering rams to break down the gates, they could start tunnelling to bring down the walls, or build up an earth ramp to enable them to reach the height of the walls and scale the ramparts.

The Celts were expert horsemen as well as skilled breeders of horses and used two-wheeled chariots with great effectiveness, but the Romans stole their horses, and in order to train them to go into battle, made a special circular enclosure called a gyrus. The cavalrymen led the horses round and round the gyrus, waving spears at them, shouting and throwing missiles so that the horses would get used to the noise and activity on the battlefield. (A similar but gentler technique is applied to police horses, without the missiles.) As stirrups were not invented until the 8th century, riders controlled horses with their thighs.

The Celtic farmer/hunters were not a bellicose lot. The people of the Brigante tribe had led peaceful, pastoral lives for century after century and were no match for the highly disciplined Roman army. Cartimandua understood this and knew that they were ill-disciplined and their tactics uncoordinated; but they were also brave and remarkably vigorous people. If necessary, they could be ferocious warriors, but as mentioned earlier, they did not protect themselves with armour. They believed that if the gods decided that they should die, no amount of armour would save them and they went into battle naked.

One weapon of choice for the average Iron Age warrior was a sling shot, which in the right hands can be formidable. The sling was made from a small rectangle of leather, gathered at the corners to create a shallow pouch which was then attached to two leather thongs. Small pebbles were used as ammunition and at a distance of 20 metres or so, this simple tool could be lethal. The sling was definitely respected and feared by the Romans who carried special tweezers in their medical kit to extract stones from their bodies.

Even more feared was the knowledge that the Celts were head hunters, and enemy heads were considered by them to be great trophies. According to the Greek writer Diodorus Siculus, the Celts cut off their enemy's heads and hung them above the doors of their huts or slung them around their horses' necks. They preserved the heads of the most high-ranking victims, or kept them in wooden boxes, or used the skulls as drinking vessels.

The Celts held the widespread belief that the head possessed the soul, so they imagined that a person's power could be obtained through the possession of their head – and hence their soul. (*See* earlier chapter.)

The Little People

The native Celts were used to the terrain and could pop up like guerrillas to attack the Romans when they least expected, then vanish without trace when pursued. They fired poison arrows, then disappeared into the hills and swamps where the invaders didn't dare set foot. The Celts became known as the little people and stories circulated that they possessed magical powers. They did in fact possess a wide knowledge of herbs and poisons that were unknown to the Romans, and this added to the growing feeling that they were truly supernatural. This is where the image of the goblin, fairy, elf, kelpie and all the other magical little beings took root; the small flint arrow heads they used that can be seen in museums today are called fairy arrows.

Despite all their training and fighting prowess, the Romans were somewhat in awe of the little people. When marching into enemy territory, the soldiers would forage and plunder but the locals knew the ground and could predict where the Romans were going to forage and lie in wait. It was rumoured that certain crops had been poisoned by the little people, a bluff no doubt generated by the Celts to protect their crops.

From this beginning, the belief in the hobgoblin continued for centuries, a spirit of nature, notorious for his mischievousness unless placated. Hob was well known to our ancestors who would leave a small quantity of food and a bowl of milk in a special place to placate this naughty spirit. Sightings of these small, imp-like creature have been reported at places with names like Hob Lane, Hob Tor and Hob Hurst that still dot the landscape. Hurst comes from the Old English *hyrst* meaning hillock or copse, so combining the two we have the dwelling of a hobgoblin in a wood. Puxhill is the hill of the goblins and Eldon is the abode of the elves.

Great Fin, the hill topped by the Iron Age fort of Fin Cop, is noted for the very green spots that dot its slopes. Our ancestors believed that these were fairy rings, owing their greenness to the moonlight revels of the little people. Many sightings were alleged of fairies dressed in green, dancing hand in hand around their rings to the music of the field cricket, grasshopper or drone bee, aided in their joyous movements by the light of numerous glow-worms. Shakespeare alluded to such widespread beliefs in many of his plays. Prospero described the elves in the Tempest:

Ye elves of hills, brooks, standing lakes and groves, and ye that on the sands with printless foot do chase the ebbing Neptune and do fly him when he comes back. You demi-puppets that by moonshine do the green sour ringlets make, whereof the ewe not bites, and you whose pastime is to make midnight mushrooms.[3]

The presence of fungi is the real, if rather less wonderful cause of the greenness of fairy rings and in Derbyshire, young mushrooms are still known as fairy buttons. When they begin to decay, local lore acknowledges that the devil has been at work on them and driven out the fairies. Could this myth have originated at the time of the Roman conquest in order for the native Celts to protect their source of food? It's a tantalising thought.

Supplying the Roman Army

Supplying the Roman army was a huge challenge, and the demand for grain alone has been estimated at 500 bushels per legion per week. While marching into enemy territory, the horses of the cavalry and the mules of the baggage train needed fodder. Usually the Romans would requisition supplies, then build secure stores so that the enemy could not get them back but this of course alienated the natives. The area's population at the time may have been mainly farmers but they were only catering for their own uncomplicated lifestyle and simple needs. They could not feed hordes of unwanted visitors. Not only was there a shortage of food for the invading armies, the native farmers were only producing enough for their own immediate needs or to provide a commodity to barter with. In times of poor harvests, they relied upon any excess to tide them over, but farmers were ordered to use their land and knowledge of husbandry to supply the needs of the Roman army. All who resisted were mercilessly put to the sword and their villages destroyed.

The Celtic animal stock would have been confiscated and slaughtered to provide meat, milk, wool and more for Roman use. How this affected the Celtic farmers can only be imagined. It surely caused widespread famine across the whole country. The Celts used hides for clothing and footwear but now the Romans demanded these things and more. It's been estimated that the invading Roman army needed the hides of 200,000 calves to make the necessary tents to provide a temporary camp.

The process of tanning to turn a skin or hide into leather had until then been a domestic role performed in the roundhouses by the womenfolk, but the demand for so many extra skins meant that it became an industry. The skins still needed to be thoroughly cleaned, softened and tanned, so the Romans soaked the skins in pits filled with an alkaline material and stale urine. This was collected in vessels placed at convenient places in residential and military areas for public use. This effluent was also used by the 'fuller' who carried out a side-line in laundry work. The Romans had interconnecting tubs for washing clothes, trampling basins to tread the clothes clean and terraces for drying. (*See* page 77.)

Many new farms were needed to grow grain and other crops, and by necessity the Romans instigated a system to produce more cereal and livestock; but that didn't happen immediately. In the meantime, they used the sea ports to bring in food for their vast armies. Ships sailed up the coast to Arbeia (modern South Shields), which became a major supply depot.

The name Arbeia probably means 'fort of the Arab troops', referring to the fact that part of its garrison at one time was a squadron of Mesopotamian boatmen from the Tigris. It was common for forts to be manned by auxiliary units originally from elsewhere in the empire. Often these men would assimilate and recruit locally.[4]

Arbeia was of prime importance to the Romans. It was a huge supply base for the Roman army, with twenty-two granaries. Its importance was due to its position at the mouth of the River Tyne where it joins the North Sea. The Tyne is generally considered to start near Hexham with the confluence of the North Tyne tributary the Rede and the South Tyne. It's navigable for at least nineteen miles, which enabled cargo ships to sail inland to Newcastle upon Tyne and further to the fort of Carpow just south of Corbridge. This is just south of where the Romans would build Hadrian's Wall in the 120s AD. (*See also* page 134.)The navigable River Tyne runs more or less parallel to Hadrian's Wall and the number of tributaries that branch from the river towards the wall was probably a major reason for choosing to build the great dividing wall here. Arbeia became the maritime supply fort for Hadrian's Wall, and here are the only permanent stone-built granaries yet found in Britain.[5]

Arbeia became a busy cosmopolitan port and two monuments in the museum at Arbeia testify to the cosmopolitan nature of its shifting population. One commemorates Regina, a British woman of the Catuvellauni tribe who occupied the area we now know as Hertfordshire. She was first the slave, then the freedwoman and wife of Barates, a merchant from Palmyra, now part of Syria. He evidently missed her greatly, and set up a gravestone after she died at the age of 30. Barates himself is buried at the nearby fort of Coria (Corbridge) Also from archaeological evidence it's known that a squadron of Spanish cavalry, the First Asturian, were stationed here. A gravemarker on display in the museum is to Victor, and records that he was of the Moorish nation. Victor was a former slave, freed by Numerianus of the Ala I Asturum, who also arranged his funeral *piantissime* (with all devotion) when Victor died at the age of 20.

The Romans built a fort here around AD120 on the Lawe Top, overlooking the Tyne, and guarding the main sea route to Hadrian's Wall. Standing where it had originally existed during the Roman occupation, the reconstruction of the fort has been accomplished using research which was undertaken following excavations. A Roman gatehouse, barracks and commanding officer's house have been reconstructed on their original foundations. The gatehouse holds many displays related to the history of the fort, and its upper levels provide an overview of the site. Arbeia remained a busy cosmopolitan port and was the Roman Emperor's HQ for the Scottish invasion. It was occupied until the Romans left Britain in the 5th century.[6]

15

THE PEACE DIVIDEND

Having seen the result of direct resistance, Cartimandua decided that rather than fighting the invading forces, she would collaborate and ally herself to the mighty Roman Empire. By negotiating to become a client kingdom of Rome she was preserving her people's tribal independence without bloodshed.

No doubt she would have donned her finery to meet the Roman generals Gaius Suetonius Paulinus and Gnaeus Julius Agricola, who began his career serving in Britain under Paulinus from AD58 to 62. Both would almost certainly have participated in the Romanisation of the Brigante tribe. To show her regal status, Cartimandua would have worn golden armlets, a heavy gold torc round her neck, and fastened brooches to her finest gown and mantle. She was a queen in her own right, and a strong-minded woman who did not consider herself to be beneath the Roman commanders. She would have negotiated terms knowing the strength of her Royal position. She would have made sure that her people would not have to suffer the humiliation of conquest. They would not be beaten down by constant abuse and were not enslaved. By making alliances with Rome, Cartimandua would retain power in her own province, and her domain would be secured by treaty. In exchange for her allegiance, as a tribal leader she would be offered the financial support and protection of the empire

Friendly kings and queens were able more or less to rule as before, so while the Romans maintained order and collected taxes, the native elite would continue to shoulder most of the burden of local

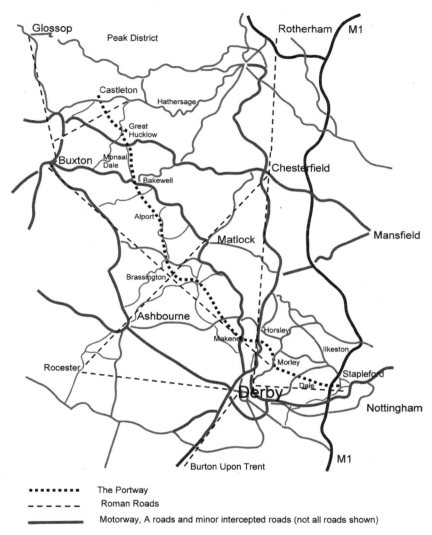

Map of Celtic and Roman roads in Brigantia.

administration. Cartimandua's collaboration would have allowed her, like the other native elite, to administer her own area as long as tributes were paid to Rome, recruits were provided for the army and slaves were always available. As a reward for unswerving loyalty, they could be granted Roman citizenship. Cartimandua may have been presented with other neighbouring domains, which is probably why the Brigante tribe was so huge.

Compliant monarchs could send their sons to Rome to be educated. This encouraged the spread of ideas and philosophies that would establish a permanent and positive link with the empire. These sons received an excellent education, formed contacts and made dynastic marriage alliances. In sending their sons to Rome, the friendly kings were not only educating them, they were forming connections which would strengthen their own positions. If Cartimandua had children, particularly boys, there is every possibility that they would have been mentioned by the Roman writers. They would have commented on them being sent to Rome, being given a Roman style education, or forming alliances with their Roman counterparts, yet there is no mention of any of this. We therefore have to assume that Cartimandua had no children.

Rome benefited in terms of additional resources and manpower at their disposal. The Roman army could not fight on multiple fronts at the same time, and could only move north or west when the tribes to their rear were either friendly or subdued by force, so compliant monarchs reduced the threat of being attacked by enemies simultaneously. The use of friendly kings/queens maintained through diplomacy, not war, formed a series of buffer zones and possible intermediaries, and it became a Claudian policy to have pro-Roman kingdoms flanking boundaries in Wales and the northern hill countries of Derbyshire and Yorkshire. Having Brigantia as a friendly kingdom held back the warring northern tribes preventing them sending sympathetic reinforcements or providing an area of retreat.

Road Systems and Vexillation Forts

As the Romans moved into an area they needed roads to move men and supplies, and obviously where the army went a massive baggage train followed in order to supply that army. The Romans are credited with giving Britain a network of metalled roads for easy movement of troops and supplies, but many of these would have been improvements on roads that the early Britons had made. We tend to think of these early roads as being tracks made with a few hacks of a reindeer antler along a contour line. They may have started in this random fashion with the holes and swampy bits filled in and firmed up with stones, bracken, branches and logs, but the Celts were experts in the use of timber.

Load-bearing timbers found at river crossings indicate the site of a bridge and some substantial roads would have been needed through marshy areas. They built log or corduroy roads made of 4–6 inch (10–15 cm) girders of fir and alder laid in the direction of the road. On these would be placed a thick layer of secured twigs, topped by cross pieces to lock and peg it all together. This would then be finished with a compacted surface of clay. There is an ancient prehistoric trackway which can be traced running from Mam Tor near Castleton in the Derbyshire Peak District to the River Erewash on the Derbyshire/ Nottinghamshire border that would have formed the southern edge of the Brigante territory. The track is known as The Portway and would have run along the high ridges wherever possible. These ridgeways and holloways were used by horse traffic for many centuries. The term ridgeway implies an elevated route; the term hollow way describes the track eroded by traffic and weather to a lower level than the surrounding land. The Roman gave us paved roads that were called *strata* from where our present name *street* originates. The Latin word *caix*, meaning limestone, used for paving roads, gives us the term causeway, meaning a pedestrian route beside a road.

The only stretch of road that still carries the old name The Portway

Towns grew up at major road junctions with buildings called mansios, the official inns or posting stations where members of the imperial post service could change horses and rest. A mansio would be the Roman equivalent of a service station complete with motel. Roads also acted as magnets for less formal settlements usually because of the trading potential they offered. As well as the *nodal* and imperial planned towns, settlements tended to grow in an organic way along stretches of Britain's major Roman roads and more may yet be discovered.

At intervals along the roads they built Vexillation fortresses. These were initially short-term bases to hold stores, and quarters for both legionaries and auxiliaries during the first century. A network of military posts were established north of the Trent during the governorship of Scapula AD47–52 but no towns. Scapula was followed by Aulus Didius Gallus AD52–57 and although the writer Tacitus is generally scornful of Gallus's abilities, he grudgingly admits that he 'advanced further into native territory, building just a few forts so that he might win the glory of having increased the area under his control'.[1]

This is the most likely context for the establishment of the fort at Strutts Park, Derby, and other sites which have yielded material datable to the 50s AD. In the Trent valley there was a twenty-acre vexillation fort at Osmanthorpe on the Nottingham/Derbyshire border. Following the Roman Road known as Rykneld Road (now large stretches of the A61), there was a vexillation fort at Pentrich and another fort 11 miles north at Chesterfield. There is little evidence of these sites now, but the forts were believed to have been established in AD55 during the governorship of Aulus Didius Gallus. Continuing on Rykneld Road, 13 miles north of Chesterfield in south Yorkshire is Templeborough, where the road crossed the River Don at a ford close to the fort built there, 12 miles north east to Danvm (Doncaster) and 15 miles west-south-west of Brough on Noe, which was a main Roman garrison fort.

Information on these vexillation forts is sparse but we have some on the Templeborough Vexillation fort. Templeborough is a suburb of Rotherham, South Yorkshire, an area that takes its name from the remains of the Roman fort found there which were mistakenly believed to be those of a Roman temple. The 1st century AD fort would have been built on the site in earth and wood and although it was cut down in size to 3¾ acres, the original fort was almost square, measuring some 495 feet by 490 feet (151 x 149 m), covering an area of 5½ acres. Defences consisted of a turf rampart, built on a foundation of gravel and clay, an average 18 feet (5.5 m) wide, with a single 18-foot-wide ditch, separated from the rampart by a 13-foot (4-m) wide berm. The newly reduced fort was surrounded by a nine-foot-thick stone wall, backed by a clay bank and fronted by a single ditch. The internal dimensions were about 380 by 440 feet (116 x 134 m).

The double bank that surrounded the fort was still visible in 1831 although stone blocks from the site were regularly carried off and re-used in nearby buildings. Archaeological excavations of part of the fort and bath house were carried out in 1877 by the Rotherham Literary and Scientific Society headed by local historians, J. D. Leader and John Guest. They found evidence that the fort had been burned to the ground and rebuilt twice. Early pottery recovered from the site confirmed that the fort was originally constructed the mid-1st century. The addition of Samian ware and later pottery from the 3rd and 4th centuries would indicate continued and uninterrupted occupation up until the Roman withdrawal from the province *c.* 410. Coins discovered during this excavation ranged in date from the time of the emperors Augustus to Constantine.[2]

In 1916 the site of the fort was acquired by a steelworks in order to expand their production to meet the demand for steel during the First World War. The site was levelled, and 10–15 feet of soil were removed from the area of the fort, destroying all archaeological remains.[3] However, before the works were constructed, an archaeologist specialising in Roman remains, Sir Thomas May, was invited by Rotherham Corporation to re-excavate the fort over the course of eight months from November 1916 to July 1917. Notable amongst the finds was a tile imprinted with the stamp of Cohors IV Gallorum dating to either the time of Domitian (81–96) or Trajan (98–117). The Fourth Cohort of Gauls are known to have occupied the fort, as evidenced by the clay tiles and carved Roman tombstones discovered on the site.

A soldier's tombstone is inscribed *DIS M CINTVSMVS M COH IIII GALLORVM POS MELISVS* ('To the spirits of the departed and Cintusmus, a soldier of the Fourth Cohort of Gauls, [this memorial was] placed by Melisus'). The tombstone of a veteran is inscribed *DIS MANIBVS CROTO VINDICIS EMERITO COH IIII GALLORVM ANNORVM XXXX MONIMENTVM FECIT FLAVIA PEREGRINA CONIVNX PIENTISSIMA MARITO PIENTISSIMO TITVLVM POSVIT* ('To the spirits of the departed and Crotus Vindex, veteran of the Fourth Cohort of Gauls, forty years old, this monument was made and its inscription set down by Flavia Peregrina, a most faithful wife for a most faithful husband'). There's also the tombstone of a Dobunni woman inscribed *DIS M VERECVD RVFI LIA CIVES DOBVNNA ANNOR XXXV EXCINGVS CONIVX CONIVGI KARISSIMAE POSIT DE SVO* ('To the spirits of the departed and to Verecunda Rufilia, a citizen of the Dobunni, thirty-five years old, her husband Excingus placed this for his dearest wife').[4] Finds from both excavations are now housed in Clifton Park Museum in Rotherham. The original stone columns from the Roman granary at Templeborough Fort were re-erected in Clifton Park in 1922.

The pre-Roman tribal organization was not obliterated by the invaders, although the boundaries were modified. There is no list of places and former Iron Age forts in the Brigante kingdom that were taken over by the Romans, but they seem to have recycled some. Towns were founded either on or close to these centres of Iron Age power to serve as the new market and administrative focus of each civitas, or tribal unit. Although they had built towns like Wroxeter (Viroconium Cornoviorum) and Lincoln (Lindum Colonia), there is little archaeological evidence to support the notion of any major towns built in the Brigante territory. For a list of towns deemed to have been in Brigante territory, see Appendix 4.

As well as the other previously mentioned forts like Isurium Brigantium (Aldborough) that undoubtedly became an administrative centre for the Brigante tribe, Cawthorne, north of Pickering, is thought to have been built as a Roman training camp where troops learnt martial skills and probably how to build Hadrian's Wall. (*See also* pages 136 and 186.) Amongst other occupied forts was Knapton, north-east of Malton, Castlesteads in the far north-west near the border with County Durham, and Eston Nab, overlooking the Tees. It may be that the Roman invasion triggered the building of other Brigantian fortifications such as at Wincobank and Whirlow Hall Farm, both on the border of Sheffield.

At Whirlow Hall Farm archaeologists have found evidence of farming taking place there dating back to the Bronze Age. In 2011 excavations revealed remains of a substantial 1st or 2nd century AD Roman estate or villa on what is believed to be a pre-existing Brigantian farmstead.[5] A geophysical survey was carried out and through magnetometry, which measures the magnetic resistance of different underground rocks, a huge rectangular enclosure entered via a timber gateway was discovered, which could indicate that this was a Roman supply base on a major military route. It has been suggested that this is the route of the lost Roman Road linking Templeborough east of Sheffield with the Roman Signal Station at Navio (Brough on Noe), and Batham Gate in the Hope Valley.[6]

Very few people were actually brought into Britain from the Mediterranean lands during the period of Roman influence except soldiers, officials and merchants. But it appears that once the initial settlements had been established, artisans familiar with the Roman style of building were brought over to build the homes of high-ranking officials both Roman and Celtic. The Romans brought new things to Britain like lavish and fashionable clothes, and a rich diet. They introduced Britons to the idea of ornamental space with gardens, trellises, fountains and fishponds where plants were grown for their beauty as much as for their usefulness. If Cartimandua had been to Rome she would undoubtedly have been in awe of her surroundings. She would have seen their education, their baths, their aqueducts and buildings. She would have marvelled at their forums, temples and theatres. As a Romanised Briton Cartimandua would have been able to benefit from this imperial sophistication and live a life of luxury. She would no doubt have received subsidies from Rome in return for her continued co-operation alongside her inherited wealth and the wealth generated through trade.

Trade and Natural Resources

We know that it was the Celts who established trading routes, not the Romans as we are often led to believe. The Greek geographer Strabo who was writing at the end of the first century BC, provides a list of British exports and hints at the complex network of gifts, exchange

Above left: The stone carving known as the T'owd Man, depicting an ancient lead miner is in Wirksworth Church.

Above right: The pub sign at Brassington shows the ancient lead miner with his pick and kibble.

and trade involved in obtaining raw materials and distributing finished products. We therefore know that by the 1st century BC British exports included gold, silver, iron, hides, slaves, cattle and hunting dogs. Salt was a vital commodity, transported in ceramic containers. Broken fragments impregnated with salt have survived and show how wide the distribution was. Salt was the main commodity used for trading by the Celts as it was a vital meat preservative. Salt was almost as highly prized as gold.

The Brigantine territory was rich in stone and metals. Stone suitable for grinding cereals and sharpening iron blades was sent over vast distances. By the first century BC decorative pots in the form of Derbyshire ware were being exported. Glass beads, pottery and small fragments of bronze that are not native to the area would suggest that the region was visited by neighbouring tribes. As a Romanised Briton Cartimandua would have traded with the Gaulish and Roman merchants who travelled the trade routes up the River Humber from the coast, or perhaps from the west with the trading ships from Erin, or overland via The Portway linking Mam Tor near Castleton with the River Erewash near Nottingham. The kind of luxury goods found would indicate that trade was an important aspect of the tribal economy.

The exploitation of the region's mineral wealth has been practised from the time of the Stone Age, and being so prominent a feature of the landscape, it's very likely that exporting stone was a major industry in Brigante territory. Apart from building in stone, the geological variation made it possible to utilise it in other ways so it would have been uncharacteristic if the Romans had not copied the Celts and put the stone to profitable use. Using stone to build huts and forts is obvious, but the range of uses and applications match the geological variety. The Romans built stone altars, guide posts, milestones and much more.

Gritstone moors and edges border the northern limestone uplands of the Peak District, and because the gritstone edges outcrop in long bands, the stone is relatively easy to quarry. Gritstone provided field walls, buildings and grindstones or millstones. Gritstone millstones were employed by the Celts and the Romans for their rotary querns and very probably for lead-ore crushing before washing and smelting.

Limestone was burnt to produce lime for agriculture and for cement. Whether the Celts used concrete is unclear although we are told that ancient Roman concrete was a mixture of lime mortar, aggregate, pozzolana (volcanic ash), water, and stones, and was stronger than previously used concretes. The ancient builders placed these ingredients in wooden frames where they hardened and bonded to a facing of rubble. A Roman bath excavated at Aquae Arnemeteae (Buxton) was found to have been constructed of limestone blocks with a lime mortar, and faced with lime cement.[7]

The hill tribesmen of the Celtic Pennine communities mined lead, which would have been an established economic concern by the time the Romans arrived on the scene in AD47, and the mineral wealth was a powerful incentive for them to stay and set up a well-organised lead mining industry. The naturalist and historian Pliny wrote: 'In Britain, lead is found near the surface of the earth in such abundance that a law is made to limit the quantity that should be gotten.' Lead ore was particularly highly prized because it was readily available (according to Pliny, although the miners would no doubt disagree), easily worked and unlike iron, was resistant to rust

A sketch of a pig of lead showing how it was inscribed.

and corrosion. It could be extracted from open workings along the outcrops of major veins, sometimes as much as 60 feet wide at the surface. Early lead mining deposits were worked by the hill tribesmen by means of shafts and galleries. The ore was obtained with hammers and chisels and gathered with wide-mouthed oak shovels into baskets. In the pre-Roman days, lead mining was probably a cottage industry where smelting of the ore was also carried out by the miners in their roundhouses.[8]

Lead was a very important commodity, the plastic of the day. Being waterproof, the Romans used it to pioneer pipe making, roofing, cisterns, weights, caskets, tanks and coffins. Our word plumber is derived from the Latin term for lead, *plumbum*. Metallurgical tests have claimed that a cistern in Pompeii, buried by the eruption of Vesuvius in 79, was made of British lead that could have come from Derbyshire. Lead bowls would have been quite common but as lead could be melted down and recycled, very few have survived.

After smelting the metal was poured into clay moulds bearing stamps in reverse which were imprinted on the resulting lumps referred to as pigs of lead. They would then be loaded into bullock carts for transportation to a central collection and distribution area, but not all made it to their destination. Twenty-six pigs of lead from this period have been found. They carry the name of the company set up by the Romano/British entrepreneurs trading as the Lutudarum Company. The cast inscription reads SOCIORVM LVTVD BRIT. EX. ARG. LVTVD is Lutudarum, and EX ARG is Ex Argentum, which means silver free, to indicate that it was not bullion. The inscription can therefore be translated as 'The Lutudarum Company, British silver-free lead.' Replicas can be seen in Buxton museum. Most give no date or evidence of exactly where they were mined or smelted, but a lead pig found near Pately Bridge is dated AD81 and is inscribed 'Imperator Caesar Domitianus Augustus, consul for the 7th time, Brigantian.'

A Roman pig of lead 17½ inches long was found on Matlock Moor in 1787. It weighs 173 pounds. Another pig weighing 126 pounds was found on Cromford moor near Matlock in 1777, with the inscription in raised letters:- IMP.CAES.HADRIANI.AUG.MET.LVT. A third reads 'Lucius Aruconius Verecundus; from the mines at Lutudarum'.

Lead ore is argentiferous, containing or bearing silver, so this mineral wealth was a great bonus to the Romans who valued silver for spoons and plating bronze objects. But dealing in a precious commodity meant that it was mined under military control and the Peak lead mines would have come under the direct supervision of the Imperial Treasury of Rome.

Unfortunately Derbyshire lead contained very little silver, which must have been a great disappointment to the treasury officials who quickly leased the mine to civil contractors who formed the Societas Lutudarum or Lutudarum Company. These private producers, known as 'conductores', worked under licence from the procurator of mines, and were taxed at a rate of 50% of ore obtained. So Derbyshire lead mining in Roman times was exploited first by the military and then by elite Romano/British entrepreneurs trading as the Lutudarum Company.[9]

For centuries historian have been searching for the lost lead mining centre of Lutudarum that's imprinted on the Roman pigs of lead. Like its neighbour Brassington and other Peak district villages, Carsington once depended heavily on lead mining, so archaeologists have speculated that Carsington could be the lost lead mining town of Lutudarum created by the Romans. But why Carsington?

The Roman name Lutudarum is thought be derived from a muddy stream. This clue puzzled scholars for years but it would be an appropriate name for a place by the Scow Brook, which ran through the Carsington valley. making the site very muddy and clayey. In the 1980s the area was completely transformed with the creation of Carsington Water, the ninth largest reservoir in England, The reservoir has a surface area of 730 acres with a holding capacity of 7,800 million gallons (35,415 megalitres).

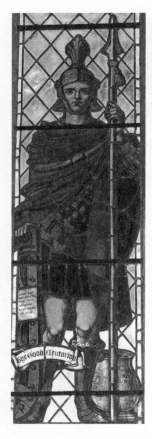

Above: Newspaper cuttings from 21 October
1983 when the Carsington reservoir inundated
the valley, obliterating all evidence of Roman
occupation.

Left: The Roman influence in Carsington is even
depicted in the stained glass window of the church.

Prior to the valley being inundated, archaeologists worked for three years excavating an area of 1½ acres and their work showed positive results. They concluded that on the west bank of the Scow Brook was a Romano-British settlement of at least 5 acres, occupied by the Romans from the last quarter of the first century to the middle of the late fourth century. That's a lot longer than most other Roman sites, yet surprisingly, there is no indication that it was ever turned into a military colony or town. Archaeologists became increasingly convinced that if this area had not been a military colony or a town, such a settlement must have been associated with an industry. As the area is rich in natural mineral deposits and lead in particular, it seemed that the lost lead mining centre of Lutudarum had been found at last. Finds at Carsington and the amenities indicate a degree of wealth and Romanisation not

The Street.

otherwise found in central Derbyshire, and that this was one of the most important locations in the area, a unique site.[10]

Not only is the area rich in natural mineral deposits, another reason to locate the centre of the Derbyshire Lead mining industry here was the fact that it was positioned directly on the old Celtic road known as The Portway giving direct access to the River Erewash, a tributary of the River Trent.

Economically the area would have flourished, and as the area's economic growth accelerated, this must have been reflected in public and private building projects. There would have been fine houses with window glass and heating systems. The home of the procurator metallorum who was in charge of the administration and supply functions would have reflected the style of a Roman villa. New important buildings would have been created along with a new road system.

No longer was the old Celtic Portway considered adequate. The Romans needed a road network that allowed merchandise to be moved freely, and here we find the junction of two major new roads, the Roman Hereward Street and The Street.

The Street ran south-east from Buxton to Derby. It still runs through the village of Brassington and has remained in continuous use since Roman times. If we assume The Street continued in a south-eastern direction, the route would be close to the modern track going down Carsington Pasture west of Carsington village and out into Carsington Water. Establishing an ancient road network is always difficult, but in this area it's made harder by the damage caused by lead mining and quarrying, and of course the flooding of the valley. Although it very probably continued to Little Chester, Derby, the southern portion of The Street is conjecture.[1]

Decline and Fall?

Humans have been mining and using lead for thousands of years, and poisoning themselves in the process. It is one of the oldest known work and environmental hazards. Lead compounds were formerly common in pottery glazing, painting, printing, plumbing and other industries. The early miners were encouraged to drink ale as it was believed to be an antidote to lead poisoning and throughout the region you will find pubs with the name *The Miner's Arms*. The T'Owd Man is the oldest representation of a miner anywhere in the world and can be found in stone carvings at the villages of Bonsall and Wirksworth.[12]

Lead poisoning is also known as plumbism. Lead interferes with a number of body processes and is toxic to many organs and tissues, including the heart, bones, intestines, kidney, reproductive and nervous systems. It also causes permanent learning and behavioural disorders. Symptoms include abdominal pains, confusion, headache, anaemia, irritability and in severe cases seizures, coma and death.

There have been many theories surrounding the decline of Rome and chronic lead poisoning was first presented as a reason by Kobert in 1909. It was re-stated by American scientist S. C. Gilfan in 1965, and the debate was re-opened in 1983 when an article by geochemist Dr Jerome Nriagu was published in the *New England Journal of Medicine*.

Dr Jerome Nriagu has estimated that wealthy Romans absorbed more than 100 times as much lead as the poor. The wealthy used lead for pots, pans and drinking vessels while the poor used earthenware. It was used in a powdered form for makeup and eye shadow. It is now realised that many leading Romans could have been suffering from accumulated lead poisoning which could have been an important factor in the collapse of the Roman civilization. From AD139 onward, luxurious licentiousness within the Empire produced a whole series of unworthy rulers. Weakness within the state encouraged invasion; so could Derbyshire lead be blamed for the downfall of Rome?

16

VENUTIUS AND CARATACUS

Tacitus refers to Cartimandua as the Queen of the Brigantine tribe with her consort Venutius. He was described as a Brigantian, but prior to his marriage to the Brigantian Queen, it has been suggested that Venutius was a prince of the Corvetti tribe whose territory was around the Lake District along the northern edge of Brigante territory. There is no evidence to support this, but it would seem that Venutius was not the leader of his tribe, or the Brigantes and the Corvetti tribe would have amalgamated. He was no doubt of noble birth but inferior in rank to his wife. Cartimandua was the rightful queen but shared power with Venutius while ever he supported her. Gold and silver coinage found in Brigante territory bears the abbreviated form CARTI-VE and could stand for Cartimandua and Venutius. If this is correct it would imply that they ruled together.

It could be that Venutius was a Roman citizen or had been sent to Rome to learn the ways of the Romans. His name sounds Roman but names could be Romanised. He could have spent time with the Roman army and acquired knowledge of military matters that he later put into practice. In exchange, he may have advised Scapula and other Roman leaders from the native viewpoint. If there was any mention of this in the Annals or the early mention of Brigante it is lost so we can only assume these things.

Perhaps the marriage was arranged to secure a Roman presence in Brigantia, or perhaps Cartimandua considered marriage to a candidate acceptable to Rome to be beneficial in such troubled times.

Initially Venutius would appear to have been the perfect consort and completely happy to support his wife.

Matrimonial trouble seemed to have started in the 50s. If the marriage was unproductive it could have been dissolved. There is no evidence of adultery, just hostility. The marriage could have ended in divorce. Perhaps Venutius did not agree with Cartimandua's decision to form an alliance with Rome. He may have been put under pressure by the many other tribal leaders who did not agree with her decision to form an alliance.

We have already come across Caratacus, the Celtic tribal leader of the Catuvellauni tribe that inhabited the area between Oxford and Cambridge. (*See also* page 163.) He had chosen to fight the Romans right from the start. In AD47 when the Roman general Publius Ostorius Scapula conquered the hostile Catuvellauni tribe, rather than accept defeat, Caratacus, heir to the Catuvellaunian throne, withdrew to fight another day. He skipped over the border into Silures territory and raised a substantial army.

In AD48 Publius Ostorius Scapula attacked the Deceangli in the north-east of what is now Wales. They appear to have surrendered with little resistance and Scapula then spent several years campaigning against the Silures and the Ordovices. Their resistance was led by Caratacus, who had set himself up as a fighting warrior chieftain of the Silures, who proved to be Rome's toughest opponents to date. They were a powerful and warlike tribe or tribal confederation occupying what is now south-east Wales. They were bordered to the north by the Ordovices; to the east by the Dobunni; and to the west by the Demetae. The Silures fiercely resisted Roman conquest but eventually, finding themselves trapped in a defensive position, they were no match for the Romans, who won a pitched battle. Caratacus' wife and daughter were captured and his brother surrendered, but undaunted Caratacus left them to their fate and escaped to the neighbouring territory of the Ordovices in mid Wales. They in turn were defeated by Scapula in AD51 but by then Caratacus had moved on again.[1]

The Silures continued to wage effective guerrilla warfare against the Roman forces and Ostorius Scapula announced that they posed such a danger that they should be either exterminated or transplanted. But even this did not subdue the Silures. His threats only increased their determination to resist the Romans.

Caratacus Moves on to the Brigante Tribe

Caratacus may have moved on to their Welsh neighbours the Deceangli in north Wales, because we know that Ostorius Scapula was on campaign against them. At around this time Caratacus headed across country to Brigante territory. He may have been just passing through hoping to do so unnoticed as he joined the tribes further north, knowing that he was theoretically in enemy territory, but he probably decided to lie low there for a time. There could have been some family link between Caratacus and Cartimandua and he may have looked to her for sanctuary, but it's more likely he was hoping to raise support amongst the anti-Roman factions amongst the Brigantes to continue his fight. Known for his cunning, Caratacus probably hoped to persuade any discontented elements and former warriors of the Brigante tribe to join him in a further uprising. He would have been aware that certain elements of the tribe were disillusioned with Cartimandua's decision to side with the Romans, so it can be assumed that he intended to undermine Cartimandua's authority. But Cartimandua was too astute to not realise what could happen. She knew Caratacus – his cunning and deceit. She knew that he would move on looking for the next opportunity, heedless of the destruction in his wake, leaving the people who had supported him to deal with the consequences of his actions. He'd abandoned his own tribe, the Silures and the Ordovices so he would not baulk when it came to using the Brigantes.

Caratacus probably taunted Venutius for being weak and not standing up to his wife. He probably said that as a man he should be the one making the decisions, he ought to be the one to lead the great Brigantian tribe with or without Cartimandua's support. Such goading may have pushed Venutius into action because in AD48, the year after Cartimandua had agreed to collaborate with the Romans we know that there was a disturbance amongst the Brigantes. This brought Ostorius Scapula hastily back from his campaign against the Deceangli in Wales in order to provide military support for Cartimandua's regime.[2] There was no reason for Scapula to have left unfinished business in the Deceanglian territory unless something major was happening in Brigante territory. His spies would have informed him that Caratacus was there, and Brigantian security was obviously crucial to Rome. If it was a threatened uprising, the ringleaders would have faced certain death, yet the names of the ringleaders were not disclosed. There is nothing more on record.

If Scapula had allowed the instigators of such an uprising to go unpunished, the might of Rome would have descended on him and the Brigante tribe as an example to others, yet the reason for this fracas has never been fully explained. Although it's been suggested that there was a major rift in their marriage and Venutius was responsible for the threatened uprising, there is nothing to support this. If it had been caused by Venutius he would have been severely punished by the Roman authorities, but he wasn't. The most persuasive answer is that the whole thing was caused by Caratacus. He had threatened the stability and peace of Cartimandua's kingdom, her position and the success of her treaty with Rome.

Cartimandua needed to assure her Roman allies of her loyalty and there was only one way that she could do that. She had to hand over Caratacus, a fellow countryman and prince of the Catuvellaunian tribe. It must have been a heart-searching decision but there would have been no doubt in her mind that he was a rebel intent upon destroying her position and the stability of her tribe. Having made the decision, Cartimandua had him imprisoned. He would not have been an easy prisoner to guard but finds at Stanwick have revealed a ritual shaft or pit, eight metres deep with a wooden pole at the bottom surrounded by traces of flesh and blood. Was this Caratacus' prison or would human sacrifices have been tied to the pole and offered to a deity, perhaps the god of the underworld? We will never know for sure. What we do know is that Caratacus was put in chains and in AD51 handed over to the Romans, giving Claudius the greatest exhibit of his triumph.

Caratacus was taken to Rome where, instead of being executed, he made a passionate appeal for his release. According to Tacitus, he spoke of how different things would have been if he had come before the emperor as a friend and ally. If Caratacus or his brother had been allowed to succeed their father on the Catuvallaunian throne, then he would not have turned rebel and would have been a friendly monarch. He fought against Rome not to better the prospects of his people but because his birthright had been taken away. 'I had horses, men, arms and wealth. Are you surprised that I am sorry to lose them? If you want to rule the world does it follow that everyone else welcomes enslavement?'³

Caratacus' emotive speech unbelievably won him a full pardon and he was allowed to remain in exile in Rome. But the repercussions for Cartimandua were great. Her enemies considered this an act of treachery and Tacitus labelled her a traitor. Whether Cartimandua's decision to hand over Caratacus was justified or not, the decision had far-reaching effects both within the Brigante tribe and elsewhere. Historians recorded that this undoubtedly changed her relationship with her husband Venutius and probably broke their marriage, although there is no firm evidence to support this.

The Roman authorities rewarded Cartimandua with great wealth and favours. It's probable that at this time she was living at Stanwick, the Celtic fort near Darlington. It's been suggested that the finest pieces of glass found there were probably diplomatic gifts, so could some of these have been her reward for handing the rebel leader Caratacus over to the Roman authorities?

Civil War in Brigante Territory

We are led to believe that it was Cartimandua who handed Caratacus over to Rome, but what if it was Venutius and not Cartimandua who did so, hoping to gain kudos with Rome? Tacitus writes about Venutius having long-standing loyalty to Rome and accepting Roman rule in the Brigante territory, so he could have been the one who handed over Caratacus. He may have seen the capture of Caratacus as his passport to power. Knowing that Rome did not agree with female rulers and looked down on any man ruled by his wife, Venutius may have only been willing to support his wife while waiting for his opportunity to take over the Brigante territory and usurp her. Rome could make that happen but despite all he had done for them, they didn't. Cartimandua remained queen and this must have infuriated Venutius. Livy wrote:

> Our ancestors would have no woman transact even private business except through her guardian; they placed them under the tutelage of parents or brothers or husbands... If you allow

them to pull away these restraints and wrench them out one after another, and finally put themselves on an equality with their husbands, do you imagine that they will be able to tolerate them? From the moment that they become your fellows, they will become your masters.[4]

Those early writers relate that tension between the royal couple led to estrangement, which led to fighting amongst the Brigantes. Things had changed and now Venutius was not going to allow himself to be ruled by a woman and was determined to change this with or without Roman help. He probably thought that he could oust his wife and take on the role of king while the Roman armies stood aside and let him. Perhaps he felt that his good standing with Rome would allow this to happen and they wouldn't interfere even if he raised an army against his wife. It wouldn't have been hard for him to do this as any tribal federation was always going to be prone to internal fighting and rival factions. It's not that he was suddenly anti-Roman, he was put out that they would not support him in his quest to take the Brigante crown. But he had misjudged the situation. Cartimandua was the rightful queen and had offered the Brigantian territory as a protectorate, so the Romans naturally sided with her against Venutius, and sent in cohorts to defend their client queen. The sides were evenly matched and the fighting was at first inconclusive until Caesius Nasica arrived with the IX Legion Hispana and defeated Venutius. Cartimandua narrowly escaped being captured but retained her throne and an unsteady peace was achieved.

This raises a rather obvious question. The Romans squashed the uprising but why were the ringleaders not named and punished? Surely that would have been something that Tacitus would have written about yet he didn't. His only comment was that Cartimandua's enemies 'invaded her kingdom because they were infuriated and goaded by fears of humiliating female rule'.[5]

As the Romans preferred to be dealing with a client king rather than a client queen, Venutius probably thought he was doing what the Romans wanted, and once the uprising had been squashed, he most likely retained their support. Miranda Aldhouse-Green, Professor of Archaeology at Cardiff University makes the point that 'He appears to have been wooed by the vicarious power, status and Roman friendship emanating from his wife, but underneath he chafed both at his own inferior rank and at Cartimandua's position as the real authority.'[6]

If on the other hand, the disturbance had been a deliberate attempt to fight the Romans, they would have made an example of him for the part that he had played in the attempted palace coup. He would have been captured and killed or lived his life in hiding and under the constant threat of Roman revenge. Tacitus said that Cartimandua lost a husband but preserved her kingdom, so what are we supposed to think? Did Venutius accept the situation and continue to support his wife? Was there a reconciliation between the estranged couple or did they agree to a compromise? The Roman writers seem to have ignored this situation. Provided she didn't give Rome the excuse to take her lands, Cartimandua remained queen and benefitted from being allied to Rome.

It's possible that theirs was a dynastic union and in order to keep it intact, Roman diplomacy encouraged the creation of the Brigantian confederation for them to rule jointly. They could have done this by nurturing a more centralised tribal structure that would be easier to deal with than countless smaller groups, so the Brigantes were formed into very large civitates, or administrative units that covered most of Yorkshire, Cleveland, Durham and Lancashire stretching from the North Sea in the east to the Irish Sea in the west. We know the names of some of the smaller tribes that made up the Brigantes at this time; they include the Setanti in Lancashire, the Lopocares, the Corionototae and the Tectoverdi around the Tyne valley.

The Brigante 'empire' covered a huge area so if we are dealing with a warring couple, it would not have been difficult for them to live separate lives within the kingdom. Unfortunately, there is no mention of where. Because neither Cartimandua nor Venutius are mentioned for the next twelve years, we can only guess at what was happening and where they were. They may have moved between a number of hillforts on a regularly basis to avoid confrontation or they may have remained together. Those early writers like Livy relate that tension between the royal couple led to estrangement, but apart from this, their domestic situation was of no interest to the Roman scribes.

Although we've considered Isurium Brigantum (Aldborough) as Cartimandua's tribal headquarters, Tacitus reports that it was the seat of Venutius.[7] J. S. Fletcher in his 1901 six-volume work *A Picturesque History of Yorkshire* confidently refers to Venutius as King of the Brigantes who was usurped from power by his wife and her lover.[8] (*See* page 225.) There is no evidence to support this. Tacitus and the other early historians never referred to Venutius as King of the Brigante tribe. Cartimandua did take her husband's armour bearer as a lover but his name was Vellocatus and there is no indication that they ruled together.

The Roman army had previously focused the area to the south of Brigantium but throughout the 50s they pushed further north. The Governor Ostorius Scapula had been wrestling with the problem of subduing rebellious tribes when he died in AD 52 and was replaced by a new Governor Didius Gallus. Two years later, the Emperor Claudius died, said to have been poisoned by his wife Agrippina to make way for her son Nero as the new teenage Emperor.[9] (*See* page 230.)

Emperor Nero and the Druids of Mona

Peace reigned in Brigante for many years, but when Nero became emperor in 54 AD, he seems to have been undecided what to do. He contemplated withdrawing his legions from Britain but was advised against doing so because it would tarnish the memory of his step-father Claudius's triumph there.[10] When weighing up the cost of occupation and maintaining a military presence it was said to be more than offset by the gains in income from the exploitation of the island's resources. For that reason Nero decided to continue the occupation and appointed Quintus Veranius as governor. His successor was Gaius Suetonius Paulinus, and in 58AD Gnaeus Julius Agricola began his career in Roman public life as a military tribune serving in Britain under Paulinus. Both Veranius and Paulinus were experienced in dealing with troublesome hill tribes. They mounted a campaign across Wales but in particular they aimed to destroy the island of Mona (Anglesey). This was a refuge for British rebels and a stronghold and learning centre administered by the Druidic religious leaders. Because the Druids were very anti-Roman, the Romans loathed them and the hold they had over the people. Tacitus describes the action. He tells how the Romans crossed the Menai Straight, attacked the people and destroyed their sacred groves:

At that time ... Paulinus Suetonius was in charge of Britain. In military science and people's talk, which allows no one to be without envy, he rivalled Corbulo, and was anxious to equal the glorious recovery of Armenia by subduing enemies of the state. For this reason he prepared to attack the island of Mona which had a large population and provided shelter for fugitives. Flat-bottomed boats were constructed to contend with the shallow water and shifting bottom, and in this way the infantry made the crossing. Then followed the cavalry, making use of fords or swimming beside their horses where the water was deeper.

Along the shore stood the enemy in a close-packed array of armed men interspersed with women dressed like Furies in funeral black, with streaming hair and brandishing torches. Round about were the Druids, their hands raised to heaven, pouring out dire curses. The Roman troops were so struck with dismay at this weird sight that they became rooted to the spot as though their limbs were paralysed and laid themselves open to wounds. Then, bolstered by the encouragements of their commander and urging one another not to be afraid of this mass of fanatical women, they advanced with their standards, cut down all they met, and enveloped them in the flames of their own torches. After this a garrison was imposed on the conquered natives, and the groves devoted to their savage rites cut down; for it was part of their religion to drench their altars with the blood of captives and to consult their gods by means of human entrails.[11]

Tacitus gives us a full description but there is more that we have learnt since. A group of 181 Iron Age metal objects were recovered in 1942 from Llyn Cerrig Bach, a small lake in the north-west of the island of Anglesey. Amongst the finds are many Brigante objects that may have been traded, plundered or captured in warfare by the local tribes. Most items are martial in function, including two slave chains, seven swords, six spearheads, fragments of a shield, iron bars, two cauldrons, part of a bronze war trumpet, blacksmith's tools, fragments of iron wagon tyres, and horse gear. The Llyn Cerrig Bach collection is of great importance to our understanding of Iron Age weaponry, metalworking, tools and the development of decorative styles, and is comparable with the famous discovery of metalwork at La Tène on the edge of Lake Neuchètel, Switzerland.

The Llyn Cerrig Bach hoard was found during the construction of the RAF airfield at Valley. The operation involved spreading peat over the sandy ground, and as workmen extracted the peat from Cors yr Ynys bog on the southern margin of Llyn Cerrig Bach, they discovered a three-metre-long chain had been caught up in the teeth of a harrow. It was not at first identified as being ancient, and was attached to a tractor used to pull lorries out of the mud, a function that it performed extremely well. Only later was it identified as a slave chain with five neck-rings to hold five captives. It weighs 6.66 kilograms and is over 2,000 years old. More items were discovered during the extraction of peat and although initially these finds were thought to be deposited all at the same time, it's now known that this important collection was built up over a long period from about 300BC to AD100.

Archaeologists looking for clues centred on the fact that the items were discovered in Cors yr Ynys, a peat bog. As we have related earlier, particularly with the story of Lindow Man (*see* pages 175–78) a sacrificial offering to the gods found in a peat bog in Brigante territory, peat bogs had special religious significance to the Celts. The fact that many of these items found at Llyn Cerrig Bach had been deliberately broken suggested that they had been placed there as votive offerings. Ritual breakage rendered the item unusable in this world, but made it acceptable as a spirit gift offered to the gods.

The fact that Llyn Cerrig Bach is in Anglesey provides the basis for an even more interesting theory. Could the offerings found at Llyn Cerrig Bach be linked to the Druids, thrown by them into the bog as a major appeal to the spirit world in response to a crisis? The presence of objects such as a war trumpet and weapons suggest that this was not simply a site of water worship of local significance. The large amount of military equipment implies that these objects had been offered before battle to placate the gods.[12]

Historians later called the destruction of the Druidic centre at Mona the Menai Massacre. The final occupation of Wales was, however, postponed because elsewhere on the mainland, Boudica, the wife of a tribal leader, was leading a rebellion against Rome.

17

THE BOUDICAN UPRISING

The fine bronze statue of Boudica in her chariot on Westminster Bridge, London.

Prasutagus was King of the Icini tribe that inhabited the area that is now Norfolk. Following Claudius's conquest the tribe had voluntarily allied themselves to Rome and were proud of their independence. They had revolted when the then governor Publius

Ostorius Scapula had threatened to disarm them, but overall the Iceni tribe were content and Prasutagus led a long life of conspicuous wealth. Prasutagus obviously found favour with Rome. His name would indicate that he was Romanized and possibly schooled in Rome. However, it was normal Roman practice to allow allied kingdoms their independence only for the lifetime of their client king, who would agree to leave his kingdom to Rome in his will. Roman law also only allowed inheritance through the male line. Hoping to preserve his line, Prasutagus made the Roman emperor Nero co-heir to his kingdom, along with his wife and two daughters. When Prasutagus died in AD61, his consort Boudica prepared to take on the role of queen.

Prasutagus' wishes were ignored.[1] Nero dissolved the tribal agreement, and the Iceni kingdom was annexed as if it had been conquered. Lands and property were confiscated and nobles treated like slaves. Roman financiers including Seneca the Younger chose to recall all the loans made to Prasutagus, and his subjects became liable for his debts. Cassius Dio wrote:

> An excuse for the war was found in the confiscation of the sums of money that Claudius had given to the foremost Britons ... Seneca, in the hope of receiving a good rate of interest, had lent to the islanders 40,000,000 sesterces that they did not want, and had afterwards called in this loan all at once and had resorted to severe measures in exacting it. These sums, as Decianus Catus, the procurator of the island maintained, were to be paid back.[2]

According to Tacitus, the procurator Decianus Catus and his men used stunning brutality in carrying out the 'provincialization' of the kingdom, seizing ancestral land and weapons, demanding huge sums of money, raping the princesses and flogging Boudica. For the Romans, the brutal excesses of Decianus Catus and his men would not have been an issue because they would have been told to use whatever means were necessary. Abuses against the natives were seen as an acceptable part of Roman occupation abroad, but these outrages, personal humiliation and the abuse their Queen and her daughters received at Roman hands were an affront to tribal honour and triggered the pent-up fury of the Iceni.[3]

While Gaius Suetonius Paulinus was leading the campaign against the people of Mona, the Iceni conspired with their neighbours the Trinovantes, and others, to revolt. Boudica was chosen as their leader and standing at the head of her followers, according to Dio Cassius, she exhorted them:

'Let us, therefore, go against [the Romans], trusting boldly to good fortune. Let us show them that they are hares and foxes trying to rule over dogs and wolves.' When she had finished speaking, she employed a species of divination, letting a hare escape from the fold of her dress; and since it ran on what they considered the auspicious side, the whole multitude shouted with pleasure, and Boudica, raising her hand toward heaven, said: 'I thank you, Andraste, and call upon you as woman speaking to woman ... I beg you for victory and preservation of liberty.'[4]

It is believed that she was originally named Breaca – Bray-ah-ca – after the goddess Briga. Her name probably changed to Boudica from the old word Boudeg meaning Bringer of Victory when she went into battle against the Romans. Boudica means victory and Boudica invoked the goddess Andraste/Andrasta/Andate who, according to the Roman historian Dio Cassius, was an Icenic war goddess and goddess of victory. The hare was considered sacred to Andraste.[5] As we related earlier, this kind of divination was common with birds and animals. To run to the left was considered unfavourable (*sinistra*) but to the right was favourable.

Gaius Suetonius Paulinus who fought Boudica and the Iceni stated that Boudica's army contained more women than men.[6] This huge force of Britons bent on revenge and led by Boudica descended on the former Trinovantian capital of Camulodunum (Colchester). According to one source, Boudica mounted in her war chariot, charged through her enemies slicing off their heads with her powerful sword. The Romans had turned towns like Camulodunum (Colchester) into *coloniae* for their own citizens, usually retired legionaries who were granted lands. Roman coloniae served two purposes, as a potential reserve of veterans who could be called about during times of emergency, and a source of future Roman citizens and therefore recruits to the Roman army.[7] The Latin name for Colchester was Colonia Claudia Victricensis Camulodunum, founded by Claudius in AD49. Roman colonies played a major role in the spread of the Latin language, Roman law and customs, and showed the surrounding native populations an example of Roman life.[8]

No doubt all this inflamed Boudica, making the city a target. The Roman occupants of the city appealed to the procurator Catus Decianus, but he sent only two hundred auxiliary troops. The poorly defended city was easily destroyed, although the temple, dedicated to the former emperor Claudius who had been declared a god after his death, was under siege for two days before it fell. The Iceni considered that making Claudius a god was an act of blasphemy so they chopped the head off his bronze statue and threw it in the river. In an attempt to relieve the city, the future governor Quintus Petillius Cerialis then commanding the Legio IX Hispana suffered an overwhelming defeat. His infantry was wiped out and only the commander and some of his cavalry escaped. Archaeologists have shown that the city was then methodically demolished.

When news of the rebellion at Camulodunum reached him, Suetonius headed for Londinium where the Celtic tribes were then heading. Londinium was then a relatively new town founded after the conquest of AD43, but already a thriving commercial centre. However, with insufficient numbers and in the wake of Petillius's defeat at Camulodunum, Suetonius decided to sacrifice the city of Londinium to save the province. Londinium was abandoned to the rebels who slaughtered the people and burnt it down in a determined effort to drive out the Romans. Archaeology revealss a thick red layer of burnt debris within the bounds of the Roman city. Tacitus:

Suetonius … with wonderful resolution, marched amidst a hostile population to Londinium, which, though undistinguished by the name of a colony, was much frequented by a number of merchants and trading vessels. Uncertain whether he should choose it as a seat of war, as he looked round on his scanty force of soldiers, and remembered with what a serious warning the rashness of Petilius had been punished, he resolved to save the province at the cost of a single town. Nor did the tears and weeping of the people, as they implored his aid, deter him from giving the signal of departure and receiving into his army all who would go with him. Those who were chained to the spot by the weakness of their sex, or the infirmity of age, or the attractions of the place, were cut off by the enemy.[9]

Boudica and her army moved on from Londinium to Verulamium (St Albans), burning and slaughtering as they went. According to legend they used the ancient crossing over the River Fleet at King's Cross, now known mainly for its huge railway station. Early reference to the original bridge uses the name Broad Ford Bridge but it became known as Battle Bridge along with the local village that also took the name. This led to the idea that this was the site of a major battle between the Romans and the Iceni tribe led by Boudica. The tradition is not supported by any historical evidence and is rejected by modern historians. But the belief that Boudica was killed and buried between platforms 9 and 10 in King's Cross Station still abounds.[10] Tacitus described the outcome of the destruction of St Albans as

> ... slaughter on a massive scale. Not only warriors but women and baggage animals were put to the sword. The Britons had no interest in taking or selling prisoners. They performed the most gruesome and bizarre rituals to the accompaniment of sacrifices, banquets and wanton behaviour.[11]

The Final Battle

The rebels had picked their time well. The Roman legions were hopelessly dispersed but it wasn't long before the well-disciplined legions were united. Suetonius regrouped with the XIV Gemina, some vexillationes (detachments) of the XX Valeria Victorix and any available auxiliaries. He was able to call on 10,000 men, but according to Dio, the rebel army numbered 230,000, although this is surely an exaggeration. The opposing forces met at an unknown site in the Midlands.

Boudica addressed her troops from her chariot, her daughters beside her. Tacitus gives her a short speech in which she presents herself as an ordinary person avenging her lost kingdom. Their cause was just and the deities were on their side. She, a woman, was resolved to win or die, if the men wanted to live in slavery that was their choice.

The British forces were at a disadvantage against the Romans skilled at armed combat. They were disciplined and had superior weapons. First the Romans used volleys of heavy javelins to kill thousands of Britons as they rushed towards the Roman lines. As the Romans advanced the Britons attempted to flee but they were trapped by the presence of their own families whom they had stationed in a ring of waggons round the edge of the battlefield to view what they imagined would be another resounding victory.

Tacitus tells us this, and in his *Germania* and again in his *Annals*, he gives detailed reports of women accompanying their men on the battlefields to provide support. He writes in detail about how the women would gather behind the war-host and show their breasts to flagging warriors while screaming that defeat that day would mean the enemy gaining these as slaves. Letting one's women become enslaved was a hideous deed. Thus the men were encouraged to fight harder.[12]

At this unknown battlefield in the middle of England, men, women and children were all slaughtered. Tacitus reported that almost eighty thousand Britons fell, compared with only four hundred Romans. There is no record of what happened to Boudica or her daughters. Whether Boudica had been killed, taken her own life or simply disappeared, she had denied Suetonius Paulinus his ultimate trophy – her. If she had escaped the battlefield the reward for her capture would have been vast. She would have been at the mercy of other tribal leaders who would consider the price of sheltering her just too great, so Suetonius Paulinus must have been 99% positive that she was dead or he would have hunted her down. Boudica would have been in no doubt as to what fate awaited her if she had been taken prisoner by the Romans, so it's assumed that she took her own life at a place of her choosing, surrounded by her own people. She would not have allowed herself to be captured, Rome had been denied a trophy queen. According to Dio, 'not a few fled the field and were prepared to fight again'.[13]

It's been suggested that the site of Boudica's final battle was Manduessedum (Mancetter) in North Warwickshire near the modern town of Atherstone.[14] Another suggested site close to the Romano/British settlement of Venonae in Leicestershire is now known as High Cross, because it's at the junction of the Roman road Watling Street and the Fosse Way.[15]

More recently, a discovery of Roman artefacts in King's Norton close to the Roman Fort of Metchley, has suggested another possibility. Was Boudica buried in Birmingham? Dr Mike Hodder, Birmingham City Council's senior archaeologist said, 'There is no doubt it's an important site and may be the lost location of the Boudica battle.' It could also indicate that this is where Boudica died and was buried.

A thorough examination of a stretch of Watling Street between St. Albans, Boudica's last known location, and the Fosse Way junction has suggested the Cuttle Mill area of Paulerspury in Northamptonshire where large quantities of human bones of both sexes, and including children, have been found over a wide area, together with fragments of Roman pottery from the 1st century.[16]

In 2009, there was the alternative suggestion that the Iceni were returning to East Anglia along the Rykneld or Icknield Way when they encountered the Roman army in the vicinity of Arbury Banks, Hertfordshire.[17] In March 2010, evidence was published suggesting the site may be located at Church Stowe, Northamptonshire.

The Aftermath

Three major settlements had been ravaged and largely destroyed, and there were many casualties. In the tribal territories of the Iceni and the Trinovantes, settlements were burned to the ground and land torched. The people were killed or taken as slaves. While hunting down any remaining rebels, Suetonius Paulinus wreaked his revenge on the whole population showing the Romans at their worst. After being held for so long by what they considered inferior forces, he ordered his army to set about a period of mass destruction. Any tribes that had sided with Boudica were to be virtually wiped out, the people killed, their homes burned. Even the tribes that had remained neutral were wiped out or suffered terribly as a warning to the rest of the country about the fate of those who rebelled against Rome.

The Romans laid waste to farms, torching crops, even going so far as to build drainage systems to take all the water from the soil, thus destroying more crops. They desecrated sanctuaries, stole property and money, and deprived the people of weapons. Tacitus wrote: 'Excellent officer though [Suetonius] was, it was feared that he would abuse their surrender and punish every offence with undue severity, as if it were a personal injury.'

But the Romans were not entirely victorious. Legions were brought in from Germany to replace the estimated 80,000 Romans and their allies who had perished during the uprising, and temporary forts and lookouts were built throughout Iceni tribal lands to keep a close watch in case they decided to rise up again. Nevertheless, according to Dio, the island was lost to Rome. Moreover, all this ruin was brought about by a woman, a fact which itself brought them the greatest shame.[18] Some historians have concluded from Dio's statement 'the island was lost to Rome' that due to all the animosity and the possibility of further uprisings, Nero was once again seriously considering withdrawing all his troops.[19]

Nero sent the new governor Publius Turpilianus with specific instructions to report on the condition of post-rebellion Britain to him directly, and in that report he criticised Suetonius for not ending the war sooner. But Nero obviously had a change of mind. The troops weren't withdrawn and Suetonius Paullinus was recalled to Rome to enjoy his triumph. The XIVth Legion was awarded 'Martia Victrix' along with a reputation for invincibility, and the XXth Legion who until then didn't have a name attached to them, subsequently won the right to be called 'Valeria'.

Poignant though their story is, the Iceni tribe have left an even more remarkable and memorable mark on history: the treasures the people buried before the Boudican revolt, intending to unearth them when they returned. They did not return and in 1948 a tractor driver ploughing his field at Snettisham, Lincolnshire, unearthed a curious piece of twisted metal. It was a gold torc dating from the 1st century AD. Over time more pieces of metal and jet were discovered; of the 150 gold torc fragments, over seventy formed complete torcs. Though their origins are unknown, they are of a high enough quality to have been the royal treasure of the Iceni.[20]

The Unknown Years AD61–69

The new procurator Alpinus Classicianus did not approve of the harsh measures employed by Suetonius Paulinus. He even appeared to make a courageous stand against Rome when he advised British rebels to wait until a new and more sympathetic governor was appointed before surrendering themselves and their arms. It took a long time before the process of recovery began, and not just for the Iceni.[21]

The Boudica revolt took place in AD60–61, just three or four years after the Brigante civil war had been stopped by the Romans, but unlike the Iceni uprising that had such a tragic end, we have no idea what happened in Brigante territory after the civil war had ended. Does the fact that it does not feature in Tacitus' Annals for another twelve years imply that the Brigantine tribe lived in relative peace? We know that Cartimandua did not side with the Iceni. She did not send an army to support her neighbour, even though other tribes did and she must have been under immense pressure to do so. If, as some historians have led us to believe, Venutius was now anti-Roman, why did he not support Boudica and the Iceni? It seems strange that he didn't if Tacitus is correct in reporting that Venutius had turned against Rome. He would have shared Boudica's view that Rome was the enemy and there was no future in a Roman world, unlike Cartimandua, who knew that she did not have a real future outside of that world. If Venutius had felt so strongly about this, he would have raised an army and ridden into battle with Boudica against the Romans. As the consort of the Brigante queen, he would probably have ridden in a chariot alongside Boudica. He would most certainly have been amongst the chiefs and he would have been mentioned by Tacitus, but he was not. We can discount the fact that Venutius had died in the meantime because he is mentioned again after an absence of twelve years. It seems that three or four years after the Civil war that he apparently instigated in Brigante territory, Cartimandua and Venutius were still married and he was prepared to accept Roman rule.

Any war is an expensive, time-consuming waste of manpower. Instead of being destroyed as the Iceni tribe and its lands were, Brigante flourished. Living conditions were good, and the people enjoyed the luxuries that Rome provided; if they had joined the Iceni revolution they would have lost everything. We are told that this is a warring couple and Venutius resented his wife's political stand. If he had been biding his time, looking for an opportunity to oust his wife and rule the Brigantine kingdom alone, surely the Boudican rebellion would have been the perfect time for him to attack Cartimandua's forces and take possession of the Brigantine tribe while the Roman army were busy fighting Boudica? At that time, Cartimandua was in effect unprotected. Yet Venutius did nothing and for almost a decade after the Brigante civil war there appears to have been peace in Brigantia. There could have been an undercurrent of grievance but little else if we can have confidence in the words, or lack of them, from the Roman historians. It may just be that in the eyes of the Roman writers, the Brigante problems were insignificant when compared to the problems nearer home, because by 64AD Rome was in trouble.

Rome Burns

The Emperor Nero had inherited the throne at the age of sixteen on the death of his stepfather/great-uncle Claudius in AD54. Nero's mother Agrippina was a scheming, ambitious woman who was determined her son would rule and did everything she could to ensure that he did (see the next chapter). Agrippina dominated Nero's young life and during the early years of his reign he was content to be guided by her, then he cast her aside, and five years into his reign, he had her murdered. After that he believed that her ghost haunted him.[22]

Nero's conduct had always been outstandingly bad and he showed reckless indifference, but after his mother's death he became shockingly malicious. He lost all sense of right and wrong and listened to flattery with total credulity. His ideas weren't just reckless they were stupid in the extreme. One of his grandest plans was to tear down a third of Rome so that he could build an elaborate series of palaces that would be known as Neropolis. Understandably the senate objected vigorously to this proposal, then on the night of 19 July AD64, a fire broke out. This was no ordinary fire; the flames raged for six days before being temporarily brought under control, then the fire reignited and burned for another three days. According to Tacitus, when the smoke cleared three of Rome's fourteen districts were totally gutted and seven others were reduced to a few scorched and mangled ruins. Two-thirds of Rome had been destroyed. Some have understandably blamed Nero for the disaster, stating that he started the fire so that he could bypass the senate and rebuild Rome to his liking.

The primary accounts did not survive, so much of what is known about the great fire of Rome comes from three secondary sources – Cassius Dio, Suetonius and Tacitus – who claimed that Nero watched Rome burn while merrily playing his fiddle, an image so memorable as to be known by all. Tacitus wrote, 'There is some support for the theory that Nero levelled the city on purpose: the *Domus Aurea*, Nero's majestic series of villas and pavilions set upon a landscaped park and a man-made lake, was built in the wake of the fire.'

During his fourteen-year rule, Nero murdered his own mother Agrippina, his first wife, Octavia, and allegedly, his second wife, Poppaea Sabina; then in AD68 he committed suicide. A brief period of civil war followed and troops were called back from all quarters of the empire. This was the first Roman civil war since Mark Antony's death in 30BC. Between June 68 and December 69, Emperors Galba, Otho, and Vitellius successively rose and fell before the July 69 accession of Vespasian, who founded the Flavian dynasty. Consequently, AD69 has become known as the Year of the Four Emperors. The social, military and political upheavals of the period had Empire-wide repercussions.

In Brigante territory in AD69 dramatic changes were taking place. According to Tacitus, Cartimandua spurned her husband Venutius for Vellocatus, his armour bearer. Webster describes him as of servile status, a servant, slave or lowly person, but that is not necessarily so. In antiquity the position of armour bearer was a prestigious one and would be held by someone of high birth and achievement. Sadly, history has not recorded Vellocatus' birth or achievements, only that unsurprisingly, he was considered inferior to the Queen.

If Tacitus is correct, by AD69 Cartimandua and Venutius had been separated and their relationship over for almost a decade. It can only be assumed that Tacitus exaggerated the situation and glossed over the in-between years to entertain his Roman audience. Painting Cartimandua as a seductress with loose morals involved in extra-marital relations made far more interesting reading than telling it as it was. Cartimandua's conduct was obviously embroidered by Tacitus to scandalise the Romans. For many years, the story of Cartimandua's alleged promiscuity was told to Roman girls by their mothers as an example of where unbridled lust would lead them.

For the Brigante queen to choose another consort was bound to evoke displeasure in some of her people and it stirred a furious Venutius into action. He may have returned to his former tribe where he started to drum up support to organise another coup as revenge against his erstwhile wife. There were elements in her kingdom that still objected to her pro-Roman stance, and there were even more who objected to her taking Vellocatus, her husband's armour bearer, as her lover. The separation of the Brigantine queen and her consort undoubtedly split the tribe, which triggered intratribal warfare.

Having been labelled immoral, self-indulgent and sexually improper, what would have happened if, in those intervening years, Cartimandua had seduced a Roman general or two instead of the lowly born Vellocatus? Her story would undoubtedly be better known. We only have to compare our 1st century AD queen to another powerful queen Cleopatra who had ruled Egypt in the 1st century BC. Her successive conquests of the world's most powerful men obviously ensured her place in history.

18

FOUR QUEENS AND
AN EMPRESS

It was not unusual for commentators of Ancient Rome to try to
diminish the status of a strong female ruler who could not be greatly
faulted in matters of state through accusations of sexual impropriety.
It was a way to try to reduce these powerful rulers to mere women,
who ruled emotionally and not rationally.

The queens who opposed Rome were either classed as promiscuous
or butch. They could be faulted for unbecoming interest and ambition.
Slanders were more or less invented. If their statesmanship could
not be questioned, then their morals were to be judged; if their
morals were unimpeachable, then the women would be criticised for
exhibiting unfeminine traits.

A strong, competent, female leader defied the boundaries that the
male world had set for her, and Cartimandua is not the only female
ruler to be traduced by the attitudes and biases of those early writers
who felt threatened, so sought to diminish their achievements. There
are clear similarities among the judgements made of these four women;
and the links between Cartimandua and Guinevere are striking.

Cleopatra

A century before Cartimandua, another native queen, Cleopatra VII
Philopator, Queen of Egypt, had a much publicised relationship with
the Roman leaders Julius Caesar and Mark Antony. Cleopatra was

Above left: A silver coin showing the head of Cleopatra (British Museum)

Above right: Bust of Cleopatra. (British Museum)

born in Alexandria in 69BC, and was the last active ruler of the Ptolemaic Kingdom of Egypt, nominally survived as pharaoh by her son Caesarian. She was also a diplomat, naval commander, linguist, and medical author. She learnt Egyptian and represented herself as the reincarnation of an Egyptian goddess Isis, but she is best remembered for her affairs with two of Rome's leading men.

She married her brothers Ptolemy XIII and Ptolemy IX as was the Egyptian custom but produced no children, then as pharaoh she consummated a liaison with Gaius Julius Caesar that solidified her grip on the throne. She was twenty-one when she met the fifty-two-year-old Julius Caesar, and one legend claims that she was smuggled into his apartment rolled in a carpet. She became his mistress and nine months later gave birth to their son Caesarian. Their relationship caused a scandal because he was married to Calpurnia Pisonis at the time.

We encountered Caesar earlier when he made an attempt to take control of Britain in 54BC. He returned to Rome where he was assassinated on 15 March 44BC. Cleopatra then aligned with another married Roman general, Mark Antony, with whom she had three children, twins Cleopatra Selene II and Alexander Helios, and another son Ptolemy Philadelphus. When the news of a barbarian queen like Cleopatra ensnaring Mark Anthony spread, it caused panic in Rome, but she was a wise woman in a strong position. She didn't need a matrimonial alliance but she wanted the political advantages a union could bring to both parties. She wanted to expand the wealth and influence of her realm. She also wanted protection from her enemies, and to remain queen of Egypt and rule alone, terms that were readily agreed.

Almost a century later, Cartimandua also negotiated similar terms. Both queens were shrewd and appreciated their own strengths and negotiated accordingly. In the case of Cartimandua, Rome couldn't fight on too many fronts and needed friendly kingdoms to act as buffer zones. Brigantia was integral to the success of Rome's conquest plan, and Cartimandua knew this. Like Cleopatra, Cartimandua wanted to expand the wealth and influence of her realm, she wanted protection from her enemies, and she wanted to remain queen of Brigantia and rule alone. Again, these terms that were readily agreed.

Cleopatra controlled the grain shipments to Rome and was often in a position to dictate terms with her political allies. There is every reason to believe that Cartimandaua had similar powers because the Brigante kingdom was rich in minerals like lead. Both women showed considerable skill in governing their respective lands, and took advantage of the natural resources to expand trade and allow their kingdoms to prosper. Both had problems yet managed to strengthen their respective economies through prudent administration and profitable foreign arrangements through Rome.

Their choice of alliances was questionable but hindsight is a great thing. Cartimandua maintained her alliance with Rome despite the rebellions led by her husband, and her fellow countrywoman Boudica and Caracatus. Similarly, Cleopatra backed Octavian and Antony rather than Brutus and Cassius. In both cases, this led to claims of treachery.

Cartimandua and Cleopatra were capable, dedicated rulers who both reigned for over twenty years, but what we think we know of these women has been coloured indelibly by the Romans. These two queens were excellent targets because they were foreigners with all the consequent connotations of depravity, dishonesty, luxury and cruelty, and they were women – capricious, weak and irrational. Even worse, the Romans saw them as unnatural women who violated accepted feminine codes to choose their own sexual partners, exercising both political and erotic power over them.

Unlike the people of Brigante who rose up in revolt against their queen, Cleopatra's own people never rose up in revolt against her. Cleopatra committed suicide on 12 August 30BC. After her death, Egypt became a province of the Roman Empire, marking the end of the Hellenistic period that had lasted since the reign of Alexander (336–323 BC), but Cleopatra's legacy survives in numerous works of art and literature and in the imagination of the world.

Agrippina the Younger

Rome played such a major part in Cartimandua's life that it makes sense to compare her to a powerful Roman lady of the time, and the most powerful woman in the Roman Empire during the first half of the first century was undoubtedly Agrippina the Younger, also referred to as Agrippina Minor. Agrippina was a Roman empress and one of the more prominent women in the Julio-Claudian dynasty. To say she was well connected is an understatement. Her father was Germanicus, a popular general and one-time heir apparent to the Roman Empire under Tiberius, and her mother was Agrippina the elder, a granddaughter of the first Roman Emperor Augustus. She was also the younger sister of Caligula as well as the niece and fourth wife of Claudius.

Her birthdate is given as 5 November AD15 and although we don't know Cartimandua's date of birth, they were probably of very similar age. Likewise we don't know about Cartimandua's childhood and youth but we know Agrippina's childhood was enough to warp even the most resilient. Agrippina's upbringing was supervised by her mother, her paternal grandmother Antonia Minor, and her great-grandmother, Livia, all notable, influential, and powerful figures from whom she learnt how to survive. After the death of the Emperor Augustus in AD14, her great-uncle Tiberius became emperor and the male head of the family.

Sources describe Agrippina's personality as ruthless, ambitious, violent, and domineering. Physically she was beautiful, and according to Pliny the Elder, she had a double canine in her upper right jaw, a sign of good fortune. Whether that proved to be true is debatable.

In AD28, just after her thirteenth birthday, Agrippina married her paternal first cousin once removed, Gnaeus Domitius Ahenobarbus. Known as Domitius, he came from a distinguished family of consular rank, but according to the Roman historian Suetonius, Domitius was a wealthy man with a despicable and dishonest character, 'a man who was in every aspect of his life detestable.' In AD37 Agrippina had a son who was to be her only child, fathered by Domitius. They named him Lucius Domitius Ahenobarbus, and this child grew up to become the Emperor Nero. Suetonius states that when Domitius was congratulated by friends on the birth of his son Lucius he replied, 'I don't think anything produced by me and Agrippina could possibly be good for the state or the people.' History was to prove him right.

That same year, Agrippina's only surviving brother, Caligula, became the new emperor, and being the emperor's sister gave Agrippina considerable influence until she was exiled by him. When Caligula was murdered in AD41 Agrippina's paternal uncle Claudius, brother of her father Germanicus, became the new emperor despite objections from the Senate. He had very little support in Rome and needed something to give him prestige so, because Britain was not under Roman control, in AD43 he sent off a Roman fleet to conquer the islands.

In Rome, Claudius lifted Agrippina's exile and she was reunited with her estranged son. In AD47 Agrippina is said to have poisoned her second husband Passienus Crispus, and in 49 she married her uncle, the Emperor Claudius. An uncle marrying his niece was considered incestuous, so this marriage caused widespread disapproval. But this was all a part of Agrippina's scheming plan to make her son Lucius the new emperor. Her marriage to Claudius was not based on love, but on power. On the day that Agrippina married her uncle Claudius as her third husband and his fourth wife, she became an empress. No woman could rule Rome, but as an empress and wife of the ruling emperor she was determined to be the authority behind the throne, and the most powerful woman in the Roman Empire.

In Britain 47–52 AD, the Romans were advancing, and Cartimandua was forced to make a decision. Having seen the result of direct resistance, she decided that rather than fighting the invading forces, she would collaborate. We know that Agrippina was aware of Cartimandua although there is no evidence that they ever met.

Agrippina was seated on a dais at a parade of captives when Caratacus, whom Cartimandua had sent to Rome in chains, bowed before Agrippina with the same homage as he accorded the emperor. In 50, Agrippina was granted the honorific title of Augusta. She was only the third Roman woman to be given this title, the others being Livia Drusilla and Antonia Minor. Also that year, Claudius founded a Roman colony and called it *Colonia Claudia Ara Agrippinensis* or Agrippinensium, because this was where Agrippina had been born. This was the only Roman colony to be named after a Roman woman, and today it is Cologne.

So while the Roman armies were systematically conquering Britain, Agrippina was being granted all manner of honours while analytically eliminating or removing anyone whom she considered was a potential threat to her position and the future of her son. Informed by an astrologer that her son Nero would murder her and become emperor while he was very young, she is reported as saying 'Let him kill me but let him rule.'[1]

Ancient sources claim that Agrippina successfully manipulated and influenced Claudius into adopting her son and naming him his successor, and in AD 50 Lucius's name was changed to Nero Claudius Caesar Drusus Germanicus and he became Claudius's adopted son, heir and recognised successor. Having achieved her goal, the ancient sources say Agrippina then poisoned Claudius on 13 October 54 with a plate of mushrooms at a banquet. This enabled her son Lucius/Nero to quickly take the throne as Emperor of Rome at just sixteen. Now Agrippina was determined to rule rather than suffer the whims of a ruler, and in the first months of Nero's reign Agrippina controlled her son and the Roman Empire. Agrippina continued to push for power and actually achieved the unthinkable for a Roman woman. She attended a meeting of the senate.[2]

Her control was short-lived. Towards AD 57, Nero had his mother expelled from the palace and she went to live in a riverside estate in Misenum. She was still very popular, powerful and influential, and Nero resented this. He sent people to annoy her and tried in every way to make her life unbearable. Rather ironically, that is what we are told was happening to Cartimandua at this time too, but in Cartimandua's case, it was her husband Venutius who was trying to remove her from power and was making her life unbearable.

Tacitus claims that Nero considered poisoning or stabbing his mother but felt these methods were too obvious. Surviving stories of attempts on Agrippina's life are generally fantastical. For example, Nero decided to build a self-sinking boat. Though aware of the plot, Agrippina embarked on the boat, but the boat failed to sink. The crew, fearful of what would happen if they failed in their quest, then sank the boat, but Agrippina swam to shore where she was met by crowds of admirers. Nero sent three assassins to kill her. Three times he ordered them to administer poison but each time she took antidotes beforehand. He then rigged up a machine in her room which would drop her ceiling tiles onto her as she slept, however, she once again escaped her death after she received word of the plan.

Finally Nero managed to get her assassinated and made it look as if she had committed suicide.³ Suetonius says that the 'over-watchful' and 'over-critical' eye that Agrippina kept over Nero drove him to murder her, an absurd rationalisation for the Emperor of Rome. His mind was undoubtedly unhinged and had been for some considerable time. Nero viewed his mother's corpse and commented how beautiful she was. There are conflicting reports on what happened to her body. Some say she was cremated that night on a dining couch, others say that during the remainder of Nero's reign, Agrippina's grave was not covered or enclosed. What they do seem to agree on is that Nero had his mother's death on his conscience, and he became 'witless, speechless and rather scared'. He was convinced that his mother's ghost now haunted him and he employed Persian magicians to scare her away.

Poor Agrippina was obviously not intended to rest in peace, yet in the cold light of day, she was a vicious, scheming, manipulative woman who had murdered at least nine people including two husbands to gain power and ultimately dominate Rome. It could be argued that it's a pity she didn't murder her son. The outcome might have been better. There is no report of Cartimandua resorting to murder, even though if she'd wanted to be rid of her husband Venutius, that would have been the obvious solution.

Agrippina married three times and it's unlikely that Cartimandua married more than once although it seems clear that in sexual relations Celtic women were much more independent than Roman women. When the wife of Argentocoxus, a Caledonian chieftain, was challenged by the empress Julia Augusta about her morals, she replied

'We fulfil the demands of nature in a much better way than do you Roman women, for we consort openly with the best men, whereas you let yourselves be debauched in secret by the vilest.'[4]

Boudica

Cartimandua and Boudica (Breaca, *see* page 217) were contemporaries. These two Celtic noblewomen possessed considerable personal status, and were recorded by classical writers as part of a tradition of autonomous and influential women. Throughout antiquity, women have always been largely defined by their relationship to men – daughter, wife, mother – dutiful roles dependent upon the male for their status, direction, and livelihood. On the other hand, we have powerful women who are not defined by their men. They had their own status, provided their own livelihood and decided what direction to take. Cartimandua achieved this to a much greater degree than Boudica, who attempted to become queen after the death of her husband Prasutagus.

Cartimandua and Boudica stood up to the superpower of Rome in two different ways. One fought their soldiers, the other fought their prejudices. They both showed the courage, ambition and political skills which Celtic noblewomen could exhibit when the opportunity arose. The Roman soldier and historian Ammianus Marcellinus comments on the valour, indomitability and sheer physical strength of such women who were as formidable in war as their husbands. They were associated with Celtic goddesses, and the Roman historian Dio Cassius (LXII, 2) refers to a war goddess named Andraste meaning the invincible one. Women like Cartimandua and Boudica were central players in the drama of the Roman annexation of Britain.

Boudica of the Iceni tribe undoubtedly led the rebellion against the Romans, but her leadership may have been in part symbolic, a result of the personal humiliation and abuse she and her daughters received at the hands of the Romans. This affront to tribal honour became the focus for the outrage felt by the Iceni tribe as a whole. Boudica represented matronly honour, fighting on behalf of her defiled daughters. Boudica and her army had stood up to a bully and lost. She was accused of leading her people to their deaths in a futile gesture yet that is the risk every leader must take when leading a people into battle. Many met a noble end worthy of songs and stories, but the Iceni tribe were devasted by death and those that didn't die become slaves. Even though Boudica was Rome's implacable enemy, in Roman culture she become a symbol of heroic resistance and was given a place of high honour that has been passed down through the centuries.

Cartimandua was the independent ruler of the powerful Brigante tribe from AD43 to 69. Her territory was the single largest Celtic kingdom in Britain, covering most of what is now northern England. Cartimandua's political skills, her leadership in battle and her influence were probably considerably greater than Boudica's, yet her story has not been chronicled in the same way, she did not fight the Romans and suffer defeat on the battlefield, so for that reason alone, she is now a far more obscure figure. Cartimandua succeeded where Boudica had failed in beating Rome at their own game.

The first English writings on Boudica appear during the reign of Queen Elizabeth I following the rediscovery of the works of Tacitus. Polydore Vergil reintroduced her to British history as 'Voadicea' in 1534.[5] Raphael Holinshed also included her story in his *Chronicles* (1577), based on the writings of Tacitus and Dio.[6] This no doubt inspired Shakespeare's younger contemporaries Francis Beaumont and John Fletcher to write the play *Bonduca* in 1610. William Cowper wrote a popular ode, *Boadicea*, in 1782.

Boudica, is known in Welsh as Buddug, and it's rather surprising to find her magnificent statue by J. Havard Thomas standing in the Marble Hall at Cardiff City Hall. To be chosen to stand alongside Welsh heroes like St David is a remarkable achievement for our Celtic Queen. Here she stands one of eleven historical figures decided by a competition in the *Western Mail*, as one of the most famous people from Welsh history. What is even more remarkable is the fact that amongst the statues, Buddug is the most ancient person here, the only female, and the only one from outside the Welsh nation. The statues made of Pentelicon marble were funded by a gift from David, Alfred Thomas, 1st Viscount Rhondda and unveiled by David Lloyd George, then Secretary of State for War, on 27 October 1916.[7]

Boudica, Queen of the Iceni, is now the most famous of all Ancient British women. In his *Roman History*, Cassius Dio described her physical appearance:

In stature she was very tall, in appearance most terrifying, in the glance of her eye most fierce, and her voice was harsh: a great mass of the tawniest hair fell to her hips: around her neck was a large golden necklace; and she wore a tunic of diverse colours over which a thick mantle was fastened with a brooch. This was her invariable attire. She now grasped a spear to aid her in terrifying all beholders...

It was in the Victorian era that Boudica's fame took on legendary proportions as Queen Victoria came to be seen as Boudica's 'namesake', their names being identical in meaning. Several ships were named after her and Queen Victoria's Poet Laureate, Alfred Lord Tennyson, wrote a poem, *Boadicea*:

Lo the colony, there they rioted in the city of Cunobeline!
There they drank in cups of emerald, there at tables of
ebony lay,
Rolling on their purple couches in their tender effeminacy.
There they dwelt and there they rioted; there – there – they
dwell no more.
Burst the gates, and burn the palaces, break the works of
the statuary,
Take the hoary Roman head and shatter it, hold it abominable,
Cut the Roman boy to pieces in his lust and voluptuousness,
Lash the maiden into swooning, me they lash'd and humiliated,
Chop the breasts from off the mother, dash the brains of the
little one out,
Up my Britons, on my chariot, on my chargers, trample them
under us.'

Lotus-eating, effeminate foreigners, so unlike the muscular Christianity of the Victorians, or even the muscular paganism of the Celts! With the encouragement of Queen Victoria's husband Prince Albert, who lent his horses for use as models, Thomas Thorneycroft worked on a magnificent statue between 1850 and 1860. He exhibited the head separately in 1864 and the whole was cast in bronze. In 1902, seventeen years after Thomas Thornycroft's death, his son Sir John Thorneycroft presented the statue to the London County Council. They erected it on a plinth inscribed with lines from Cowper's poem: 'Regions Caesar never knew, thy posterity shall sway.' Boudica's magnificent statue is on the Victorian Embankment next to Westminster Bridge and the Houses of Parliamant, standing guard over the city she razed.

Patricia Southern in *Roman Britain: A New History* links Boudica to Cleopatra and Zenobia as the most powerful female enemies of Rome. She finds another similarity:

> Boudica also shares with them another feature, in that their fame obscures the fact that there is precious little information about them. At least Cleopatra and Zenobia are known by their real names.

The same can be said of Cartimandua.

Queen Guinevere

Cartimandua's behaviour as an adulteress is said to have inspired one of the greatest legends of all, the story of King Arthur and his Queen Guinevere. It is widely accepted that Arthur was a real person but there is little agreement as to who he was, what he did or even where he lived. None of the early sources call him a king, although he is likely to have been a Celtic war-chief or a Romanised cavalry commander in the image of Cartimandua's first husband Venutius. Just as Venutius led the combined forces of several British tribes against the Romans, Arthur led the combined forces of several British kingdoms against the invading Saxons. Even the dating is uncertain but the name Arthur, or variations of it, suddenly appears amongst several royal houses in Britain around AD600 suggesting that Arthur was already a renowned paragon of war-like courage by that date.

History of the Britains attributed to Nennius is a 9th-century rag-bag of material assembled from earlier sources including a list of Arthur's battles. Arthur became a folk figure, a generic Celtic hero surrounded by myth and magic. The first real creator of the medieval King Arthur was Geoffrey of Monmouthshire whose *Historia Regum Britanniae* (History of the Kings of Britain) published around 1136 included much freely invented material. It is in this pseudo-historical chronicle of British history that Guinevere first appears as *Guanhumara* (with many spelling variants in the manuscript tradition) Her name translated as 'The White Enchantress' or the white fay, or ghost, from Proto-Celtic *Windo,* 'white, fair, holy' + *sēbarā,*'magical being' (cognate with Old Irish *síabair,* a spectre, phantom, supernatural being, usually in a pejorative sense).[8]

In the *Historia Regum Britanniae*, she is described as well educated and one of the great beauties of Britain, descended from a noble Roman family. In this story, Arthur leaves her in the care of his nephew Modredus (Mordred) while he crosses over to Europe to go to war with the (fictitious) Roman Emperor, Lucius Tiberius, but during Arthur's absence, Mordred crowns himself king and lives in an adulterous union with Arthur's wife Guinevere. Geoffrey does not make it clear how complicit Guinevere is in Mordred's actions, simply stating that the Queen had 'broken her vows' and 'about this matter... [he] prefers to say nothing.' This forces Arthur to return to Britain to fight at the Battle of Camlann, where Mordred is ultimately slain. Arthur, having been mortally wounded in battle, is sent to Avalon.

Early chronicles tend to portray Guinevere inauspiciously or hardly at all but later authors use her good and bad qualities to construct a deeper character who played a larger role. She is portrayed as everything from a weak and opportunistic traitor to a fatally flawed but noble and virtuous lady. In Chrétien de Troyes' *Yvain, The Knight of the Lion*, she is praised for her intelligence, friendliness, and gentility, while in Marie de Frances's *Lanval* and Thomas Chestre's Middle English version, *Sir Launfal*, she is a vindictive adulteress, disliked by the protagonist and all well-bred knights. In most versions she is childless but in the Alliterative *Morte Arthure* Guinevere willingly becomes Mordred's consort and bears him two sons.[9]

Guinevere's lover in a nearly forgotten tradition mentioned in Béroul's *Tristan* and reflected in the later *Roman de Yder* is Isdernus, believed to be an incarnation of a Celtic hero named Yder. The Welsh poet Dafydd ap Gwilym alludes to Guinevere's abduction in two of his poems; the medievalist Roger Sherman Loomis suggested that this tale shows that 'she had inherited the role of a Celtic Persephone'.[10]

In medieval romances, one of the most prominent story arcs is Queen Guinevere's tragic love affair with her husband's chief knight, Lancelot. This story first appeared in Chrétien de Troyes' *Lancelot, The Knight of the Garter* and became a motif in Arthurian literature, starting with the Lancelot grail of the early 13th century and carrying through the Post-Vulgate Cycle and Thomas Malory's *Le Morte d'Arthur*. In *Lancelot, the Knight of the Garter*, the abduction sequence is largely a reworking of that recorded in earlier works, but here the queen's rescuer is not Arthur or Yder but Lancelot. It has been suggested that Chrétien de Troyes invented their affair to supply Guinevere with a courtly extramarital lover. Yder had been forgotten entirely, and Mordred was classed as a traitor whose name was synonymous with treason, so his reputation was beyond saving.[11]

Just as Cartimandua ended her first marriage to Venutius and had an affair with his armour bearer Vellocatus, Queen Guinevere replaced her first husband Arthur, and substituted his nephew Mordred. It's possible that Cartimandua had other affairs, just as Guinevere reputedly did. Each queen obtained help from an external source to retain power, Cartimandua from the Romans, Guinevere from the Saxons, but both stories end in civil wars. Both women were blamed for the misfortunes that ensued, and the overriding message was quite clearly, that the consequences of infidelity are death and destruction.

The Arthurian romances retain echoes of ancient, pre-historic themes and motifs, with perhaps the most striking being when the dying king returns his magic sword Excalibur to The Lady of The Lake. Sacrificing fine metal work, especially swords, in rivers and pools was an ancient custom stretching back into the Bronze Age. Although not a uniquely Celtic practice, the scale of Celtic water sacrifice was phenomenal.[12]

19

THE ROMANS TAKE OVER
BRIGANTE TERRITORY

Auxiliary cavalryman of the Imperial period carrying an oval cavalry shield.
(Artwork by John R. Travis)

Tacitus is our only source of information, and his account in the *Histories* which describes the Brigantian conflict of AD69 is remarkably similar to the account in the *Annals* which describes the Brigantian Civil War in AD52–57, so we must be wary. Tacitus' reports are known to be unreliable and people have suggested he told the same story twice, but with a different ending. In the Civil War of the 50s Cartimandua was returned to her position as queen. The later uprising had a different ending.

Cartimandua had obviously grown tired of Venutius, the disagreements and the hostile opposition to her decisions, and fell for the charms of her husband's armour bearer Vollocatus. She is said to have conducted an open affair with him, and such behaviour by a Celtic noblewoman scandalised the Romans (or was supposed to). According to Tacitus, who always seemed to view Cartimandua in a negative light, the Brigante tribe were not in favour of her liaison:

> Her house was at once shaken by this scandalous act... Her husband was favoured by the sentiments of all the citizens; the adulterer was supported by the queen's passion for him, and by her savage spirit.

Rather surprisingly, in his moralising narratives, Tacitus mentions Cartimandua scheming in rejecting Venutius. It would have been most enlightening to know what form her scheming had taken, yet there is nothing to back his comment.

When Cartimandua decided to divorce Venutius in favour of Vellocatus, the furious Venutius responded by raising a force against his former queen. Campaigning with all the fury of a cuckolded husband as well as the anger of a deposed consort/king, he persuaded the Druids, and through them the rest of the huge Brigante tribe, that Cartimandua was no longer fit to govern. The scorned Venutius used this anti-Roman sentiment amongst the other Celtic tribes to build alliances and to incite a rebellion. According to Tacitus, the Brigantes were 'goaded on by the shame of being yoked under a woman', and they revolted against her. Venutius had been biding his time as he formed alliances with other Celtic tribes, and inter-tribal tensions were high when Cartimandua took Venutius's brother and other relatives as hostages in an attempt to prevent conflict. It seemed a sensible move to prevent unnecessary blood shed rather than a cunning strategy. It did not stop the queen's erstwhile husband, and several skirmishes occurred. Venutius grew stronger as he gained more sympathisers, and the further north he moved the more followers he gathered. Wheeler spoke of 'tribes rallying from the north and north west – from those borderlands whence most of the auxiliary tribesmen of Venutius must have come'[1] In 'Roman Britain in 1964' *(The Journal of Roman Studies)*, D. R. Wilson and R. P. Wright also refer to these northern tribes as being part of Venutius's forces, but they could have been repeating Wheeler and Tacitus.

Within weeks, a full-scale Brigantian civil war was in progress. Venutius had picked his time well because after the Emperor Nero's death and the major struggle to decide who would be Nero's successor, the Roman Empire was hit by civil war (see page 225). Venutius took advantage of Roman political instability knowing that Cartimandua could not rely upon help from her Roman protectors. This time when he made a full-scale attack on his former wife he intended to take control of the Brigante tribe. He was not only waging war against his ex spouse, he was also waging war against Rome. When Cartimandua appealed for help from the Romans, their armies were so depleted they were only able to send auxiliary troops who were inadequate and incapable of fighting Venutius and his forces.

All the Romans could do was extricate the Queen. Tacitus pithily commented that 'the throne was left to Venutius, the war to us,' implying that civil war continued in the Brigantine province until the Roman army's arrival the following year. There is no record of whether Cartimandua took any further part in this conflict.

Venutius had overthrown his former wife and taken the throne but at what price? He had alienated Rome so the people could no longer rely upon Roman backing, and like many ambitious individuals who crave power, he was to find that it was easy to be popular when he didn't have the responsibility of providing for the tribe. Throughout her reign, Cartimandua had taken that responsibility very seriously. Her lands remained unoccupied by Imperial forces and her people remained largely unmolested thanks to the Queen's political manoeuvering. Hers was an independent kingdom but one able to rely on Roman subsidies or assistance in times of bad harvests or conflict.

With Cartimandau no longer in control all that changed. The tribe had supported an insurgency against Roman rule and as an immediate consequence, Rome would have withdrawn their subsidies. They could have blocked all the Brigante trading routes. It was obvious that Rome was not going to allow this situation to continue indefinitely. They would not put up with rebels and guerrillas in their midst and would not permit a known dissident to be in control.

Stanwick as Venutius's Headquarters

It is assumed that Cartimandua left Brigantia. Popular opinion held that Venutius took over the fort at Stanwick that had previously been Cartimandua's stronghold. Sir Mortimer Wheeler, the archaeologist who worked on Stanwick, has suggested that having exiled Cartimandua, Venutius moved into Stanwick. Wheeler was heavily influenced by Tacitus's account of the intrigues at the Brigantian court, and suggested that Stanwick was the rebel stronghold of Venutius after their final separation. According to Wheeler it was here that Venutius rallied his anti-Roman tribesmen and allies for his revolt against the Romans. He suggested that Stanwick was central to Venutius's resistance from AD69 to 74. It that is so, the tremendous earth shifting and stone walling would have been the work of Venutius, fortifying his stronghold against Roman attack because there must have been no doubt in his mind that the Brigante tribe would be punished for their uprising.

It was not until after AD70 that the Roman armies were able to turn their attention to the British frontier problem and advance into the north. The decision was made to invade, conquer and absorb Brigantia, which meant the whole of Derbyshire, Cheshire, Yorkshire, Lancashire, and beyond.

The Final Push and the Building of York

Agricola had returned to Rome in AD62 after the Boudican rebellion and after Vespasian had established himself as emperor, Agricola was appointed to the command of the Legio XX Valeria Victrix stationed in Britain. He replaced Marcus Roscius Coelius, who had stirred up a mutiny against the governor, Vettius Bolanus. Agricola reimposed discipline on the legion and helped to consolidate Roman rule until AD71, when Bolanus was replaced by Quintus Petillus Cerialis, a more aggressive governor, a seasoned soldier and son-in-law of the Emperor Vespasian. Agricola was able to display his talents as a commander in campaigns against the Brigantes as Petillius Cerealis moved the Ninth Legion north from Lincoln to a new base in York.

The history of the walled city of York begins with the Romans who founded the city they called Eboracum around this date to serve as a main operating base from which to confront the hostile Brigantes tribe. It was the ideal spot to launch attacks against Brigantian resistance in the North York Moors and the Pennine valleys, and being at the boundary of the Brigante and Parisi territory made it neutral territory from which to supervise both tribes.

The Roman fort stands at the confluence of the Rivers Ouse and Foss. It was a perfect site to build a fortress, although there is no evidence that this was a former Brigante settlement. The Roman fort was built on a slightly raised plateau at the confluence of the rivers making it a transportation link for men and supplies via the River Ouse to the North Sea. It also offered a land transport route along what is now largely the A64 road.

The original Eboracum Roman fortress could hold 5,000 men and was built from earth and timber. It established the centre of York and a pattern of streets that still exist today. Remains of the city walls of the legionary fortress and up to five metres of deposits and other structures survive below ground over much of the city's historic core.

While establishing their major fort at York, to extend their control the Romans built satellite forts across the wider region. According to Tacitus, after a series of bloody battles, Petillius Cerialis had overrun if not actually conquered the major part of the Brigantine territory. Bent on final conquest, a second thrust from Cheshire up the west coast to the Solway followed and by AD78 Brigante territory was occupied by the Romans.

Venutius's strategy was to keep moving, attacking and raiding when and where he could. There is no report of a final decisive battle or the death or imprisonment of Venutius. The Romans would have boasted of such an event, so Venutius might have died of his wounds or natural causes, and without a charismatic leader the fighting was over. It had taken four years for the Roman army to finally conquer Brigante and Petillius Cerialis's campaign is thought to have ended with the capture of the fort at Stanwick. It's believed that the remnants of Venutius's forces who had been at Stanwick melted away to Ingleborough and other Brigante strongholds. Sir Mortimer Wheeler believed that the northern ramparts had been slighted by a Roman attacking army rather than falling down naturally through decay. If this is correct, did Venutius make his last stand at Stanwick, despite the fact that there is no record of a battle in the archaeological records?

Archaeology has placed the abandonment of Stanwick at around 70AD, which fits in with the general timeframe implied by Tacitus. Between 1981–86, a new series of major excavations were carried out at Stanwick by a team from Durham university led by Percival Turnbull and Professor Colin Haselgrove (see page ***). One of their most mysterious and unfathomable discoveries was found at the rear of a rampart in the fortifications. This was an adult male burial, and a horse's head had been carefully placed upon the body. It is certainly stretching credulity to suggest that this was the remains of Venutius but it is almost irresistible. In the end, Venutius had proved no match for Roman might. Rome had lost one of its major allies and its buffer zone in the north that prevented the far northern tribes from attacking. Now they had to take full control of the former Brigante territory.

The Development of Aldborough

As we have seen, the Celtic settlement of Stanwick fell out of use and was never an important township again. Trading operations were moved to Piercebridge at the river crossing to the north, or to Almondbury (see page ***), or to Catterick where the Romans established stations linked by what is now called Dere Street. This ran between York and Corbridge (*Corstopitum*). The road would later extend all the way to Perthshire, but initially it ran through Isurium Brigantum (Aldborough) as this was the optimum point to cross the River Ure.

The name Oppidum is a Latin term for a town or urban agglomeration, by extension applied in documentary sources to some late Iron Age, Celtic proto-towns and fortified sites. Isurium Brigantum would have been referred to as an oppidum. Being sited within easy reach of the legion stationed at York, it became a new capital for the compliant Brigantes. Roecliffe Fort, one mile west of the site, was decommissioned and replaced with a new outpost at Aldborough in AD79, which according to Tacitus marked the final subjugation of the Brigantes. The earlier settlement was flattened and buried under sand to create a platform for the new town. Like other planned Roman towns, the new Aldborough was laid out in a grid pattern structured around a central road. Key administrative buildings would have included the forum and basilica, and there would have been substantial public infrastructure such as sewers. A public bath house was located near the west gate and an amphitheatre was built to the north-west of the town. When it was originally founded, the settlement had no defences but an earthwork rampart and ditch was added around the end of second century AD, probably for taxation and administrative purposes, such as preventing burials within the town boundary.

Roman town defences had an irregular layout as they were adapted to the terrain, the existing street pattern and any outlying assets that also needed to be enclosed. The total area of the defended town of Aldborough was around 138 acres. The walls were rebuilt in stone during the late third century AD, and around the mid-fourth century, a number of semi-circular bastions were added to them. To make more space the town ditch was moved further out.

Roman occupation of England ended in the early fifth century AD and Aldborough's role as a regional administrative centre came to an end. The town reduced in size as the population returned to a more subsistence-based existence, although the site seemingly remained occupied throughout the Dark Ages. One thousand years after the Roman invasion, the Normans converted the former Roman amphitheatre into a small castle, and in the Domesday survey of 1086 it is recorded as being the centre of an administrative area called Burghshire. It was probably also at this time that the road network shifted to the east when a new bridge was built at Boroughbridge, thus marginalising Aldborough.

The modern village now retains part of the Roman street plan and the church stands on the site of the forum. In 2011, geomagnetic scanning revealed the existence of an amphitheatre, emphasising Isurium's importance as a major Roman town.[2] Aldborough's Roman remains are in the care of English Heritage and consist of a stretch of the massive town wall constructed in the 2nd century with its defensive towers and two in-situ mosaic pavements, once part of a Roman townhouse. An exhibition of archaeological finds from the site are on display in the museum providing an insight into the lives of Roman civilians in its most northern capital.[3]

20

ROMAN TOWNS AND FORTS IN BRIGANTIA

Once the Romans had taken control of Brigante, they had to crush any resistance, so forts were built to house the legions and the auxiliaries. Overall was a governor, chosen by the emperor, who would be in control of the legions in the provinces. A Roman legion had just over 5,000 Roman citizen infantry soldiers. Their ranks were swelled by the addition of auxiliaries, who were recruited from amongst newly conquered people. The auxiliaries would have been posted to distant parts of the Empire for duty unless they were the sons of wealthy families, when a bribe was paid to avoid service. Once any resistance was crushed, auxiliary troops were left to garrison and police the newly captured lands. With the chance of being allowed to return home if they worked well, the auxiliaries would have had no sympathy with the locals and would have stamped out any rebellions. As an incentive, after twenty-five years' service, they would be awarded Roman citizenship.

Initially, the Romans built timber forts with turf ramparts that needed extensive refurbishment and rebuilding after twenty or thirty years. It was during Agricola's governorship 77–84 that the first permanent Roman forts were built. Most early building has been obliterated by urbanisation and where its possible to investigate a site, archaeology can provide a ground floor plan but not much more. However, we know that the usual British home was round, the settlements free form and irregular, while Roman forts were rectangular, planned and standardised. The footprint of each fort resembled a playing card with rounded corners. Each straight side was inset with a gateway, and each gateway was protected on either side by two tall gate towers, their bases holding guardrooms and the upper stories acting as sentry and observation posts. Above the central spina or gate arch and fronting the approaching traveller was a slab giving the name of the fort, and leading from the four gateways were roads to the next Roman forts.

The forts were packed with buildings, roads and streets, and the *intervallum* roadway circulated the whole fort. In the centre were the three main buildings. The commander's house (*praetorium*), headquarters (*principia*) and granaries (*horrea*). The front (*praetentura*) and back (*retentura*) contained accommodation, stables, workshops, sheds and sometimes a hospital, cooking ovens, latrines and sheds.

Outside the fort walls were other buildings, chiefly the bath house, the balneum, which was a stone building because of the fire risk. Any flat convenient space was used as the fort parade ground, and lining the roads would be cemeteries. Outside most fort cantonments grew up, Romanised villages – vici – that often developed into thriving townships covering an area greater than the fort itself. They were important centres of Romanisation in often wild and scarcely inhabited country. The vici attracted the families of the soldiers and traders. There were workshops, inns, bars, temples and brothels. The local population was encouraged to settle and engage in trade and manufacturing so not only did the people serve the garrison, good housing, education, cultural amenities and markets were all designed to lock the locals into a Roman way of life. They even had local self-government with their own council.

The Romans built many of their forts at sites previously inhabited by the Celts and although new finds mean that the list is never complete, of great significance are the forts that administered the Brigante areas greatest asset – lead. This was found in the south and west of Brigante in the area we now know as the Peak District, and the importance of this region is indicated by the Roman construction of a major east-west road crossing the Pennines through the Hope valley. Spurs from this road criss-crossed the area to provide for rapid troop (deployment and here the Romans built Melandra Castle near

Glossop and Brough on Noe near Hope. Each fort covered an area of 2–3 acres and would hold 500–1,000 auxiliary troops as distinct from the legionaries' fortresses at York (Eboracum) and Chester on the Dee (Deva).

Anavio

The Romans build their fort at Brough-on-Noe and called it Anavio, which means place by the river. It was one of a line of forts stretching across the country, and Anavio is now the best known in the Peak District. Anavio is mentioned on a milestone found at Silverlands and now in Buxton museum. Now known as Navio, this Roman fort near Hope lies beside Brough village in the angle of the River Noe and the Bradwell Brook, which meanders round the site. The fort platform is discernible in the fields called the Halsteads, although little remains to be seen on the ground, the lines of external walls and gateways can be traced and stones visible on the ground represent the site of the headquarters building.

This was a fort built to house auxiliaries, and Navio was garrisoned by a unit of French irregular cavalry, the 1st Cohort of Aquitanians, recruited in south-west France. Auxiliaries wore lighter armour than the regular legions and often retained their own regional speciality in weaponry. In the case of the Gauls at Navio, these were a light javelin, a large two-edged sword and a small round leather shield. Navio would have housed an auxiliary infantry cohort of 500 men, and although built along the same template as the legionary bases, auxiliary forts were usually much smaller, covering an area of some three acres.

The first fort built around AD70 was the typical Roman design surrounded by two rings of stout walls with ditches outside. The innermost walls were of earth and wood, which were eventually replaced with stone when the wooden fort was demolished 50 years later. In time, a vicus or civilian town would have grown up outside its walls, where the local population were encouraged to settle and engage in trade and manufacturing. In times of danger, the villagers (vicani) were under the jurisdiction of the fort commander but generally each vicus had local self-government with its own council.

The chief purpose of the fort at Brough-on-Noe was to police and supervise the adjacent lead mining areas, but as well as a policing

The footpath sign at the former Roman camp of Brough-on-Noe; the ledge gives the only evidence of the outer walls of the fort.

point, it would also have been a mining depot and a transit centre. Navio was strategically positioned at the junction of newly constructed Roman roads where the east/west route along the Hope valley connected the fort at Melandra, Glossop, with Chesterfield. The road running north-north-west to south-south-east joined the

Left: A plaque to mark the Roman roots of Chesterfield after its redevelopment in 2002.

Below: A plan of Chesterfield showing the distinctive 'playing card' shape of the town's outer walls, the two predominant Roman roads, and the present roads.

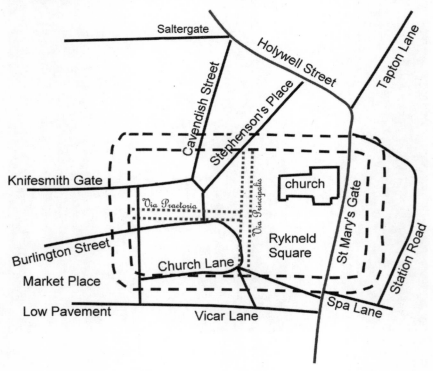

south-west route through Batham Gate and Bradwell valley to Buxton (Aquae Arnemetia). Later a spur was constructed to join the main east coast highway near present day Rotherham. Anavio was abandoned early in the 2nd century AD as the army pushed northwards to consolidate Hadrian's Wall.

Large quantities of lead were mined throughout the Peak District, and in excavations carried out at Navio in 1938 and 1967, lead ingots were found in an underground room (aerarium) at the fort site. Not only was this secure room used to store ingots, it was where the regimental pay and savings chests were stored.

There have been numerous excavations at Navio since the beginning of the last century and many reports in the Derbyshire Archaeological Journal. The site has yielded important finds including several altars, one to the goddess Arnomecta, a local water goddess, another dedicated by Aelius Motio, and others in favour of the gods Mars, Hercules, Augustus. Another important item is the 2nd-century building inscription set up to commemorate the rebuilding of the reoccupied fort by the 1st Cohort of Aquitanians. This fragmentary inscription is the most important epigraphic evidence of Roman fort construction found in the region and is on view in Buxton museum. Other artefacts like a votive altar found nearby are at Weston Park Museum.[1]

Melandra Castle

It is thought that the Roman name for the fort built at Gamesley near Glossop was Ardotalia meaning the place of the high dark hill, taken from the Celtic word 'talia' meaning steep hill, but Melandra is a relatively recent name and so far no-one has agreed what it means. Melandra Castle/Ardotalia was built by the specialist craftsmen needed to perform the skilled work assisted by the *Cohors Primae Frisiavonum* – the First Cohort of Frisiavones, who would have accumulated the building materials, gathered fuel, and cleared the land for grazing and the establishment of small farmsteads. Evidence for the existence of this unit exists not only from the building stone found at the site but from various other Roman writings.[2]

This unit was probably assisted by the 3rd Cohort of Bracara Augustani from the colony of Braga in Portugal, and it's unsure which of these two units, both attached to the XX Legion Valeria Victrix in Chester, manned the fort that housed 1,000 men.

Inside the fort, the HQ (*principia*) was oblong containing two L-shaped rooms enclosing a square open courtyard. The rooms accommodated stores and the armouries. Beyond was a covered cross hall (basilica) where the fort commander could address the unit officers from his ceremonial chair (*tribunal*), dispense orders and issue punishments. The central room was the *aedes* or regimental chapel containing the legion's insignia, altars and symbols of Rome – the eagle and the bust or statue of the reigning emperor. Next to the HQ was the commander's house (*praetorium*), a fashionable Italian-style house containing private rooms for the officer, his family and staff, who enjoyed such luxuries as centrally heated rooms, frescoed walls, a private latrine and bath suite. The granaries stored cereal, meat, wine and vegetables in bins and barrels raised from the flagged floors.

The bath house at Melandra has been excavated outside the north gate. The barracks would have been equipped with receptacles for the men to urinate, but many forts had a communal latrine building where the men sat around a square on wooden unpartitioned seats. The building, like the baths, was supplied with piped water for 'flushing' and for wetting sponges held on sticks, the Roman equivalent of toilet paper.

Cremation burials have been found along one of the roads leading from Melandra, and the vicus covered an area of nineteen acres. This was on a plateau spreading round three sides of the fort and is now under the Gameley Estate where excavations have established the presence of a village set within its own defences of stockaded ramparts and a ditch. Inside were timber booths, shops and a mansion, or inn. These vici provided the off-duty soldiers with bars, gambling dens and brothels. On market days the fort vici would have been full of traders, farmers and peasants producing a fair-like occasion with food and drink, market trading and the provision of blood sports like cock-fighting and bear-baiting. Trade would have been brisk in these village markets in cattle, horses, dogs, slaves, pottery and brooches.

Pentrich Auxiliary Fort

The district of Pentrich in the south of Brigante territory covers a large area and at its heart is a small village; but our interest lies in the auxiliary fort that stood on the Roman road still known as Rykneld Road. This was a major commercial highway that runs north/south. The long, straight stretch called Street Lane still runs north from Denby near Derby until its course disappears beside the A38 at Ripley, then continues through Hartshorn, Pentrich and on to Chesterfield. The fort's Roman name is unknown but based on the *Ravenna Cosmology* of the seventh century it could have been Varatino. *The Ravenna Cosmology* is the only classical source to give the name and although listed as unidentified, Varatino is after the entry for Derventio, Derby, which is just over 12 miles away. The fort at Pentrich was built midway between the forts at Derby and Chesterfield. The elevated site called Castle Hill is currently occupied by Coneygrey Farm and gives no evidence of its former use or the fact that the site was once a busy hub at the intersection of many tracks. The area around Pentrich was not just rich in lead, coal was also mined in this area. It was so plentiful that the compacted slack was used for road building. The Pentrich fort would have been an administration centre for both lead and coal mining.

Aquae Arnemetiae (Buxton)

Most Roman towns in Britain started life as military bases for the Roman legions but Aquae Arnemetiae (modern Buxton) was different. It was never a military town and the civilian street layout is totally unrelated to military planning. There is little evidence of any significant Roman towns in the Brigante area, but Aquae Arnemetiae was very special to the Romans. This was a Celtic religious centre of some significance, a sacred grove used by many generations of native Britons, and the Romans were quick to realise what the Celts had understood for centuries – Derbyshire Water is special. It's been estimated that nine natural thermal springs surfaced in the valley and here the Celts worshipped a water-goddess called Arnemetiae 'the goddess beside the sacred grove'.

In Latin, the Aquae means water, a prefix used by the Romans to denote natural spas or springs, and they added the name of the Celtic goddess to honour her and no doubt to placate the Celts. The popularity of Buxton became second only to the only other recognised Spa-town in Roman Britain, Aquae Sulis which we know as Bath. The water from Aquae Arnemetiae was held in such high esteem that it was sent out in barrels for the treatment of scrofula and other skin complaints. Gradually the Celtic goddess Arnemetiae became Saint Anne. She was the Christian representative of the ancient mother earth goddess Artemis, widely worshipped in Roman times as a symbol of fertility and motherhood. Like the Celts before them, the Romans would worship at the sacred shrine.

St Anne's spring still flows in the heart of Buxton and it's possible to take the waters as our ancient ancestors would have done. The thermal water percolates through the limestone and is stored in some subterranean source from where it is piped or springs up. The water is radioactive and gaseous; mostly carbon dioxide and nitrogen with a little argon and helium. It lacks odour, is tasteless, free of organic matter and a striking blue colour.

The Romans built a bath at the thermal spring site, enclosed it and added all the extras they enjoyed. Bathing for the Romans was a social thing and they recognised hydrotherapy as a medicinal treatment. Aquae Arnemetiae would have been a provincial town where the clients were prevalently military integrated with the local population. The town would have been fairly large with civilian camp followers to provide the facilities for the soldiers' varied pleasures. The bath would be supplied with the natural spring water which still flows at 82°F (28°C). It would have been controlled by a hydraulic water wheel and heated further with a furnace. Hot water would be pumped through underfloor pipes for heating, and hot air would also circulate around the air space between the walls. The actual bath would be divided into two opposing non-communicating sectors, one for men and one for women, flanked by rooms for washing before entering the pool. There would be a *Natatio* – swimming pool, *Laconicum* – sweat bath, *Frigidarium* – cold bath, *Tepidarium* – lukewarm bath, and *Calidarium* – hot bath.

The bath house needed constant servicing, a boiler man to keep the fires full of charcoal or wood, attendants to arrange towels and plentiful supplies of olive oil to rub down or massage the bathers. Here off-duty soldiers perspired amid the graded temperature rooms equipped with their olive oil bottles and strigils (body scrapers). They would relax, gossip, throw dice and socialise.

The building would also house public toilets that were flushed by the waste water from the baths. The toilets would have been a simple affair with wooden or stone seats in multiple units without discrimination, over a constructed open sewer. A gutter in the floor in front would have carried flowing water to rinse the communal sponges fixed to wooden handles.

Bathing was just one aspect of the Roman way of life enjoyed by the soldiers, traders and the new Romano-British leaders. Not only did they take great interest in hygiene, grooming and cosmetics were important too. A favourite accessory for a Roman was a 'pocket set' consisting of tweezers, nail cleaner, nail file, tooth pick and ear scoop, all made of bronze and suspended on a metal loop like a large key ring attached to the belt.

Cosmetics were not new to the Britons but the Romans brought a new repertoire of beauty treatments. Fashionable Roman ladies whitened their faces using either poisonous white lead or chalk. The whitened complexion was designed to make the upper classes stand out, as a natural sun-tanned complexion was a sign that the person spent their days toiling in the fields. The eyes were made up in contrasting black pigments – black antimony mixed with fat, soot with olive oil, burnt rose petal or even squashed flies. Rouge in the form of red earth was applied to the cheeks. These pigments would be mixed in shells or on slate palettes and stored in wooden boxes.

Rich Roman women wore perfume ranging in price from myrrh mixed with spices, through to perfume made from rose-petals. The Romans cleaned their teeth with a preparation made from burnt eggshells and whitened them with powdered pumice stone. Wigs were worn and hair was coloured and worn in many different styles. Pliny mentions a depilatory cream made from the blood of a she-goat mixed with dried viper's blood. There must have been many such preparations. The Celts had polished metal mirrors which were objects of beauty in their own right, but with their glass making techniques, by the 3rd century the Romans had glass mirrors.

It's difficult to say just how large any protohistoric settlement may have been because although the baths continued to flourish, successive development between the 16th and 20th century has disturbed much of Buxton and most of the region where the springs emerged. Archaeological and hydrological exploration have revealed much of interest including the fact that the Roman ground level was some three metres below the current ground floor levels. This would mean that the cellars, vaults, apses and unexplored voids in the foundations of places like the Old Hall Hotel are of special interest. Cornelius White who ran the baths in the late 17th century made an attempt in 1695–6 to restore them to Roman standards and in the process discovered a large, ancient, smooth stone bath 20 m x 7 m and a lead cistern 4 m under the earth.

When the foundations were being dug to build The Crescent in 1780–84, modelled on Bath's Royal Crescent, a wall made of red plaster was discovered; 'a Roman wall cemented with red Roman plaister, close by St Ann's well where we may see the ruins of the ancient Bath, its dimensions and length. The plaister is red and hard as brick … a possible mixture of lime and powdered tiles cemented with blood and eggs.' The bath referred to was a rectangle 13 ft x 15 ft. It had a floor of lime and coarse sand, and limestone walls overlaid with a coating of cement. It was fed by a spring at the west end from which rose bubbling warm water. Opposite, a type of floodgate could be operated to adjust the depth of water or to drain the main tank. Built into the eastern end was a cavity shaped to resemble a boat and fed by water from a lead pipe.

At the same time that these finds were being excavated (1787), a solidly built podium of well-dressed stone with a packed clay infill situated about 80ft from the Roman Bath site was investigated. The platform measured 22½ ft wide by 46 ft long and stood about 4 ft in height. Oriented north-south there is a possibility that this was a temple. Finds of iron nails and roofing tiles suggest that the superstructure was of timber. In 2009, previously unknown underground cisterns were discovered in front of the Crescent. The old Court House in George Street is built directly over the river. The massive pillars and arches inside this building once made it ideal as the town jail but of interest to us is the fact that it's believed to stand on the site of a watermill used in Roman times for grinding flour. Two historic water mills are recorded in Buxton in Ernest Axon's papers at the Buxton Museum – this one in George Street and one at Ashwood Dale.

The Romans built a bath house and all the necessary extras in the sacred grove, but they built their town on a plateau overlooking the valley. Evidence of this is found in the road alignments and in 2005–6, the Market Place alteration scheme enabled the road layouts to be examined using computer graphic technology. It was found that eleven Roman streets converged on a single point at the Market Place.

As a Roman town, Buxton would have been protected by a wall. There are a few visible stretches although in general, the wall now forms ancient foundations to more modern buildings. It is quite possible that a suburban settlement would have existed outside the walls and there would have been gates positioned along the town wall to serve the roads. From the site of the north-east gate it is possible to look down the slope towards the curve of the Roman amphitheatre, which would have used the hillside to provide natural seating for the spectators.

The Town Hall's southern elevation dominates the northern end of the Market Place and its northern elevation looks down into the former grove. It was built on the foundations of the s the basilica/odeion and it's possible that the Roman basilica also had a dual aspect, north towards the recreational and bathing area, and south towards the residential town centre. Many Roman remains were found when the central section of the present town hall was built in 1811. A large number were food-related items including bones and a Roman tankard that would seem to confirm that this area had a fair share of inns (tabernae) and restaurants. It would also have been a central hub for trade.[3]

Many of the current churches in Buxton are built on sites that were considered to be sacred, and as religious observance was an important daily activity, the Roman town would have had numerous temples. It's been suggested that the Methodist Chapel on the Market Place was the site of a Roman Temple – possibly dedicated to Apollo. Conversion work has uncovered many buried Roman surfaces including the south wall and a likely entrance passage and doorway to the baths exercise hall (*Palaestra*), fine mosaics, cobbled streets and floor slabs buried under concrete. Other finds include a large number of dressed stone blocks, red clay roof tiles, wall tiles, hearths, fine Samian and coarse pottery, glassware, coins, metalwork and charred bones. The most significant find is a Roman milestone discovered in a garden on Silverlands, a residential suburb of Buxton. It is inscribed 'TRIB POT COS II P P A NAVIONE M P XI' – 'Tribunician Power, Consul two times, Father of this Country, eleven thousand paces from Navio.'

Professor Boyd Dawkins is of the opinion that the name Buxton comes from bawkstone or big-stone, which formed the stone abutment to the timber Roman Bridge over the River Wye.

Poole's Cavern

Most of us like to take home a souvenir from our holidays and the Romans were no exception. For the Romans, Aquae Arnemetiae was a holiday destination and when the legionnaires were not participating in the social life of the bath house, or wining and dining, they could enjoy a spot of retail therapy. It's believed that the Hill Road between the lower and upper town was lined with shops. Poole's Cavern on the southern outskirts of Aquae Arnemetiae was a factory supplying these shops.

Like many of Derbyshire's natural caves, Poole's Cavern was formed by the action of rainwater percolating through cracks and joints in the limestone rocks over thousands of years. There have been many archaeological finds which are now on display in Buxton Museum, but recent finds of molten and copper alloys have painted a very interesting picture of the activities that took place in Poole's cavern during the Roman occupation.

Amongst the finds are brooches dating back to the 2nd century that have been described as unusable, and when the experts call something unusable there is generally a reason. An unusable item is not fit for purpose because it's unfinished. Why were a number of unfinished brooches amongst the finds at Poole's Cavern? The lugs behind the head of one unusable brooch are not perforated to take a pin-spring assembly; the catch plate is unfinished, there's a rib along the edge where the return would normally be, and the items show no sign of wear. There are fragments of wire, some of which are cut, coiled and pointed like pins, and these are all clues to the true purpose of the unusable brooches. They were either rejects, work in progress or prototypes which would indicate that this was the site of a Roman factory making brooches. They are made of lead, which would have been an ideal material to make a model or prototype brooch. It's easy to work, taking fine detail. The prototype would then be pressed into clay from which a mould would be made. When the clay was hard-baked, the lead brooch would be removed, and the mould cleaned ready to make copies.

A small crucible found amongst the Victorian discoveries at Poole's Cavern confirms that metals were cast and wrought here. Metal would be melted in the crucible, then poured into the clay moulds to cast brooches, a fact supported by the finding of an identical brooch to the lead one, but this time made in copper alloy. Over sixty leaded bronze brooches with a Polden-Hill-type head were analysed. These brooches are similar in design to a modern safety pin and were used to fasten clothing. There are some brass examples with areas of tinning that is used to attach repoussé silver foil bands and rosettes, but in some cases the tinning appears to be a decorative effect in its own right. Among the finds are disc brooches enamelled in red and blue, bow brooches, wheel brooches, umbonate brooches and penannular brooches that are normally wrought, not cast. Leaded alloys can't be wrought.

With the amount of finds and the variety of brooches there is no doubt that Poole's Cavern was an early example of a Roman factory. There have been almost identical finds at Thurst Hole Cave which is nearby, indicating that this also was used by metalworkers in Roman times. They would have undoubtedly found a ready market for their trinkets at the spa town of Aquae Arnemetiae.[4]

21

WHAT HAPPENED TO CARTIMANDUA?

It is more or less assumed that after the AD69 overthrow, Cartimandua was forced to leave her tribal lands because her ex-husband and his victorious rebels would have shown her no mercy. There was scope for an honorable suicide, like Boudica possibly and Cleopatra unforgettably. Sadly, there is no record of what happened to Cartimandua who had worked so hard to maintain the independence of the Brigantes outside the Empire. Was she exiled or ejected, or was she given a safe haven to live out her days? When order was restored in Brigantia in 70AD we do not know what new arrangements were made for Cartimandua. She could have remained and continued as before but that obviously hadn't worked previously. Remaining in Brigantian lands still left her vulnerable and a target for Venutius to capture, but if Cartimandua was to be reinstated on the throne of Brigantia, it would make sense to keep her protected somewhere near her territorial borders.

Earlier writers have speculated as to what might have happened to a displaced royal. Once she was ousted, annexation was inevitable. We have no record of her family, but family relationships do not guarantee loyalty or approval. She may have been a mother but any grown-up children would surely have been mentioned. It is hardly likely that she was totally alone. Her position as a royal queen would ensure a royal household and loyal supporters. But how strong was her royal position? Cartimandua remained a queen loyal to the Empire, which should have given her untouchable strength. Her position would have affected her sense of identity and entitlement. Cartimandua may have been forced to leave her throne but it's unlikely that she was ready to leave her kingdom and abandon her supporters entirely. It's doubtful that Rome would have wanted that, but with the likelihood of further serious disturbances in the client kingdom, change was clearly necessary. Brigantian territory had to be under constant Roman surveillance and control; would the added pressure of shoring up Cartimandua's position be just too much?

Tribal relations were fractious, so it's unlikely that she would have been offered asylum in another Celtic tribe, although according to Ellen Castelo, Cartimandua fled to the newly built Roman fort at Deva (Chester). According to Ptolemy, Deva Victix was in the lands of the Cornovii tribe bordering that of the Brigantes in the north.[1] Deva was a strategic site for a fortress, overlooking the bridge crossing the River Dee which gave access to the sea, and close to the natural harbour which is today occupied by Chester Racecourse. The River Dee also divided the Brigante territory from the Cornovii/ Ordovices, so Cartimandua would have been on the very border of her tribal lands. But there is no evidence to support the theory that Cartimandua fled to Chester. Castelo has based her suggestion on the word of writers like Braund (1984) and Reed (1977) but they give no evidence to support this assumption either. There is no link between the two tribes and there is no reason to believe that the Cornovii welcomed Cartimandua, the exiled queen of the Brigantes into their midst. There is also a date discrepancy because the legionary fortress was not built until AD74, which is at least four years after the Brigantian conflict of 69-70.

With Roman citizenship and having been a loyal ally of Rome for many years, Cartimandua might have gone to Rome. She might have spent her remaining days settled comfortably in Italy. But if she had gone to Rome she would have been nothing – a stranger in a strange land without friends or family – a ruler with no one to rule, a queen without a crown. She may not even have been accepted in Rome. The Roman writers had not exactly sung her praises or made her appear to be a likeable person, but they would surely have followed her progress and written about her if she had gone to Rome. It may not have been a flattering or a true report but it would have given us some idea of what eventually happened to our Celtic queen.

Was Cartimandua taken to Strutts Park?

With no written evidence we can only speculate as to what happened to Cartimandua, and I have a theory. Cartimandua was not taken to Chester, but to Little Chester on the outskirts of Derby on the very southern boundary of Brigantine territory. Didius Gallus established a military fort on the west bank of the River Trent in the 50s, but it was evacuated in order to establish a new fort at Little Chester on the east bank of the river just thirty years later. One question that has puzzled archaeologists is why. It was not unusual for early forts, especially the wooden structures, to be rebuilt, but not on a different site unless that site was to be used for a different purpose. None of the post holes at the earlier fort showed any signs of rotting timber and many had damaged edges indicating that the timbers had been rocked loose or levered out, no doubt to be re-used elsewhere. Salvaging usable timbers would indicate deliberate and systematic demolition of the site and in view of material of Flavian date which has been recovered from Little Chester, these materials were transferred across the river in a move thought to have taken place in the early 80s during the governorship of Agricola.

The earlier site on the sandstone ridge on the west bank of the river was known as Strutts Park and was probably a Brigantian stronghold originally. It stood on The Portway giving easy access

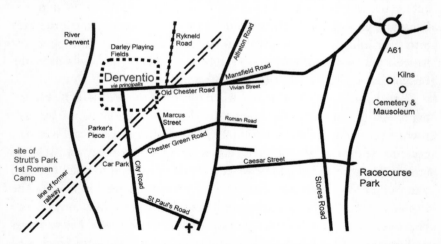

A plan showing the site of Strutts Park on one side of the river, and its replacement fort of Little Chester on the other. Could this have been where Cartimandua spent her final days?

to the trade routes in the north-west of Brigante country and the river systems of eastern England, and the upper limit for sea-going vessels. The Portway was used for centuries by the Celtic people and traders, and by the Romans both before and during the construction of their road network. As the Romans advanced north, they fortified strategic and defensive sites and were not averse to taking over former Celtic strongholds for their own use and this is what they undoubtedly did at Strutts Park. This area is now mostly covered by Darley Abbey Park on the northern approach to Derby, but 2,000 years ago it would have been on the southern boundary of Brigante territory, the Vale of Trent, Sherwood Forest and the River Don. The Romans constructed a series of frontier forts in defensive river positions along the Trent Valley connected by an east to west road. In the upper Trent Valley was Chesterton; Rocester was at the confluence of the Rivers Churnet and Dove; Strutts Park overlooked the River Derwent, and Broxtowe was adjacent to the River Leen at Nottingham.

It is likely that Strutts Park served as a store and supply base for the advancing armies during its thrust to the west, obtaining supplies from Letocetum (Wall near Lichfield). Unlike its neighbour Broxtowe, which was large and probably extended further during the Brigante uprising, Strutts Park was small, which would imply that it was not occupied by a garrison. Perhaps it was used as a detention centre if a person's crime did not justify them being killed outright, or before they could be transported back to Rome. Excavations have shown evidence of an early structure or structures at Strutts Park. A single main building is aligned north-south 29 ft (9 m) wide with a carefully laid floor of red marl. The width would indicate a 1st-century timber barrack block, the men's sleeping quarters with adjacent smaller rooms for storing equipment. Rather surprisingly, a further phase of building with associated industrial activities *c.* 55–70 is civilian rather than military. This could be a clue: because more than one phase of activity is represented, and it is not military, so is it possible that this site could have been expanded for the use of Cartimandua? Its position with support from Broxtowe, Rocester and Chesterton was secure, making this a good place to keep Cartimandua safe but on the very edge of her former territory.

There is not a lot of information available on Strutts Park as most of the land has been disturbed by post-medieval pits, modern land drains and tree roots. There is evidence to support the theory that it was only occupied for a relatively short period, the earliest account of which is in Stephen Glover's *History of the County of Derbyshire* (1829). He wrote 'In the year 1820, when Darley Grove was broken up, skeletons, coins and various Roman relics were discovered.' According to George Bailey, local historian and artist writing in *The Derbyshire Archaeological and Natural History Society Journal,* a hoard of about ninety silver and bronze Roman coins was found by workmen while making a road through the lower part of Strutts Park. The coins varied in date from before the Roman invasion to AD77.

Of even greater interest, in 1924, an ancient stone footing was discovered by workmen next to the cricket pavilion on the Derby School cricket ground. It proved to be the wing of a substantial building, the bulk of which still lies sealed under the railway embankment which forms the southern boundary of the playing field and covered the area of Strutts Park. There is no Roman masonry but that was often robbed for other sites, and although earth banks were often preserved, these would have been flattened by later development. Roofing tiles and painted wall plaster were found, then foundations of a room with walls that were three feet thick. The overall dimensions remain unknown but a wall 35 ft long is recorded. The building was at first referred to as a Roman bath house because alongside the footings a Roman hypocaust, an underfloor ducted heating system supplying hot air, was discovered. But the idea that this was a bath house has been challenged and it's now believed that the hypocaust served a substantial building that was more likely to be civilian rather than military.

In the following years, finds included coins, beads, a bronze pin and needle, a lead spindle whorl, lead or sheet bronze, some bronze objects distorted by heat, a spillage of lead, and a decorated brooch. In 1974 excavations produced structural evidence of 1st-century Roman occupation in the Strutts Park area,

Is it conceivable that in the aftermath of the AD69 uprising, Cartimandua was moved to Strutts Park where a garrison was placed, poised for intervention in support of the exiled queen? If she was housed at Strutts Park, was the fort at Little Chester built to protect the client queen while allowing her to live out her life without a constant military presence, or was Little Chester built to house her while military occupation continued at Strutts Park?[1]

Cartimandua had shown unswerving loyalty to Rome, and she had done her best to foster pro-Roman attitudes in the early years of the conquest. In return, the Romans respected her authority, and as a Romanised Briton she would have lived a life of luxury and benefitted from Rome's generosity. This was not necessarily going to change because she was no longer a client queen. We can compare her to another successful client king, Cogidubnus.

Cogidubnus (Togidubnus) King of the Atrebates tribe, became a client king in 43–44AD under Claudius and took a Roman name and citizenship. According to Tacitus he was 'one who maintained his unswerving loyalty down to our times'. We know that Cogidubnus's loyalty was rewarded with the magnificent palace at Fishbourne, the area on the Sussex coast that he governed. The first building on the site in the early years of the conquest was a military supply depot dating to AD43, but this was cleared and sometime in the late 40s or early 50s a timber house with a separate building, perhaps a servant's range, was constructed. It had clay or mortar floors and there were traces of painted plaster, so a person of some status must have lived there.

In the 60s the first masonry building was erected. It was no ordinary building but its magnificence was far outstripped when sometime after AD75, a great palace constructed of four wings around a formal garden was built on the ten-acre site. This house was vast with the main rooms arranged round a rectangular courtyard more than 90 metres across. There was a colonnaded garden, much of which was probably laid to lawn, with a stream, fountains and basins fed from a network of underground pipes. To enhance the view from the principal rooms, parts of the garden would have been adorned with plants popular in Roman times such as lilies, roses and acanthus and the whole was screened with trees. The interior would have been equally impressive with a bath suite, a set of living rooms and servant/slave's quarters. The whole was elaborately decorated with stucco, painted and unpainted; its floors were paved in mosaic and marble. The owner of such a palace would be a high ranking Roman official or a local landowner of great distinction and it's now believed that this was the home of Cogidubnus. Could Cartimandua expect anything less?

Because evidence of a large building equipped with the latest heating and bathing facilities was discovered at Strutts Park further investigations were carried out. Finds indicate that this building was decorated in the Roman fashion with mosaic floors and plastered walls decorated with painted frescoes, but not enough has been unearthed to say for certain that this was a luxury villa, and it's sheer guesswork to say it was the home of Cartimandua. But it's a possibility. Fishbourne was not discovered until 1960 and that was totally by accident. If one of the most outstanding sites of Roman Britain has laid undiscovered all those centuries, there is always a possibility that other finds will be made, and if Strutts Park was to undergo more vigorous investigations who knows what conclusions can be drawn?

It would be an appropriate location for our courageous Celtic queen.

Appendix 1

ARCHAEOLOGY – THE DIG

The late 19th century was the heyday of amateurism in the administration and supervision of local excavations by archaeologists like Thomas Bateman and John Fossick Lucas, in association with Llewellynn Jewitt, who carried on a series of barrow digs in the 1880s. Llewellyn Jewitt was an artist, author and publisher who illustrated most of Thomas Bateman's archaeological finds and the engravings, which he published in *Bateman's Ten Years' Diggings in Celtic and Saxon Grave Hills* (1861). An enthusiastic excavator, Jewitt founded the *Derby Telegraph* newspaper in 1853, and was the brains behind Britain's first archaeological magazine, *The Reliquary*, published as a quarterly from 1860. It was edited by Jewitt until 1886 and survived well into the 20th century. The Derbyshire Archaeological Society was founded in 1878 to examine, preserve and illustrate the archaeology of the county, and Celtic sites are well documented.

It is often farmers who initially spot the signs, but they don't tell the local archaeologists because they are worried about their ability to continue to work the land. Metal detectors have of course made a huge difference. If there's a large amount of evidence archaeologists can be persuaded to pursue further work on the site and go for a full-scale dig. This is costly and time-consuming. It needs permission from various local authorities, the county conservation officer, the county building archaeologist, the English Heritage archaeological officer, English Heritage structural engineers and often an environmental specialist from the local museum who will oversee the operation.

An early 20th-century poster alerting farmers and others to the need to be vigilant and report finds. (Courtesy Buxton Museum)

Above and below: A hoard of mainly broken jewellery and a hoard of silver coins.
(British Museum)

Even the government need to approve a scheme of work. A licence is needed to excavate or do any geophysics surveys. The licence needed for an excavation also specifies such details as who is working on a site and their qualifications, how an excavation will be recorded and what experts will be consulted. At the end of the day, it boils down to cost, so people or organisations are always needed to sponsor a dig.

First, the area is gridded into squares marked by canes, and field walkers and metal detectors are used to collect any surface material. Each stone, lump and bump is charted as these often indicate a network of walls, and there could be more substantial foundation walls beneath them. Over the centuries buildings have usually been quarried and the stones used in other projects, so walls alone can't be dated. Dating evidence comes from finding evidence of occupation, and for this, a trench is dug to section a ditch or earth works.

Removing material at a site has to be done in layers so that replacing it follows an ecologically sound plan approved by the authorities. This material may look insignificant to the untrained eye, but it is highly sensitive. Exposing the lower surface which may date back to the Bronze Age or earlier, shows a vulnerable archaeological deposit that could give detailed information about the types of plants and fauna that were around in the prehistory period. Sometimes these finds make no archaeological sense but even the smallest find justifies the belief that some earlier civilisation did exist. However small and ephemeral, it is essential that everything must be mapped and accounted for so that at some time in the future, others will be able to examine what has been done and draw their own conclusions using more advanced technology.

Occasionally, archaeologists will find what is referred to as a hoard, a group of valuable objects deliberately gathered together and buried in the ground. It may have been to keep the objects safe during times of war or uncertainty, or perhaps they were offerings to the gods. Hoards often contain coins and jewellery. The most important hoard containing objects of British prehistory, buried around 100BC, was found at Ken Hill, Snettisham, Norfolk (Iceni territory). Occupying a wooded hillside near the north-west coast of Norfolk, near Hunstanton, this key site first began to reveal its secrets in 1948 when five torcs were uncovered during ploughing. Further finds were made at the site in subsequent years, and at least twelve hoards have been found at the site. One of the hoards known as hoard L contained 21 torcs placed in a small hole in the ground. Archaeologists found seven torcs carefully placed in the ground, then below a layer of soil, they found another 14 torcs placed on top of one another along with two bronze bracelets. In addition to complete and broken torcs, many of the hoards included objects such as coins, rings, bracelets and ingots. Sometimes these objects were strung together. Other objects were deliberately deformed by cutting, and some were partly melted, possibly being prepared for re-cycling. The objects in the British museum were discovered in 1950 and 1990, and others are now in Norwich Castle Museum.

Appendix 2

DATING ARTEFACTS

We are working on the very edge of prehistory when very little was written and even if it was, has not survived. Discovering the history of the Celts is therefore rather like piecing together a giant jigsaw puzzle with pieces from archaeologists, archaeological conservators, forensic archaeologists, philologists and historians who record the latest archaeological, anthropological and social studies. Even so, much of it is postulation.

Arial photography can give a bird's eye view of an area and identify marks in the landscape that are under the surface and not seen clearly at ground level. Electronic theodolite and distance measure (EDM) are effective on sites. Radiocarbon analysis has revolutionized the dating of artefacts, but margins of error in dating the Iron Age period are sometimes too great for this form of analysis to be of much value. Dendrochronology has been used since 1901, and works on the principle that the seasonal growth rings of trees create a permanent record in timber which is as unique as a fingerprint. By this method, wooden objects can be accurately dated as far back as 7000 years, but wooden artefacts from the Iron Age are rarely found in well preserved condition.

Geophysics plotting is Ground Penetrating Radar (GPR) which finds any anomaly below the surface through magnetometry, which measures differences in magnetic strength. Any activity that disturbs the natural bedrock will subtly change the magnetic signal. If a fire is lit on the floor of a prehistoric hut, the original signal is changed.

Above: Bones found in an early Celtic bowl. (British Museum)

Below: Quality drinking vessels. (British Museum)

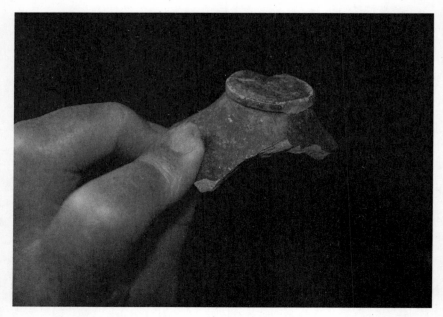

Above: Even the smallest piece of pottery must be handled with care as it can give a bigger picture.

Below: Armlets. (British Museum)

Fires, hearths, kilns and ditches contain slag or metalworkings which give stronger magnetic signals. If a ditch is dug for foundations, drains or a pit, it will eventually be filled with a material that has a different magnetic signal to the original surface. If through GPR archaeologists find a blocked-up well or sullage pit, it is like finding a time capsule buried in the earth.

Portable artefacts give us our best clues, and there is widespread archaeological evidence in the form of raw materials, waste, tools and finished goods for a variety of specialist crafts; metal working in gold, silver, bronze and iron, enamelling bronzes, ornaments in glass, shale and jet, and of course coins.

Metalwork more often than not survives as rusted iron or corroded bronze, so artefacts from the Iron Age such as shields or chariots are rarely found in good condition. Organic materials like wood, cloth and bone rarely survive after 2000 years in the ground except in exceptional conditions such as at water-logged sites like bogs where the tannic acid and anaerobic conditions act to preserve the material. The peat acts like an antiseptic to preserve bodies and clothing. Even then, bone evidence is fraught with problems. Although some were used as tools and tool handles, bones were usually roasted or boiled for glue or stock before being thrown away, or given to the dogs or pigs.

A number of handmade pots containing sheep bones and dating back to 350-100BC have been found in graves at Rudston, Burton Fleming and Danes Grove, East Yorkshire. It's a mystery as to why these bones were put in the pots, especially when it's only the left humerus or forelimb of sheep that were obviously specially selected. Analysis of the sheep bones from these pots tells us that Iron Age sheep were smaller in size than modern-day breeds. In other graves found in East Yorkshire, people were buried with the remains of pigs, possibly to give them sustenance in the afterlife.

Because of the corrosive nature of acid soil, the most frequent archaeological finds such as spindle whorls, whetstones and flint flakes from earlier periods are made from stone or pottery. Even in tiny fragments, pottery gives the archaeologists evidence of occupation during specific periods. Pottery finds dating from the Iron Age would imply that was the main period of activity on the site. Often, even from a small piece of pot, it's possible to tell the size of the original piece from the curve of the shape. A terracotta pot could have been a piece of an amphora or storage jar, and would be proof that our Iron Age ancestors had access to luxury imports like wine and olive oil. Had the jar come up the River on an Iron Age boat that had perhaps made contact with a Mediterranean vessel or more likely a trader from France who had carried the amphora across the channel? Luxury items like silver drinking cups were popular across the Roman Empire between 100BC and AD100.

Glass beads, pottery and small fragments of bronze that are not native to the area would suggest that the region was visited by neighbouring tribes and might have been part of a much bigger trading network.Personal ornaments like glass beads and bangles of coloured glass were well liked, with blue being the most popular colour for glass beads in the Iron Age. Often single beads were threaded onto bronze rings or bangles. Some were marvered with scroll or spiral patterns into which opaque glass was inlaid. Bangles found at Burton Agnes, East Yorkshire, were in different widths, embossed with blue beads and white spirals, dating from 500 to 300BC. A beaded collar dating from AD100–250 was found inside a bronze bowl during peat cutting in Dumfriesshire. It consists of a flat, cast segment complete with an articulated section composed of fluted beads with concave spacers originally threaded onto bronze or iron wire.

Dating from AD50–200 is a dragonesque brooch in cast bronze with blue, red, yellow and white enamel inlay, found at Norton, North Yorkshire. Cast copper alloy belt mounts were found in Cumberland. Matching pairs of cast bronze armlets ornamented with enamelled discs in red and yellow are massive, each weighs over 1600 grams. Dating from AD100–250, the enamelled roundels were made separately and fixed in place with iron discs.

These are just a few of the documented finds we have scattered in many museum collections across former Brigante territory and in the British Museum. Finds are sporadic and most come from grave goods buried with the dead or at special sites were religious offerings were made, usually in rivers or lakes.

Appendix 3

STRUTTS PARK AND MAM TOR FINDS

According to Josephine Dool's report DAJ 1985/86, scraps of Samian ware indicated an initial occupation of Strutts Park not later than AD60 (Forrest, 1967). All the Samian pottery sherds were from vessels made by La Graufesenque in South Gaul. Because most are

A near complete Samian ware bowl at Little Chester Museum

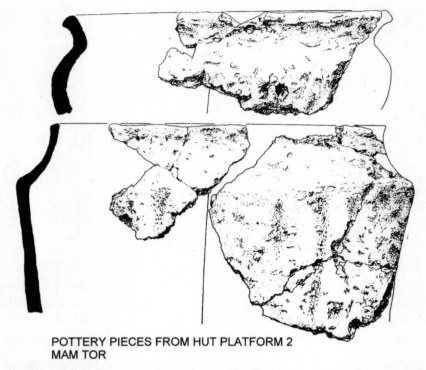

**POTTERY PIECES FROM HUT PLATFORM 2
MAM TOR**

Above and below: Pottery finds at Mam Tor 1965-69, and how it is pieced together for identification.

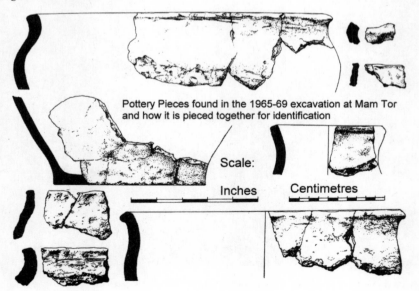

Pottery Pieces found in the 1965-69 excavation at Mam Tor and how it is pieced together for identification

Scale:

Inches   Centimetres

Grave goods, including an urn and miniature cup were found in a burial mound on Stanton Moor near Bakewell, and illustrated by writer and antiquary Samuel Pegge in 1784.

so small it is difficult to date them accurately but none have the high gloss which is characteristic of the Neronian period. Where dating is certain it is Claudian, which means that none are later than AD60. Some of the coarser pottery fragments were probably an imitation of the Samian ware. Some were a soft, micaceous, orange fabric with buff or grey core, others were a thick white fabric, fairly hard with a few small inclusions of limonite and haermonite, or hard, sandy, light grey fabric with a darker grey core. The decoration shows sprays of vegetation, delicate tendrils, petalled rosettes spirals and cordate leaves, volutes or curved gadroons and straight gadroons (The straight gadroons were common in Claudian and Neronian times), scrolling, curved fronds, long pendant leaves, cordate leaf with serrated edges, medallions, and bold, wavy lines. There were slight traces of orange slip coat with abraded surfaces; later imported potters brought new forms and exotic techniques like lead glazing.

Pottery from the 1965–69 excavations of Mam Tor conducted by Manchester University, is described generally as course and thick, and roughly hand-worked. Pottery known previously from the site has been termed Brigantian Ware (Bartlett and Preston 1965: p.113). Its variations are known as Derbyshire ware. It ranges from orange to blue-grey in colour with abundant quartz inclusions creating a pimply surface and making it extremely hard. The pottery can be divided according to eight criteria; colour, feel, hardness, fracture, frequency of inclusions, sorting of inclusions, average sizes of inclusions and petrology.

Virtually all the pottery is coaurse and poorly finished, which would indicate that it was manufactured by individual domestic groups. It is therefore assumed that the pastoralist subsistence strategy practised by the Mam Tor community was unlikely to have produced the surplus necessary to support pottery specialists. All the grits used in the coarse ware would have been available close-by and the clay probably came from the Derwent river bank.

The range of jars and bowls encompass common methods of manufacture. Most jars have a simple S shaped profile with rims that are slightly thickened and occasionally flattened. Other jars have slightly out-turned rims, sloping necks and rounded shoulders. There are plain concave sided jars with hooked-over or bevelled rims. The commonest vessel form is the lid-sealed jar – 25 examples of which have been identified. The bulk of the pottery sherds found are from the body and are without features making identification a problem, but the amount of pottery found on a site is done by counting the different rims, ranging from large jars to beakers.

Coarse, heavily gritted wares are typical of the early period of occupation with denser, thinner and better fired wares occurring in later phases. This shows multi-phase development and might indicate the work of a part-time specialist craftsman, but again the grits used were available locally. (Challis and Harding 1975: 34) The Mam Tor hillfort report is taken from The Derbyshire Archaeological Journal Volume CIII 1983, page 43. The 1965–69 excavations conducted by Manchester University have provided critical information about the chronology and nature of hillfort settlements in Northern England (Coombs. 1967, 1971; Coombs and Thompson, 1979).

Appendix 4

ROMAN/CELTIC TOWNS AND THEIR MODERN NAMES

Aldborough – Isurium Brigantum
Anglesey – Mona
Bath – Aquae Sulis
Brough on Humber – Petuaria
Brough-on-Noe – Anavio
Buxton – Aquae Arnemetiae
Canterbury – Durovernum Cantiacorum
Carmarthen – Moridundum Demetarum
Colchester – Camulodunon
Corbridge – Corstopitum
Dorchester – Durnovaria
Glossop – Melandra
Ilchester – Lindinis
Leicester – Ratae Corieltauvorum
Little Chester – Derventio
Manchester – Mamvcivm
Silchester – Calleva Atrebatum,
St Albans – Verulamium
Winchester – Venta Belgarum
York – Eboracum

The following towns are deemed to have been in Brigante territory.

Aquae Arnemetia, Buxton, Derbyshire
Bremetenacum Veteranorum, Ribchester, Lancashire
Calatum-Burrow, Lonsdale, Lancashire
Calcaria, Tadcaster, North Yorkshire
Cambodunum, Slack, West Yorkshire
Cataractonium, Catterick, North Yorkshire
Coria, Corbridge, Northumberland, perhaps a settlement of the Lopocares
Danvm Doncaster, South Yorkshire)
Derventio Littlechester, Derby, Derbyshire
Eboracum, City of York, North Yorkshire
Epiacum, Whitley Castle, Northumberland
Isurium Brigantum, Aldborough, North Yorkshire
Luguvalium, Carlisle, Cumbria. probably a settlement of the Carvetii
Olicana, Ilkley, West Yorkshire
Rigodunum, Castleshaw, Greater Manchester
Vinovium, Binchester, County Durham
Wincobank, on the border of Sheffield.

Appendix 5

SMALLER HILLFORTS AND PLACES OF INTEREST IN BRIGANTE TERRITORY

There are hundreds, possibly thousands of hillforts in Britain yet only a handful have been excavated. Evidence found by excavation is sporadic and most comes from grave goods or at special sites were religious offerings were made, usually in rivers, lakes or water-logged sites like bogs. Metalwork usually survives as rusted iron or corroded bronze. Organic materials such as wood, cloth and bone rarely survive after 2000 years in the ground except in exceptional conditions such as water-logged soil. In boggy conditions, the tannic acid and anaerobic conditions act to preserve organic material. Because of the corrosive nature of acid soil, the most frequent archaeological finds are made from stone or pottery such as spindle whorls, whetstones and flint flakes from an earlier period. In the hilly terrain of the Peak District, there are plenty of stone lumps and bumps. There are upright stones and stone walls, but they do not give any clue as to what era they were built in. A series of walls may link with others to give some form and order, and a network of walls may have more substantial walls beneath them, but walls alone can't be dated. Stone is likely to be re-used time and again so it's necessary to find evidence of occupation – a piece of pottery, a bit of broken window glass, a jug handle or some object that shows evidence of early occupation. To make a complete list would be impossible but this is to show how many diverse and interesting Celtic related places and items can be found today.

ARBOUR LOW combines two names that give some indication of its past use. Arbour and harbour are derivations from 'here-barge' and could mean 'army camp/shelter', and burh means fortification so there was probably a fortification here. 'Low' is derived from the Old English *hlaw* meaning hill particularly one that was noticeably higher than others nearby. These high places were frequently used by early man as burial mounds and hillforts.

BALL CROSS is near Bakewell just off the road behind Bakewell's former railway station leading to Chatsworth. It is without public access. It is significantly smaller than Fin Cop or Mam Tor and was probably little more than an enclosed farmstead. The defences seem to have been deliberately destroyed.

BINCHESTER ROMAN FORT, NEAR BISHOP AUCKLAND, COUNTY DURHAM was built around AD75 on the north-eastern edge of Brigante territory for Roman legionary and auxiliary soldiers, and although no fort buildings have survived, there's the remains of the commander's house, and a fine preserved example of a Roman bath house with its amazing 1,700-year-old underfloor heating system. It was while excavating the bath house that the carved stone head of the Celtic/Romano god Antenociticus dating from the 2nd or 3rd century was found close to the site where a small altar dedicated to him was discovered in 2011.

BRASSINGTON The Roman road between Buxton and Derby ran through the wild, bleak environs of Brassington and Carsington. There are extensive quarries and particularly lead mines.

BURR TOR HILLFORT at Great Hucklow overlooks the limestone plateau between Eyam and Hazelbridge 396 m (1300 ft) above sea level. It is now part of the site of the Great Hucklow Gliding Club. It's not one of the usual Celtic 'tourist destinations', but for a bird's eye view of the site and particularly the defences, you could get get air-borne.

CASTLE NAZE The hillfort high above Chapel en le Frith is a triangular shape. It has multiple ramparts on one side while the other two are precipitous natural slopes.

CARL WARK is one of the smaller Iron Age hillforts situated in the Longshaw Country Park above Hathersage, Derbyshire, occupying a grit-stone plateau, about 1,250ft above sea level. Its rectangular shape approximately 173 yards by 53 yards encloses almost two acres. The natural rock edge acts as a defence along the south and eastern sides, but with evidence of additional stone emplacement. The western side has a large stone wall 150 ft (45 m) long by 20 ft (6 m) wide and almost 10 ft (3 m) high. Some of the stones in these ramparts are impressive, over 5 ft (1.5m) long. Remains of round houses with enclosures have been found in the Longshaw Country Park.

CARSINGTON is believed to have been the lead mining centre of Latudarum. In the 1980s the area was excavated before being flooded to create Carsington Reservoir. Archaeologists discovered the remains of Roman buildings and a settlement comprising a group of buildings covering around 2 hectares. Finds now in Buxton Museum include spindle whorls, glass and pottery fragments, a bronze stud, iron nail, lead amulets and jet beads, a ring and bracelet.

CASTLE RING – HARTHILL MOOR is without public access but go and find someone at Harthill Moor Farm and request to visit. This tiny hillfort enclosing ¾ of an acre has a good bank, ditch and counterscarp. A small section is missing in the south east. In the 18th century archaeologist Major Rooke described an entrance in the south east, but there's no evidence of this today. If you follow the Limestone Way round the farm, it looks like the remains of what might have been an outer bank over 2 m high in places.

CELTIC CROSSES Many early Celtic crosses were positioned at crossroads. These were not just to mark territory and provide location markers, they were where itinerant priests and monks would preach when in the area. Most were removed and destroyed by an Act of Parliament in 1643 when it was decreed that all crosses in public places had to go. But many local citizens circumvented the wishes of parliament by concealing these crosses with the intention of re-erecting them when the government policy changed, which it was likely to do at short notice during the Civil War. Many were then taken to churchyards for safekeeping. Examples of early Celtic crosses can be found in the churchyards at Bakewell, Eyam, Hope and Chapel. One fine example is still positioned by the roadside at Wheston near Tidewell.

CONKSBURY HILL FORT lies just south of the river at Over Haddon. This area is littered with evidence of primitive man's passage. At SK 203652 is Conksbury Cairn Circle, also known as Meadow Place. The cairn was almost totally destroyed when a wall was built and a generator sited here, but a stone circle is still visible – just. Thomas Bateman the Derbyshire archaeologist uncovered two disturbed burials here in his 1848 dig. A little further south is Bee Low, another round cairn sited at SK192648.

GARDOM EDGE was once interpreted as a hillfort but is now thought to be much older. A pollen analysis shows that by 500BC the weather was much colder and wetter, causing bogs to form on the high ground and marshy conditions in the valleys. The area was not well drained, the hillsides were composed of sticky clay and the valley bottom was subject to floods. Cup and ring marks would indicate that here was a lost village.

HADDON HALL has the remains of a Roman altar and a Sheela Na Gig. At Haddon Fields a round barrow was discovered at SK217662.

HADRIAN'S WALL was built to guard the wild north-west frontier of the Roman Empire and stretches 73 miles from coast to coast. At over twenty English Heritage sites you can see the remains of the forts, towers, turrets and towns that once kept watch over the Wall, and see rare Roman artefacts that show what life was like for the men, women and children on the edge of Roman Britain. Hadrian's Wall is a UNESCO World Heritage Site.

HARBORO ROCKS The Roman road between Buxton and Derby has been traced as far south as a point north east of Brassington (SK237548) just below Harboro Rocks. This outcrop of dolomitic limestone on a 1,000ft plateau is exceptional because most of the Peak District is carboniferous limestone. Harbour or Harborough is a name found often on Roman and pre-Roman roads. (See Arbour Low.) What was once the home of prehistoric man is now a popular place for climbers. It could have been a Druidic circle. A few years ago, two barrows were opened and in one a cist was found containing skulls and bones. Depressions in the ground on the terrace may be the remains of the hut-platforms of the Iron Age settlement site. It was excavated by Ward in 1890, then the cave and rocks were excavated in 1907 by W Storrs Fox. Finds are now in either Derby or Buxton Museum and include remains of early mammals, Iron Age pottery, a coral-mounted bronze brooch with rayed foot, iron spear heads, awls, a pin and a needle of bone.

HOLBROOK, HAZELWOOD, DERBY Large production centres for pottery, they produced Derbyshire Ware, which developed from serving a local market to having a wide circulation supplying the northern Roman military garrisons. New kiln sites are continually being discovered. Several kilns were found near the racecourse playing fields at Derby in 1967/8, manufacturing jars, bowls, flagons, beakers and mortaria. Go to Derby Museum and Little Chester Museum.

OLD WOMANS CAVE – TADDINGTON Excavated in 1909. Finds include two early Iron Age shards.

PENTRICH ROMAN CAMP On the old Roman Road near Pentrich there was an Iron Age enclosure on a hill within which a small Roman fort was built at an early date in the occupation. Now the site of Coney Grey Farm.

PORTWAY The possibility of a prehistoric trackway through Derbyshire and called the Portway running from the north west to the south east, was first proposed by the eminent local historian R. W. P. Cockerton (1904–1980), a Bakewell solicitor involved in many excavations and an expert on the Roman period in Derbyshire. He published articles in the *Derbyshire Countryside* between 1932 and 1936. The actual name Portway is Anglo-Saxon and there is written evidence of its existence throughout the medieval period and even in the 18th century sections were still in use as a route from Derby to Manchester. Its name survives on a stretch between Holbrook and Coxbench. The construction of turn-pike roads led to the demise of the old road, which was closed to prevent people avoiding the tolls, yet this pre-Roman road that has been in use for more than 2,000 years can still be followed on footpaths and green lanes. In places it has been obscured and obliterated and it can't be guaranteed that the exact line of the original route can be fully traced but my book *Discover Celtic Derbyshire* (Sigma Press 2013) follows the route and uncovers Celtic finds on the way.

RAVENSCLIFFE CAVE SK17397356, north of Cressbrookdale and south of Wardlow. Finds include pottery from the early Bronze Age and two Roman gold bands.

RIBER CASTLE Standing above the market town of Matlock and commanding views of all the surrounding countryside. It is also known as Smedley's Folley because this was the home of John Smedley who introduced hydrotherapy to the area. In 1868, John Smedley wrote: 'Here is the site of a Druidical temple, the remains of which, standing on the summit of the hill, were by barbarous hands removed but a few years since... The mind is led back to the time, probably more than 2,000 years ago when the inhabitants of the surrounding district, far and near, might be seen on the first day of November ascending the steep mountain side from the surrounding district, bringing their offerings to the priests, and carrying back the sacred fire to relight their family hearths which had all been extinguished by the priests' command the evening before; and no doubt also often to witness human sacrifices. This worship was put an end to by the Romans, who came into this country BC55, and who on this hill in aftertimes, made large fires when the south wind blew, not for sacrifices but to smelt the lead ore so abundantly found in this locality.' Kelly's directory of 1891 concurs: 'Large masses of gritstone found on the highest point of Riber Hill, 900 feet above sea level are the remains of an ancient cromlech, thought by some to have been a Druidical altar still intact in 1822, but broken down by 1834.'

ROYSTON GRANGE VALLEY The Roman road between Buxton and Derby ran just to the west of Royston Grange Valley, through the bleak environs of Brassington and continued through or near Rainster Rocks (SK218549). This is the site of a Romano/British settlement which could have developed a small market to judge from the considerable number of coins found here. It is still possible to see the enclosure walls, earthworks and remains of a road.

SCARCLIFFE PARK near Langwith was a Romano/British site where round and rectangular huts have been plotted in the open countryside.

WETWANG SLACK Three cart burials. One is of an Iron Age woman interred with a dismantled vehicle. The grave pit was probably once covered with a mound built from the spoil of the surrounding square ditch. Other objects buried with her included an iron mirror and a mysterious bronze 'bean can' of unknown purpose. Excavations took place in the parishes of Garton, Wetwang, Rudston and Burton Fleming revealing some 700 graves.

Appendix 6

MUSEUMS

Although we have concentrated mainly on museums and places of interest in Brigante country, we also include a small selection of other interesting places displaying Celtic artefacts.

ALDBOROUGH ROMAN TOWN North west of York. On-site museum and Roman mosaics.

ANDOVER MUSEUM OF THE IRON AGE Danesbury near Andover was an Iron Age hillfort. Excavations from the site are on display in the nearby Andover Museum.

ARBEIA was a large Roman fort and supply depot in South Shields, Tyne & Wear. It was first excavated in the 1870s and is now a museum and archaeological park with three full-scale Roman reconstructions and a spring/summer season of events. With some important objects from Roman Britain including the Regina tombstone, it is managed by Tyne and Wear Museums as Arbeia Roman Fort and Museum. Arbeia is A UNESCO World Heritage Site.

BAGINTON near Coventry airport on the southern outskirts of Coventry is not in Brigante territory but is well worth a visit. A 1st-century fort that has had an ambitious reconstruction scheme, turning a blank field into one of the most instructive military sites of Roman Britain.

Tombstone of Regina found to the south-west of the fort at South Shields (Arbeia).

BRITISH MUSEUM, LONDON There are many Celtic and Roman artefacts on display including the Lindow Man. There's the Waterloo helmet, shields and swords; the Snettisham hoards (also in Norwich museum), mirrors, weapons, pottery coins and grave materials. A very elaborate, detailed tombstone was found at South Shields, Co Durham on the northern edge of Brigante territory and is now in the museum. This finely sculpted piece looks like a classical building entrance with Regina seated in a highbacked wicker chair holding a distaff and spindle in her left hand and opening a jewellery box with her right. (See previous page.) Sadly her face has completely worn away to show no details at all. It was commissioned by her husband Barates, from Palmyra, and the epitaph along the bottom is in Latin and his native tongue. It reads 'To the spirit of the departed Regina, his freedwoman and wife – a Catavellaunian by tribe, aged 30.'

BUTSER ANCIENT FARM near Petersfield south of Guidford displays agricultural farming techniques and has impressive reconstructions of round houses.

BUXTON MUSEUM houses a considerable amount of material from excavations carried out in the town and at Poole's Cavern. At the time of writing, the bath complex is undertaking ongoing rebuilding work. Finds assembled over a period of years were originally exhibited at Poole's Cavern Museum but the artefacts were removed to Buxton Museum along with items excavated during the Peakland Archaeological Society dig 1981–84.

BUXTON – POOLE'S CAVERN is owned and operated by Buxton Civic Society. More than 400 items dating from the 1st century AD have been found inside the cave, and there is a Roman chamber dedicated to the use of the caves in Roman times when it was used as a factory producing brooches. Finds assembled over a period of years were removed to Buxton Museum. There is still a small museum on site, and a tour of the caves with enthusiastic, knowledgable guides is highly recommended.

CAMBRIDGE UNIVERSITY MUSEUM OF ARCHAEOLOGY AND ETHNOLOGY holds La Tène metalwork.

CHESTERFIELD The Roman town on the main road, known as Rykneld Road. Rykneld Square beside the church of the Crooked Spire has a plaque to mark the site of the Roman camp. A few finds in the local museum.

COLCHESTER CASTLE MUSEUM contains finds from the Iron Age oppidum and the Roman city including traces of the Boudican revolt. The castle stands on the podium of the Temple of Claudius.

DERBY has two major sites of interest either side of the River – Little Chester and Strutts Park. St Paul's Church on Mansfield Road, Chester Green houses a Heritage Centre. Manned by volunteers, it is open every Sunday between 2 p.m. and 4.30 p.m. from April to October. Derby Museum also has items of interest.

HULL MUSEUM has displays of Iron Age and Romano-British archaeology including reconstructed chariot burials and dioramas.

LIVERPOOL MUSEUM has items of La Tène metalwork

NEWCASTLE UPON TYNE The University Museum of Antiquities and the Society of Antiquaries contain some Iron Age material and important collections relating to the Roman military occupation in the area.

NORWICH CASTLE MUSEUM houses part of the Snettisham hoard.

ST ALBANS The newly refurbished Verulamium Museum tells the story of the Iron Age and the Romano/British town

STANWICK At the large Brigantian site of a section of the earthwork defences has been reconstructed.

THE NATIONAL MUSEUM OF WALES in Cardiff houses the finds from Llyn Cerrig Bach in Anglesey as well as other extensive collections from pre-history. Cardiff City Hall has a fine, Victorian stone statue of Boudica and her daughters.

Appendix 7

FEASTS AND FESTIVALS OF THE CELTIC YEAR

There were four seasonal festivals that marked the Celtic year: Imbolc, Beltane, Lughnasadh and Samhain. They are believed to have pagan origins, are mentioned in early literature and mythology, and were widely observed throughout the Celtic world. These were times when the barriers between real and supernatural worlds were frail, and were favoured times to practise divination.

IMBOLC OR IMBOLG, 31 January/1 February
Although traditionally celebrated on 1 February, because the day was deemed to begin and end at sunset, the Imbolc celebrations, as with all the other celebrations, would begin the previous evening. The festivities would start on what is now 31 January, but the date was fluid. They would celebrate the festival when the first stirrings of spring were felt, or on the full moon nearest this, or with the onset of the lambing season, which could vary considerably, or about halfway between the winter solstice and the spring equinox. This was a celebration of the lengthening days and the early signs of spring, so people lit candles and bonfires to represent the return of warmth and the increasing power of the Sun over the coming months. Celebrations often involved divination or watching for omens, and visiting holy wells. Visitors would pray for health while walking sunwise around the well, then they would leave offerings. Water from the well was used to bless the home, family members, livestock and fields.

The 1st of February was believed to be the birthday of St Brigid so she is strongly associated with Imbolc and it's sometimes called Saint Brigid's Day. St Brigid is the former fertility goddess Brigid. On Imbolc Eve, Brigid was said to visit virtuous households and bless the inhabitants. Special food would be eaten on Imbolc Eve and some of the food and drink would be set aside for Brigid. Ashes from the fire would be raked smooth and in the morning, the people would look for some kind of mark on the ashes as a sign that Brigid had visited. They made Brigid's crosses usually from rushes or occasionally from straw woven into a square or equilateral cross. A Brigid's Cross was thought to keep evil, fire and hunger from a home where it was displayed and was generally left there until the next Imbolc.

BELTANE, 30 April–1 May

May eve in the old Celtic calendar, Beltane marked the end of winter and the beginning of summer just as Hallowe'en marked the end of summer and beginning of winter. This was the first fire festival of the year, the purpose of which was to purify the earth and free growing crops from witch's spells. Bones were often burnt because the foul smell of the smoke was supposed to drive evil spirits away. That is where the name bon fire comes from, bone-fire.

THE SUMMER SOLSTICE AND THE FESTIVAL OF JOHN THE BAPTIST

Midway between the festivals of Beltane and Lugnasadh was the summer solstice, the longest day that marked midsummer. Although this is 21 June, the day for celebration was often 23 June, designated as the day John the Baptist was born. The eve of the festival of St John the Baptist was a night when witches were thought to ride abroad so special measures were taken to protect people, cattle and crops. Bonfires lit on midsummer's day had special significance as the ashes mixed with seed that was then scattered on the fields had great potency, especially if the plant known as St John's wort was burnt on the fire. St John's wort (hypericum perforatum) is a yellow-flowered plant with red spots that symbolise the spilled blood of the saint. The oil glands in its leaves generate a pungent smell and when burnt on the Midsummer bonfire, this oil scented the smoke, through which people had to jump to insulate themselves against evil. St John's wort was also hung on doors and windows and placed round the home and cowshed to protect from illness and evil.

LUGNASADH, 1 AUGUST

Lugnasadh, sometimes called Lammas, is named after the god Lug or Lugh. This pagan festival commemorates the start of the harvest, especially the corn harvest. The gathering of other fruits usually don't start until September. The Celts believed that all natural objects had souls/spirits, so the last portion of the crop was left standing. It was universally believed that this was where the corn goddess Demeter had taken refuge, so the last ears of the harvest were woven into an effigy of the corn goddess. The effigy shaped roughly into the form of a human figure was called the corn dolly, the word dolly being derived from the word idol. They believed that the spirit of the corn would be preserved in the dolly during the winter as it hung in the farm kitchen where it served to protect the household throughout the winter months, then in the spring it was broken up and mixed with the seed corn in order to transfer the spirit back into the soil to ensure a good harvest.

SAMHAIN, 31 OCTOBER/1 NOVEMBER

Samhain, a name that means summer's end, is a Celtic, pagan festival that was later absorbed into the Christian festival of All Saints or All Hallows better known as Hallowe'en. It was the Old Year's Eve in the Celtic calendar and marked the time when the great tribal god Dagda and Morrigan, an earth mother and goddess of fertility came together. Their intercourse ensured the renewal of the fertility of the land. At Samhain, the Celts celebrated the gathering in of the crops and the people gave thanks to the gods for a good harvest to see them through the winter. Farmers would walk round their barns and granaries with a lighted brand chanting a magical spell intended to protect their stores during the winter months.

Because the Celts thought that death was only a bridge between one existence and another, they believed that at Samhain, when the veil between the world of the living and the dead was temporarily drawn away, the dead would return to visit the living. Samhain incorporated the ancient Festival of the Dead, and was not entirely a sorrowful occasion. At dusk, the *Sluah,* the ghost of the dead were said to go drifting by on the wind. They revisited their families, warmed themselves by the fire and partook of refreshment to help them face the long winter months. It was believed that at Samhain mortal men could communicate with the inhabitants of the Otherworld to seek their advice and guidance on the course of events for the coming year. Samhain is the time when it's believed that a major crack appears between the worlds, and mortals may see the fairy *sidhe*, those beings that dwell in the parallel universe of the supernatural. Between sunset and cockcrow of Samhain, it was possible to gain entrance to a fairy hill by going round it seven times, then a door would open and admit the visitor to the fairy world. It was considered quite natural that the process should also work in reverse so supernatural creatures would all be free to visit. That's the theory on which our modern hallowe'en tradition is based. It was also the night when evil spirits were free to wander the world of man, but the activities of the evil spirits could be deterred by the lighting of bonfires.

NOTES

Chapter One
1. Phillips Guy Ragland. *Brigantia*. Routledge & Kegan Paul 1976, p 41
2. Ibid
3. Ibid
4. Ross A. 'The Horned God of the Brigantes', *Archaeologia Aeliana* 4 1961, p 85
5. Henig M. *Roman Sculpture from the Hadrian's Wall Region*. Durham University, Hadrian's Wall Research Framework. Available on line.
6. Ziegler M. 'Brigantia, Cartimandua and Gwenhwyfar', *The Heroic Age* Issue 1. 1999. Available at www.mun.ca/mst/heroicage/issue/1.
7. Creighton, John. *Britannia; The Creation of a Roman Province*. Routledge. 2006
8. *Britannia on British Coins*. Chards.co.uk
9. Thomas James. *The Works of James Thomas*. 1763, Vol II. P191 gives the original version of the poem.

Chapter Two
1. Phillips. Guy Ragland. *Brigantia*. Routledge & Kegan Paul, 1976 p 5
2. Phillips. Guy Ragland. *Brigantia*. Routledge & Kegan Paul. 1976 p 6
3. Burgess Colin. *Bronze Age Metalwork in Northern England. c. 100 to 700BC,* 1968.
4. Simon James. *Exploring the World of the Celts*. Thames & Hudson 1993, p 52
5. Diodorus Siculus 5.31
6. Hyatt, Derek. *The Alphabet Stone,* 1997
7. 'The Memory of Trees', *Only Time* by Enya, lyrics by Roma Ryan
8. Piercy, Joseph. *The Story of English*. Michael O'Mara Books 2012, pp 16-21

9. Cornelius Nepos, a writer of chronicles and short biographies made this comment after the death of his friend and contemporary Cicero who would have shaped it into a worthy literary form.
10. The most complete range of English translations of Roman historians is now in the Penguin Classics series. Especially good are those of Tacitus' *Annals,* M.Grant, and *Histories,* K Wellersley. Significant earlier translations of Tacitus include those of A. J. Church and J. Brodribb (London 1882) and W. Fyfe (Oxford 1912).

Chapter Four

1. Elizabeth Ewing. *Fashion in Underwear*. Batsford 1971
2. Anon. *The Complete Book of Fortune; The secrets of the past, present and future revealed.* Blaketon Hall 1988
3. The Letters of James Joyce, Vol. 2, Faber and Faber 1957, p. 183
4. Diodorus Siculus. 5. 30
5. Elizabeth Ewing. Fashion in Underwear. Batsford 1971
6. *Letters of James Joyce*. Volume 2, Faber & Faber 1957, p 185
7. Strabo 4, 4-6
8. *Letters of James Joyce*. Volume 2, Faber & Faber 1957, p 177
9. *Letters of James Joyce*. Volume 2, p 176
10. *Letters of James Joyce*, Vol. 2, p 183

Chapter Five

1. Polybius 2.17. 9-12
2. The Greek scientist and inventor Archimedes (287–212BC) discovered a method of measuring the density/purity of gold and silver by immersing them in water.
3. Julius Caesar, *De Bello Gallico*, 5.12
4. The basic details on coinage are taken from *The Journal of Ancient Numismatics*, 'Britain's First Coins' by Chris Rudd. Vol 1. Issue 4
5. Henig, M., *Religion in Roman Britain*, London, BT Batsford Publishers 1984
6. Pliny the Elder. *Natural History* (trans. Bostock, J., Riley, H. T.). London: Taylor and Francis. 1855, Chapter 36
7. Jones, Allason. *Roman Jet in the Yorkshire Museum*, York, 1996. pp 8–11
8. Ford, Trevor D. *Derbyshire Blue John*. Landmark Publishing 2000
9. *The Religion of the Ancient Celts*, Chapter III. 'The Gods of Gaul and the Continental Celts'. Sacred-texts.com
10. Piggott, Stuart, *Early Celtic Art from its Origins to its Aftermath*. Routledge 2008

Chapter Six

1. Bríd Mahon, *Traditional Dyestuffs in Ireland*, pp 116-122

Chapter Seven

1. Cooper, Irving Steiger. 'Reincarnation: The Hope of the World'. *Theosophical Society in America.* 1920, p.15
2. Schibli, S., Hermann, *Pherekydes of Syros*, OUP 2001, p 104
3. Diodorus Siculus v.28.6; Hippolytus *Philosophumena* i.25
4. Julius Caesar, *De Bello Gallico*, VI 102
5. Evans-Wentz, W.Y. Belief in reincarnation is expressed as an on-going Celtic tradition in *The Fairy Faith in Celtic Countries*.
6. Numrich, Paul David. *The Boundaries of Knowledge in Buddhism, Christianity, and Science.* Vandenhoeck & Ruprecht 2008, p 13
7. *Primitive Man.* The George Washington University Institute for Ethnographic Research.
8. Borthwick, Joy. 'Past Life Birthmarks'. Paranormal.lovetoknow.com
9. Caesar VI, 19
10. Green, Miranda. *The Gods of the Celts*, p 120
11. *The Religion of the Ancient Celts*: Chapter III. 'The Gods of Gaul and the Continental Celts'. Sacred-texts.com
12. James, Simon. *Exploring the World of the Celts.* Thames and Hudson 1993, p 102
13. Matthews, John. *The Celtic Oracle.* Ivy Press 2005, p 130
14. Koch, John T. *Celtic Culture: A Historical Encyclopedia.* ABC-CLIO 2006. p 1671
15. Mackillop. James. *Dictionary of Celtic Mythology.* OUP 1998, pp 21, 205, 270, 322–3, 346, 359–60
16. Mircea, Eliade. *Rites and Symbols of Initiation: the mysteries of birth and rebirth.* Harper & Row 1965
17. James, Simon. *Exploring the World of the Celts.* Thames and Hudson 2002, p 88
18. Shaw, Judith. feminismandreligion.com 2015.
19. Green, Miranda J. *Exploring the World of the Druids.* London: Thames & Hudson 2005, p 30
20. The head of Antenociticus and three temple altars were formerly displayed at the Museum of Antiquities at Newcastle University, but can now be seen at the Great North Museum, Newcastle. Binchester Roman Fort, near Bishop Auckland, County Durham was built around AD75 on the north-eastern edge of Brigante territory, for Roman legionary and auxiliary soldiers. History of Benwell Roman Temple: the Temple and its Dedications from www.english-heritage.org.uk by Paul Bidwell.

Chapter Eight

1. Green, Miranda. *Animals in Celtic Life and Myth*. London: Routledge 1992
2. Diodorus Siculus. 22.9. 4
3. The phrase 'The Seven Wonders of the Peak' comes from Michael Drayton, the Tudor poet in the third edition of his *Poly-Olbion Or A Chorographical Description of Tracts, Rivers, Mountains, Forests and other Parts of this renowned Isle of Great Britain*, 1622.
4. Phillips Guy Ragland. *Brigantia*. Routledge & Kegan Paul 1976

Chapter Nine

1. Paul Screeton's 2010 book *Quest for the Hexham Heads*. Anne Ross's *Archaeologia Aeliana* article (1973). *The Fortean Times* 294 and 295 (November/December 2012) by Stuart Ferrol.

Chapter Ten

1. McNeill, Marian, F. *The Silver Bough*, Vol. 2, 1959
2. Green, Miranda J. *Exploring the World of the Druids*. London: Thames & Hudson 2005, p 29
3. Marcus Annaeus Lucanus. *Bellum civile*, Book I, ll.498-501, c. AD61-65
4. Gallic Wars, 6.16
5. Koch, John T. *Celtic Culture: A Historical Encyclopedia*. ABC-CLIO 2006, p 1350
6. Green, Miranda J. *The Celtic World*. Routledge 1996, p 448
7. World Tree, in the *Encyclopedia Britannica*.
8. Alwyn & Brinley Rees, *Celtic Heritage: Ancient Tradition in Ireland and Wales*. New York: Thames and Hudson 1998,. p.120.
9. Pliny *Natural History* 16 95. We are now aware that mistletoe is poisonous.
10. Lindow Man is on display at the British Museum, London.
11. Clarke, David & Roberts, Andy. *Twilight of the Celtic Gods: An Exploration of Britain's Hidden Pagan Traditions*. Blandford 1996, p. 96
12. Collyer, Robert & Turner, J. Horsfall. *Ilkley: Ancient and Modern* (W.M. Walker & Sons 1885, p. 26
13. Ross, Anne. *Pagan Celtic Britain*. Routledge & Kegan Paul 1967, p 279
14. Collingwood, R.G. and Wright, R.P. *The Roman Inscriptions of Britain* (RIB) Vol. I 'Inscriptions on Stone'. Oxford 1965
15. PastScape entry for Coventina's Well. English Heritage. 2007. Many of the artefacts recovered by John Clayton are preserved in the Clayton Collection currently curated by English Heritage at Chester's Museum.

Chapter Eleven

1. *The Oxford History of England: Roman Britain*, Peter Salway with additional information by Edward Dawson and Rhys Saunders.
2. Caesar, Gallic Wars 6.19
3. Tacitus: *Agricola* c. AD98
4. Dobinson, C. *Aldborough Roman Town*. English Heritage 1995, p 3
5. The Derbyshire Archaeological Journal for the year 1979 (December 1980) Excavation of the Hill fort of Mam Tor.
6. See note 3, Chapter 8.
7. Bowden, M. C. B., Mackay, D. A. & Blood, N. K. 'A New Survey of Ingleborough Hillfort, North Yorkshire', *Proceedings of the Prehistoric Society*. Vol 55, 1989, pp 267-271 White, Robert. *The Yorkshire Dales. A Landscape Through Time*. Ilkley: Great Northern Books 2002
8. A. D. Brook; J Griffith; M. H Long. *Northern Caves Volume 2: The Three Peaks*. Dalesman Publishing Co. 1991, pp 232-234
9. Historical England 'Camulodunon' (47459) www.castlesfortsbattles.co.uk/yorkshirecastle_hillalmondbury.html
10. Historical England 'Cambodunum' (1005804)
11. Halsgrove, C. 'Stanwick Oppidium'. *Current Archaeology* 1989, p 385

Chapter Twelve

1. Caesar. *Commentaries on the Gallic Wars*, Chapter 18
2. Bede, *Historia Ecclesiastica Gentis Anglorum c.* 701 AD, Chapter 2
3. Ackroyd Peter. *Thames, Sacred River*. Chatto and Windus 2007, p 67
4. Olivia Fairfield. https://people.elmbridgehundred.org.uk/biographies/julius-caesar/
5. Strabo, *Geography* 4.5
6. Dio Cassius *Roman History* 49.38, 53.22, 53.25
7. Cunliffe, Barry. *Client King Togidubnus*. Tempus 1998. Tacitus(http//heritage-key.com.volumes) Fishbourne Roman Palace is open to the public. An archaeological dig in July 1996 unearthed many of its secrets and in 2006 it underwent a multi-million pound redevelopment. It now offers a computer graphic reconstruction of the palace.

Chapter Thirteen

1. Matthews, Caítlin. *Celtic Wisdom Sticks. An Ogam Oracle*. Connection Book Publishing 2001, p 12
2. Parts of this article have been extracted from *Celtic Visions: Seership, Dreams and Omens of the Otherworld* by Caitlín Matthews, Watkins, 2012.

3. *The Element Encyclopedia of the Psychic World.* Harper Collins 2006, pp 384–385
4. Green, Miranda J. (2005) *Exploring the World of the Druids.* Thames & Hudson 2005, p 24.
5. Stead 1986
6. Turner & Scaife 1995
7. Morgan and Morgan 2004

Chapter Fourteen
1. Vegetius. *The Military Institution of the Romans.* Book II
2. Tacitus, *Histories* 4.14.
3. William Shakespeare *The Tempest,* Act 5 Scene 1
4. Bruce, John. *'Handbook to the Roman Wall', Newcastle upon Tyne: Society of Antiquaries* 2006
5. 'Feeding the army', *Archaeology* 70. (3): 33. May–June 2017
6. *'About Arbeia, South Shields Roman Fort', arbeiaromanfort.org.uk*

Chapter Fifteen
1. Didius Gallus. *Agricola* 14)
2. Armitage, Ella Sophia. *Roman Remains,* 'A key to English antiquities: with special reference to the Sheffield and Rotherham District', London: J.M. Dent 1905
3. May, Thomas. *The Roman Forts of Templebrough near Rotherham.* Rotherham: H. Garnett and Co 1922.
4. R. G. Collingwood and R. P. Wright, ed. 'Funerary inscription for Cintusmus' 1965. *The Roman Inscriptions of Britain, RIB 619,* Volume One (online).
5. Waddington, Clive. 'Discovery and Excavation of a Roman estate Centre at Whirlow, South west Sheffield', Archaeological Research Services. Council for British Archaeology 2012
6. Inglis, D. H. 'The Roman Road Project', The Roman Roads Research Association 2016
7. *The Industrial Archaeology of Derbyshire* p 78
8. *Derby Evening Telegraph* Friday 21 October 1983
9. Armitage, Jill. *Discover Celtic Derbyshire.* Sigma Publishers 2013
10. Ling, Roger & Terry Courtney. 'Map of main Roman sites in Derbyshire, forts, roads and the settlements at Carsington', *Derbyshire Archaeological Journal* Vol C1 1981. p58
11. Armitage, Jill. *Discover Celtic Derbyshire.* Sigma Publishers 2013
12. Armitage, Jill. *Derbyshire History Walks.* Country Books 2012

Chapter Sixteen
1. Tacitus *Annals* 12.35.
2. Tacitus *Annals* xii.32. 40
3. Tacitus *Annals* 12. 37
4. Livy *The History of Rome* 34. 2-3
5. Tacitus *Annals* 12-40
6. Aldhouse-Green. Miranda Jane, *Boudica Britannia*. Pearson. Harlow 2006 p127. Miranda Jane Aldhouse-Green, FSA, FLSW is a British archaeologist and academic who until about 2000 published as Miranda Green or Miranda J. Green.
7. Tacitus *Agricola, c.* AD98
8. Fletcher, J. S. *A Picturesque History of Yorkshire: Being an Account of the History, Topography, and Antiquities of the Cities, Towns and Villages of the County of York, Founded on Personal Observations Made During Many Journeys Through the Three Ridings,* Vol 3 1901
9. Suetonius, *Claudius,* 44; Tacitus *Annals,* 12. 66-67
10. *Nero* 18
11. Tacitus, *Annals* XIV, 29-30
12. These important items found at Llyn Cerrig Bach can be seen in the National Museum of Wales, Cardiff, which holds all but four of the objects discovered. National Museum of Wales page 'Artefacts from Llyn Cerrig Bach' has links to pages on key objects.

Chapter Seventeen
1. Braund 1984, p 144
2. Dio, *Roman History* 62.2.1
3. Tacitus, *Annals* 14.31
4. Dio. *Roman Histories,* 62. 6. 1-2.
5. Kightly, Charles. *Folk Heroes of Britain.* Thames and Hudson 1982, pp 36-40
6. Hingley, Richard. *Boudica: Iron Age Warrior Queen.* Hambledon Continuum 2006, p 60
7. Rodgers, Nigel. *Roman Empire.* Lorenz Books 2006
8. 'History of Europe – Romans'. *Encyclopedia Britannica.*
9. Tacitus, *Annals* 14-33
10. Spence, Lewis. *Boadicea — Warrior Queen of the Britons.* Robert Hale 1937
11. Tacitus, *Annals,* 14–37.
12. http://library.flawlesslogic.com/tacitus.htm
13. Dio, *Roman History,* 62. 12. 5-6
14. Frere, Sheppard. *Britannia: A History of Roman Britain.* Routledge 1978, p.73

15. Carroll, Kevin K. 'The Date of Boudicca's Revolt', *Britannia*. 10, 1979. pp 197–202

16. British History Online, Paulerspury pp 111-117, http:// www.british-historyhistory.ac.uk/rchme/northants/vol4/p111-117

17. Appleby, Grahame. 'The Boudican Revolt; Countdown to Defeat', 2009 *Hertfordshire Archaeology and History* 16, 2009, pp 57–66

18. Dio. *Roman Histories*, 62.1.1

19. Suetonius, *Nero* 18, 39-40

20. 'The Snettisham Treasure'. *Current Archaeology*. Archived from the original on 9 May 2006.

21. Tacitus, *Annals* 14.38

22. Tacitus, *Annals* XIV.3; XIV.5; XIV.8

Chapter Eighteen

1. Tacitus, *Annals* 14.9

2. Tacitus, *Annals* 13.5.

3. Tacitus, *Annals* XIV.3; XIV.5; XIV.8

4. Dio 77, 16.5.

5. Polydore Vergil. *English History*, Book 2, pp 69–72

6. Raphael Holinshed, *Chronicles: History of England*, 4.9-13.

7. Chappell, Edgar L. *Cardiff's Civic Centre: A Historical Guide*. Priory Press. 1946, pp. 21–6

8. Koch, John T. *Celtic Culture: a Historical Encyclopedia*. ABC-CLIO 2006, p 861

9. Abigail Wilentz. *Relationship Devotional: 365 lessons to love and learn by*. Sterling 2009, p 215

10. Loomis, Roger Sherman. *The Development of Arthurian Romance*. Dover Publications 2000

11. Chrétien de Troyes. *Lancelot The Knight of The Cart*. University of Georgia Press 1990

12. James, Simon. *Exploring the World of the Celts*. Thames & Hudson 1993, reprinted 2002, p 94

Chapter Nineteen

1. Wheeler, M. 'The Stanwick Fortifications, North Riding of Yorkshire'. Oxford University Press for the *Society of Antiquarians* 1954

2. Wainwright, Martin. 'Archaeologist digs into grandad's tale to uncover lost Yorkshire amphitheatre'. guardian.co.uk 17 August 2011

3. Chisholm, Hugh, ed. 'Aldborough'. *Encyclopædia Britannica* 11th ed. 1911, pp 530–531

Chapter Twenty

1. Garlick Tom. *Roman Derbyshire*. Dalesman Mini Book 1975
2. Brown, M H. *Melandra Castle Roman Fort*, 1986
3. Evans Eric. *About Buxton*. Kinder Press 1947
4. Poole's Cavern, Buxton is owned and operated by Buxton Civic Society. More than 400 items dating from the 1st century AD have been found inside the cave, and there is a Roman chamber dedicated to the use of the caves in Roman times. There is a small museum on site.

Chapter Twenty One

1. Ptolemy Book II Chapter 2 trans 1992. 'The Celtic Tribes of Britain'. Roman-Britain.org. Archived from the original.

BIBLIOGRAPHY

Ackroyd, Peter. *Thames, Sacred River.* Chatto and Windus, London 2008

Adler, Margot. *Drawing Down the Moon: Witches, Druids, Goddess-Worshippers, and Other Pagans in America Today.* Beacon Press, Boston 1979

Alcock, Lesley. *Arthur's Britain* Allen Lane, London 1971

Allen, Thomas. *History of the County of York* 1828

Armitage, E.S. 'Early Norman Castles of the British Isles', *English Historical Review* Vol 14, 1904

Ashe, Geoffrey. *From Caesar to Arthur.* Collins, London 1960

Aveni, Anthony F. *The Book of the Year: A Brief History of Our Seasonal Holidays.* Oxford University Press, USA 2004

Bailey, Stephen. *The Derbyshire Portway, Pilgrimage to the Past.* Scarthin 2008

Barnat, J, Reeder, P, 'Prehistoric Rock Art in the Peak District', *Derbyshire Archaeological Journal* Vol. 102, 1984

Barrett, Anthony A. *Agrippina: Sex, Power and Politics in the Early Roman Empire.* Routledge 1999

Berger, Pamela. *The Goddess Obscured: Transformation of the Grain Protectress from Goddess to Saint.* Boston, Beacon Press 1985

Bede. *Historia Ecclesiastica Gentis Anglorum, c.* 701 AD. Chapter 2

Bedoyere, G. *Roman Britain: A New History.* Thames and Hudson Ltd, London 2010

_____*Defying Rome: The Rebels of Roman Britain.* The History Press 2008

Berggren, J. L. and Jones, A. *Ptolemy's Geography.* Princeton University Press 2001

Bitel, Lisa M. *St. Brigit of Ireland: From Virgin Saint to Fertility Goddess* https://monasticmatrix.osu.edu/bibliographia/st-brigit-ireland-virgin-saint-fertility-goddess 2001

Bohn, Henry G. 'The Life of Cnaeus Julius Agricola' in *The Works of Cornelius Tacitus*. The Oxford Translation, revised. London *1854*

Bord, Janet & Colin Bord. *Mysterious Britain*. Garnstone Press 1973

Bowden, M. C. B., Mackay, D. A. & Blood, N. K. 'A New Survey of Ingleborough Hillfort, North Yorkshire'. *Proceedings of the Prehistoric Society* Vol 55 1989, pp 267-271

Branigan, Keith. *Rome and the Brigantes: the Impact of Rome on Northern England*. University of Sheffield 1980

Breeze, D.J. *The Frontiers of Imperial Rome*. Pen and Sword Books Ltd 2011

Brook, A.D., J. Griffith; M. H. Long. *Northern Caves* Volume 2, 'The Three Peaks'. Dalesman Publishing Co. 1991

Briggs, Katharine. *An Encyclopedia of Fairies*. New York, Pantheon Books 1976

Bruce, John. *Handbook to the Roman Wall*. Newcastle upon Tyne Society of Antiquaries 2006

Brown, I. *Beacons in the Landscape: The Hillforts of England and Wales*. Windgather Press 2009

Burgess. Colin and Tylecote, R. F. *Bronze Age Metalwork in Northern England. c 1000–700BC*. Oriel Press 1968

Burrow, J. A. *Sir Gawain and the Green Knight*. Hammondsworth, Penguin 1972

Chadwick, Nora. *The Celts*. London, Penguin 1970

Champlin, Edward. *Nero*. Harvard University Press 2005

Christian, Roy. *The Peak District*. David & Charles 1976

Clarke, D. & Roberts, A. *Twighlight of the Celtic Gods*. Blandford 1996

Coombs D. G. & Thompson, F.H. 'Excavation of the hillfort of Mam Tor, Derbyshire'. *Derbyshire Archaeological Journal* 99, 1979

Collingwood, R. G. *Roman Britain and the English Settlements*. OUP 1937

Collingwood, R. G. and Wright, R. P. *The Roman Inscriptions of Britain* (RIB) Vol. I 'Inscriptions on Stone' 1965

Cottrell, Leonard. *The Great Invasion*, Coward–McCann 1962

Creighton, O. H. *Castles and Landscapes: Power, Community and Fortification in Medieval England*. Equinox 2002

Cunliffe, Barry. *The Ancient Celts*. OUP 1997

_____*Client King Togidubnus*. Tempus 1998

Dando-Collins, S. *Legions of Rome*. Quercus 2010

D'Arcy, Joan. *A City Within a City – Little Chester, Derby AD80–AD2000*. Little Chester Local History Group 2005

Dio Cassius. *Roman History.* Loeb 1989

Dixon, Suzanne. *The Roman Mother.* Routledge 1988

Dobinson, C. *Aldborough Roman Town.* English Heritage 1995

Douglas, D. C. and Rothwell, H. (eds). *English Historical Documents Vol 3 (1189-1327).* Routledge 1975

Douglas, D. C. and Greenaway, G. W. (eds). *English Historical Documents Vol 2 (1042-1189).* Routledge 1981

Dowden, Ken. *European Paganism: The Realities of Cult from Antiquity to the Middle Ages.* Routledge 2000

Drayton, Michael. *Poly-Olbion Or a Chorographical Description of Tracts, Rivers, Mountains, Forests and other Parts of this renowned Isle of Great Britain.* 1622

Derbyshire Archaeological Journal for the year 1979 (December 1980). Excavation of the Hill fort of Mam Tor.

Ellis, Peter Berresford. *Dictionary of Celtic Mythology.* OUP 1994

Fairfield Olivia. *Walton Bridge and Coway Sales, Walton on Thames.* Local history society

Fields, N. *Rome's Northern Frontier AD 70–235.* Osprey 2005

Fleming, R. *Britain after Rome: the Fall and Rise 400 to 1070.* Penguin Books 2010

Forder, Simon. *The Romans in Scotland and the Battle of Mons Graupius.* Amberley Books 2019.

Foster, Herbert Baldwin. *Translations of the Complete Works of Cassius Dio.* Delphi Classics, books 59-62, 2014

Frazer, James. *The Golden Bough.* Canongate Books Ltd 2004

Freisenbruch, Annalise. *The First Ladies of Rome: The Women behind the Caesars* .Jonathan Cape 2010

Gallagher Ann-Marie. *The Wicca Bible: The Definitive Guide to Magic and the Craft.* Godsfield Press 2005

Garlick, Tom. *Roman Derbyshire.* Dalesman Mini Book 1975

Ginsburg Judith. *Representing Agrippina: Constructions of Female Power in the Early Roman Empire.* OUP 2005

Goldsworthy, A. *The Complete Roman Army.* Thames and Hudson, London 2003

Graves, Robert. *I, Claudius.* Penguin Modern Classics 2006

_____*Claudius the God.* Penguin Modern Classics 2006

_____Translation of Suetonius' *The Twelve Caesars* (Penguin Classics, 2007

Green, Miranda. *The Gods of the Celts.* The History Press 1986

_____*The Celtic World.* Routledge 1996

_____*Celtic Goddesses.* British Museum Press 1995

_____*Exploring the World of the Druids*. London: Thames & Hudson. 2005

_____*Animals in Celtic Life and Myth*. London: Routledge.

Halsgrove C. 'Stanwick Oppidium', *Current Archaeology* 1989

Harding, D.W. *Hillforts. Later Prehistoric Earthworks in Britain and Ireland*. Academic Press 1976

Hart, C.R. *North Derbyshire Archaeological Survey*. The North Derbyshire Archaeological Trust 1981

Hartley, Brian. *The Brigantes*. Sutton Publishing 1988

Howarth, Nicki. *Cartimandua Queen of the Brigantes*. The History Press 2008

Hutton, Ronald. *Stations of the Sun: A History of the Ritual Year in Britain*. OUP 1996

Ingham, Bernard. *Yorkshire Castles*. Dalesman Publishing Co Ltd 2001

Inglis, D. H. *The Roman Road Project*. The Roman Roads Research Association 2016

Jackson, Sidney. *Celtic and Other Stone Heads*. Published in association with Lund Humphries 1973

James, Simon. *Exploring the World of the Celts*. Thames & Hudson 1993

Jewitt, Llewellyn. 'Some Additional Notes on the Tissington Well Dressing', *The Reliquary and Illustrated Archæologist,* London

Joliffe, Norah. 'Dea Brigantia', *Archaeological Journal* 98, 1941

Kendrick T. D. *The Druids*. Merchant Book Company Limited 1994

Kightly, Charles. *Folk Heroes of Britain,* Thames and Hudson 1982

Koch, John T. *Celtic Culture: A Historical Encyclopedia*. ABC-CLIO 2006

MacCana, Proinsias. *Celtic Mythology*. Feltham Hamlyn 1970

MacKillop James. *Dictionary of Celtic Mythology*. OUP 1998

McGrath, Sheena. *Brigantia: Goddess of the North*. Lulu Books 2015

McNeill, F. Marian. *The Silver Bough*, Vols 1–4. William MacLellan 1959. 1961

Manley John. *AD43: The Roman Invasion of Britain*. Tempus 2002

Matthews, Caitlin. *Celtic Visions: Seership, Dreams and Omens of the Otherworld*. Watkins 2012.

_____*Celtic Wisdom Sticks. An Ogham Oracle*. Connection Book Publishing 2001

Monaghan, Patricia. *The Encyclopedia of Celtic Mythology and Folklore*. Infobase Publishing 2004.

Moore A. W & Terry, John F. 'Water and Well-Worship in Man', *Folklore* 5 (3), 1894

Ó Catháin, Séamas *Festival of Brigit*. DBA Publications 1995

Preston F L. 'The Hill-Forts of the Peak', *Derbyshire Archaeological Journal* Vol. 74, 1954

Pryor, Francis. *Britain AD*. New York, HarperCollins 2004

Pryor, F. *The Making of the British Landscape*. Penguin Books, London, 2010

Phillips, Guy Ragland. *Brigantia*. Routledge & Kegan Paul 1976

Pliny *Natural History* John Healey trans. Penguin Classics 1991

Raine, A. *Medieval York*. John Murray 1955

Raistrick, Arthur. *Green Tracks on the Pennines*. Dalesman Publications 1962

_____*Prehistoric Yorkshire*. Dalesman Publications 1964

_____*The Romans in Yorkshire*. Dalesman Publications 1972

Rees, Alwyn & Brinley. *Celtic Heritage: Ancient Tradition in Ireland and Wales*. New York, Thames and Hudson, 1998

Reynolds, A. J. *Later Anglo-Saxon England: Life and Landscape*. NPI Media Group 1999

Rivet, Albert Lionel Frederick & Smith, C. *(1979), The Place-Names of Roman Britain*. Batsford 1979

Rivet A. L. F. *Town and Country in Roman Britain*. Hutchinson 1958

Ross, Anne. *Pagan Celtic Britain. Studies in Iconography and Tradition.* Routledge & Kegan Paul 1967

Russell, M. and Laycock, S. *Un-Roman Britain: Exposing the Myth of Britannia*. The History Press 2010

Saklatvala, Beram. *Arthur. Roman Britain's Last Champion*. David & Charles 1967

Salter, M. *The Castles and Tower Houses of Yorkshire*. Folly Publications 2001

Salway, Peter. *Roman Britain*. OUP 1986

Scott-Giles. C. W. *The Road Goes on*. Epworth Press 1946

Sheppard Sunderland Frere. *Britannia: A History of Roman Britain.* Routledge & Kegan Paul 1987

Shipway, George. *Imperial Governor*. Cassell Military Paperbacks 2002

Smith, Rev. William. *Old Yorkshire*. 1881

Southern, Patricia. *Roman Britain: A New History 55BC–AD450*. Amberley Books 2011

Strabo, *Geography* 4.5

Tacitus. Trans. J. H. Sleeman. *De vita et moribus Julii Agricolae*. CUP 1914

Tacitus. Trans. Michael Grant. *The Annals of Imperial Rome*. Penguin Classics 2003

Travis, Hilary & John Travis. *Roman Shields*. Amberely Books 2014

Underwood, Guy. *The Pattern of the Past*. Museum Press 1969

Varley, W.J. *A Summary of Excavations at Castle Hill Almondbury 1939-72*. Academic Press 1976

Vegetius. *The Military Institution of the Romans*. Book II

Waddington, Clive. 'Discovery and Excavation of a Roman estate Centre at Whirlow, South West Sheffield', Archaeological Research Services, Council for British Archaeology. 2012

Waite, J. *To Rule Britannia*. The History Press 2011

Waltham & Dixon. 'Movement of the Mam Tor Landslide, Derbyshire UK', *The Quarterly Journal of Engineering Geology and Hydrogeology* Vol. 33 No 2, May 2000

Watkins, Alfred. *The Old Straight Track*. Simpkin 1927

White, Robert. *The Yorkshire Dales. A Landscape through Time*. Great Northern Books 2002

Wilkinson, Philip. *What the Romans Did for us*. Boxtree 2000

Wilson, Roger. *A Guide to the Roman Remains in Britain*. Constable 1975

Wright, Brian. *Brigid: Goddess, Druidess and Saint*. The History Press 2011

Wood, Juliette. *The Celts: Life, Myth, and Art*. Thorsons 2002

Young, Arthur. *A six month's tour through the North of England*. London 1771

On Line

Celtic Coin Index available at www.finds.org.uk/CCI/

The academic journal *Britannia,* published annually by the Society for the promotion of Roman Studies, covers the most recent developments in the archaeology of Roman Britain

Websites – www.24hourmuseum.org.uk www.thebritishmuseum.ac.uk www.english-heritage.org.uk www.britainexpress.com/History/ www.ancientsites.co/-Lucius_Aelius www.frommers.com/destinations/chichester/A25101.html

About Arbeia, South Shields Roman fort: arbeiaromanfort.org.uk

INDEX

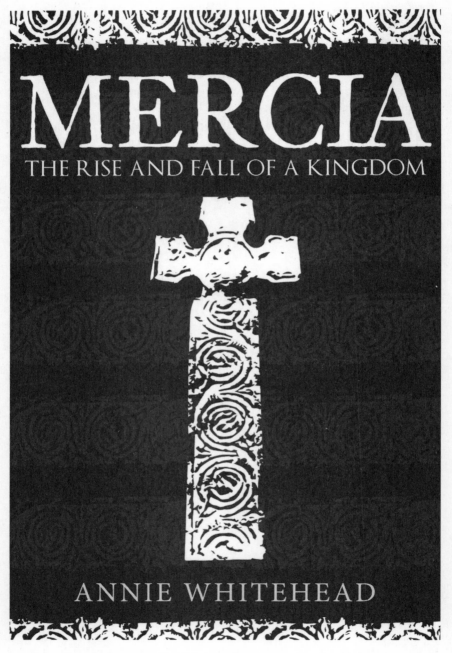